Managing Microcomputer Technology as an Organizational Resource

Mehdi Khosrowpour
Penn State University at Harrisburg

Donald Amoroso
University of Colorado at Colorado Springs

 *IDEA GROUP PUBLISHING*

Senior Editor: Mehdi Khosrowpour
Managing Editor: Jan Travers
Copy Editor: Karen Cullings
Index Editor: Cheryl Dunn
Printed: Jednota Press

Copyright © 1991 by Idea Group Publishing
4751 Lindle Road, Suite 116
Harrisburg, Pennsylvania 17111
(717) 939-7320

Printed in the United States of America

Library of Congress Card Catalog No: 90-082961

ISBN: 1-878289-07-1

Preface

The advances in information technology in our lifetimes has been nothing short of incredible. Perhaps a better word would be amazing. The microcomputer, scarcely 15 years old, has truly revolutionized our society, our businesses, and individual participators. The phenomenal pace of change initiated by microcomputers has been both upsetting to organizational planners while also beneficial to corporate managers, work teams, and organizations as a whole. The emergence of end-user computing, an environment where a computer user can utilize information technology to develop an application or to enhance the effectiveness of a task, has furthered the need for microcomputers in business in the next decade.

Although end-user computing has been pervasive within organizations in the 1980s, it has not been concentrated in one location or functional area. The distributive nature of the microcomputer has given each user a high degree of autonomy and independence. Individuals have reported increases in efficiency, effectiveness, and productivity. In the past ten years there has been a shifting of emphasis from using the microcomputer to improve efficiency to increasing effectiveness.

With the increase in independence has come the linking of users, forming work groups. Interdependence among users of information technology has created the need to develop organizational strategy and reshape organizational structures to accommodate the variety of growing systems.

All areas of organizational management have been impacted by the microcomputer, including the full spectrum of functional areas. Approaches to managing the microcomputer, and the areas affected by it, have ranged from creating an information center to establishing policies to govern purchases and data administration.

There appears to be a common thread running through the literature in past years, namely that of recognizing microcomputer technology as an organizational resource. That is, microcomputer technologies are recognized by managers as providing an extraordinary value to the organization. With that realization follows the need to address a variety of issues in order to more effectively manage these resources.

The goal of this book is to blend a variety of research studies that address the issues known and yet emerging with respect to managing microcomputer resources. Since the organization is in such a state of transition with respect to the planning of new and emerging microcomputer technologies, we welcome research studying its assimilation and management. The authors of the chapters discuss a variety of management issues from strategy formulation to end-user training to microcomputer security. Each of the chapters represent a different perspective existing in organizations with respect to the microcomputer resource.

We have organized the chapters into six categories:

1) microcomputer technology as a strategic resource
2) managing microcomputer technology
3) microcomputer technology and end users
4) artificial intelligence and microcomputer technology
5) microcomputer security and protection
6) microcomputer education and training

Finally, we would like to thank each of the authors who contributed a chapter to this book. Their insights are especially valuable, we believe, both to practice and to stimulate future research.

Mehdi Khosrowpour
Donald Amoroso

Managing Microcomputer Technology as an Organizational Resource
Table of Contents

Part I
Microcomputer
Technology as a
Strategic Resource

Technological advancements of computer technology in the past decades have added a new dimension to strategic management in organizations. Microcomputers have come to be viewed as more than just simple machines. They are now accepted as important information resources that strongly impact strategic planning and management. In Managing the Use of Microcomputers as a Strategic Tool, Lawrence Oliva, Mehdi Khosrowpour, and Donald Amoroso investigate how the proliferation of microcomputer technology has enabled end users to acquire, analyze, and act on information in a timely and effective fashion. It discusses the value of microcomputers as strategic tools and provides directions for the successful strategic utilization of microcomputers in support of business goals and objectives. In the next chapter (Mapping the Corporate Microcomputer Strategy), Oliva takes this evaluation one step further by discussing the human factors involved in the micro environment and the importance of viewing the whole picture of the organizational information technology resources .

Chapter 1

MANAGING THE USE OF MICROCOMPUTERS AS A STRATEGIC TOOL

Lawrence M. Oliva
Sun Microsystems, Inc.

Mehdi Khosrowpour
Pennsylvania State University at Harrisburg

Donald L. Amoroso
University of Colorado at Colorado Springs

An unprecedented surge in information technologies (IT) within the past two decades has presented many new challenges for organizations in meeting the demands of decision makers in the effective and timely management of information in the organization. Advancements in computer technology, telecommunication technology, and office automation technology of the past decade have also led many businesses to recognition of their information resources as one of the mainstream organizational resources needing to be effectively managed (Bryce, 1983; Burk & Horton, 1989; Henderson & Treacy, 1986; Kubicki, 1985; Thrieaf, 1984; Trauth, 1984).

The growth in end-user computing is producing some of the most pronounced changes in organizations today. For example, organizations have grown to

Previously published in the Journal of Microcomputer Systems Management, Vol. 1, No. 1
© Idea Group Publishing

view their information technology resources as a major strategic asset and to utilize them in support of maintaining a competitive edge in the world market (Belohlav & Raho, 1987; Ives & Learmonth, 1984; King, 1988; McFarlan, 1984; Nolan, 1982; Rockart & Scott Morton, 1984; Sullivan, 1985). In recent years, IT resources have come to represent the single most important competitive weapon available to corporate management for corporate growth and survival. Corporate executives, in turn, has begun to realize that they cannot afford to surrender management of this valuable corporate asset. Organizations now have the opportunity to utilize information technology in ways that could lead them to the discovery of new markets, products, or services - or an entire new way of managing a firm.

Even with the tremendous growth in end-user computing in the past decade, little attention has been given to the management of these issues. Many of the firms investigated in a variety of empirically-based studies reported a lack of integration of end-user issues into the corporate strategic framework (Amoroso, 1987; Rivard, 1988; Rockart, 1983). Consequently, disjointed environments exist with respect to services and the policies needed to manage those services.

Background

Traditionally, information systems have relied on the mainframe computers which utilized central information processing centers. But, in the past decade alone, with the proliferation of technological advancements achieved in microcomputer technology, there are now innovative ways of managing corporate information. Today end users can perform a full range of information processing with their desktop microcomputers, in a very timely and effective fashion, without relying on their centralized systems. End users are defined as users and/or developers of computer-based information applications using desktop workstations.

The growth in end-user computing and microcomputer use has been staggering, with more than 10 million microcomputers expected to be used by 1990 (Business Week, 1984; Guimaraes, 1986). In 1985, Strassman projected that over the next fifteen years the number of microcomputer workstations in offices world-wide will increase to 200 million. One can hypothesize that the dramatic surge in the use of microcomputers in the past few years is underestimated. In support of this argument, Manzi (1989) forecasts that by the middle of the next decade, there will be a microcomputer for every three white collar workers, with company payrolls predicted to include more than 50% white collar workers. Now as we approach the new century, we are beginning to see personal computing integrated into all areas of the workplace.

Information management for the 1990s increasingly stresses flexibility, performance, and standardization in microcomputer hardware and software. These new directions allow end users the opportunity for using this technology to support strategic, tactical, and operational functions of the organization. In the 1990s, microcomputers will increasingly provide the "glue" linking customer and vendor, supplier and users, managers and employees in organizations.

This article focuses on determining the strategic value of end-user computing, the management issues involved in exploiting microcomputing applications, and discusses various opportunities that businesses will have in the effective utilization of end-user technologies.

Assessing the Situation

Early in the past decade there was only one long-distance telephone company, a bar code was something concerning taverns, and microcomputers were sold as kits to be assembled at home by electrical engineering hobbyists. Today, there are dozens of long-distance carriers, bar codes appear on every manufactured retail product, and microcomputers are as common a business tool as the calculator was. Microcomputers have survived doubts and criticisms regarding their potential to provide for a variety of useful tasks.

In the 1980s, tremendous technological changes in microcomputer technology occurred concurrently with such factors as increased large city traffic congestion, increased real estate rental costs, raised expectations about product quality and customer service levels, integrated supplier-customer relationships, and demands for more active employee involvement in the management of organizations. The tremendous advancements achieved in the telecommunication industry linking autonomous systems together have contributed to the acceptance of microcomputers as a potential tool for facilitating organizational communications.

With the declining cost of microcomputers, coupled with greater availability and higher productivity gains reported (Applegate, Cash, & Mills, 1988; Lay, 1985; Malone, 1985; Mautz, Merten, & Severance, 1984; Raymond, 1983), organizations of all sizes and types can now employ this technology to increase their competitive posture (Business Week, 1985; Delone, 1988; Lee & Lee, 1987; McFarlan, 1984). As a result, organizations should strive for increasing gains using end-user technologies to support organizations' strategic goals and objectives.

The Impact of Microcomputer Use By End Users

Application development and use by end users has grown in proportion to increases in microcomputer sales. The change in use has occurred in two distinct ways. First, end users are using microcomputers to accomplish current tasks more efficiently. Second, microcomputer users have been able to develop applications to perform new types of analysis never before possible or even imagined. The result has been a dramatic increase in end-user effectiveness, especially in the area of decision making. In turn, end-user effectiveness leads to improved performance, individually and organizationally.

In recent years, there has been a dramatic increase in the use of microcomputer applications throughout the business functions of the firm (Saarinen, Heikkila, & Saaksjarvi, 1988). The popularity of microcomputers with end users is partially explained by the fact that microcomputers permit users to have a sense of control over their own data and applications. Often brought in the office "back door" to bypass mandates concerning the use of large systems, users have played increasingly important roles in defining the future directions of microcomputer technology and directing how management should deploy this technology in the organization. It is this degree of user involvement which has pulled the microcomputer industry from infancy into relative maturity in less than ten years.

Strategic Use of Microcomputers

A major question facing business managers today is how to develop and apply computer-based technologies that will better their strategic position. An integrated approach involves consideration of both the internal and external environments (customers, suppliers, vendors, employees, competitors, and management). Among the major advantages of using IT strategically are creating linkages and saving costs.

An examples is in the customer service area where microcomputer applications can significantly improve telemarketing, complaint response, survey analysis, data entry, sales order entry, and sales leads. In these areas, immediate response is essential to handle every call or request in order to avoid a loss of potential sales and to seize advantage of a new marketing trend or product production.

Creating Linkages. Microcomputers can be linked together to exponentially increase the potential strategic impact over stand-alone workstations. Organizational linkages increase communications and facilitate group interactions. A typical local area network makes use of electronic mail bridging time and space. Electronic mail offers a different way of communicating with advantages of multiple addressees and potentially rapid exchanges. This helps reduce communication delays (telephone tag) and opens up direct dialogue between any or all employees. Organizational linkages can change the very structure of reporting relationships as information becomes accessible and actionable.

Furthermore, many businesses these days are providing their customers with microcomputers to permit direct on-line order entry and order status checking abilities. To many businesses this arrangement can be considered a strategic move, but the tactical benefits include reduced in-house order entry labor and improved customer services relationships. The organization should establish a clear direction and policy as to how this service can be managed and integrated into other functions and services of the organization. Managers should realize that management of organization end user computing planning and control has proven to be much more complicated than expected (Karten, 1987).

Proper and effective management of microcomputers can enable an organization to integrate organizational activities, including those with a centralized data processing. Decision makers can make decisions in a more accurate and timely fashion by having the needed information available to them through the use of microcomputers with the ability to communicate to other personnel in upward, downward, or horizontal directions within the organizations.

Saving Costs. An important advantage of microcomputers is their cost savings to the firm. One example where costs have been significantly reduced is in the area of inventory reduction. Office or manufacturing inventories is problem of the 1990s driven by the issues of customer configurable products, the increasing cost of office and storage space, and the cost of inventory purchases. Management is constantly seeking ways to minimize the cost of obtaining and storing inventories. For some businesses, costs of maintaining adequate inventory is considered to be a significant portion of their assets. Edwards (1987) states that most small businesses have 75-90% of their assets invested in their inventory. In many cases this drives a change to just-in-time inventory replenishment services. Establishing direct computer connections with suppliers to communicate purchase orders for supplies and inventory items can reduce errors and paperwork costs. Electronic orders can be placed using communication networks, which also allow payments to be made directly to a supplier's bank account. Likewise, customer invoicing and direct customer payment can be made via microcomputer linkages. The advantages include avoiding mail and telephone delays, elimination of inaccurate or missing paperwork, and much faster receipt of receivables.

Among the many cost savings and productivity advantages of the work-at-home concept include a reduction in office overhead costs and increased workforce flexibility (e.g. mothers with young children and the physically handicapped). In cases when the organization, because of additional staffing levels, is considering an expansion of its physical facilities by moving to a larger office, management should first consider the option of having certain employees perform some of their work at home via communications and coming into the office one or two days a week. With a rotating schedule for office attendance, the need for expansion space might be avoided for several years.

Limitations

Despite the fact that microcomputers have matured to the performance levels of most mainframe computers of a few years ago, they still have certain limitations. Human interaction is still needed during meetings, in making customer telephone calls, establishing personal relationships, and in making decisions and judgments. In addition, microcomputers lack the processing power of modern large mainframes for solving extremely large, complex, computationally intense problems. Those types of problems usually exist mainly in the engineering and scientific areas, and even then, only a very small percentage of the time. Another area that microcomputers are poorly equipped to handle is massive database applications such as found in financial institutions or insurance companies. For these applications, mainframes or minicomputers are considered to be much more appropriate than microcomputers. Karasik (1984) states that managers should attempt to understand microcomputer systems capability with regard to the everyday demands of the business.

Creating a Strategy for Managing Microcomputers

The growth and competitive advantages of microcomputer use indicate the need for a strategy that manages them. Ideally, the strategy addressing end-user computing issues should be integrated within the information systems strategy, which in turn should be an integral part of the corporation's overall strategy. Figure 1 illustrates this concept.

The scope of an end-user computing strategy should be sufficiently broad to include all of the appropriate information technologies which play an important role in the computing environment. In recent literature, four distinct components of an EUC strategy have unfolded:

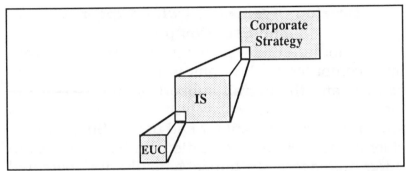

Figure 1. Integrated Strategy for End-User Computing

1) Identify the "right" software tools for end users;
2) Develop organization-wide support of end-user computing;
3) Manage corporate data as a resource;
4) Create end-user policies that support the corporate strategy.

Identify the "Right" Software
Tools for End Users

Selection of the right software development tools is one of the most important keys to a successful end-user strategy. The quality of an end-user tool in terms of its friendliness, power, and flexibility is crucial to the quality of the application. Using inappropriate software tools in the development of end-user applications on stand-alone microcomputer workstations could lead to disastrous results. The evaluation criteria for selecting software must focus on end user needs for modeling, analysis, forecasting, statistics, data query and manipulation, graphics, report building, text writing and communications (Amoroso, 1987). Other criteria which should be considered include vendor support, hardware and operating system characteristics, user-friendliness, and command language capabilities.

Develop Organization-wide Support of End-User Computing

Another critical factor in fostering successful microcomputer applications is the allocation of resources and the overall support of end users. Top management must be involved in order to build a supportive environment for end users. Support considerations include information centers, microcomputer managers, in-house consultants, personal computing groups, and scheduled training programs.

Information centers provide centralized support facilities for decentralized end users. Information centers are often responsible for a variety of activities, including data administration, software evaluation, debugging assistance, information clearinghouse, and documentation support.

In organizations with many microcomputers, management should consider the funding of a microcomputer manager position to help guide users to the most efficient methods of using and learning about the systems. Having a person responsible for the technology permits the appropriate features of the technology to be deployed where needed. Management should also recommend the creation of microcomputer support and trouble shooting groups to assist end users with critical installations and problems related to the utilization of microcomputers. In addition, this group can assist users in developing various applications such as order processing, clients' information processing, inventory processing, or production management. Forward thinking organizations should send out signals that microcomputer use is generally encouraged by top management as demonstrated by the level of organizational support (Amoroso, 1989).

Manage Corporate Data As a Resource

The management of the data resource underlies the effectiveness of end-user computing. The quality of an application is only as good as the quality of the data. Data, a corporate resource, is crucial to the development and utilization of end-user applications and must therefore be properly managed to ensure integrity, accuracy, and reliability. Data management issues must be incorporated into the end-user computing strategy. Data policies should be aimed at reducing the data management risks and enhancing accessibility, integrity, and security of the data (Amoroso, 1990).

From a practical standpoint, management should ensure that data entered into one microcomputer can be used by another microcomputer to avoid duplication of effort. To accomplish this goal, management should develop a corporate-wide policy to inform end users of the issue of data duplication and provide remedies to reduce data entry redundancy.

Create End-user Policies that Support the Corporate Strategy

Operating policies tend to evolve from the overall corporate strategy. An effective end-user computing strategy must include policies aimed at assessing the quality of microcomputer applications. Specific policies should be considered when planning for an effective end-user computing environment include: purchase justification, hardware and software standards and usage guidelines. Standards promote communications and sharing of data between applications and among end users. An integrated strategy addressing end-user issues should be implemented in a top-down fashion to avoid a fragmented ineffective approach to microcomputer management.

Conclusion

An enormous potential in cost savings, productivity increases, and significant flexibility are available through the use of microcomputers technology. With many social and environmental problems increasing the costs of business, microcomputer technology offers a significant strategic advantage to many organizations. No longer can management afford to view microcomputers as limited data processing tools; instead, a careful strategic analysis and recognition of its value must be given to the applications microcomputers can produce. It is incumbent upon management to understand and apply this technology toward the realization of corporate objectives. The advantages and realistic applications of this technology, as described in this chapter, are only a few of the major, strategic features of these systems. Information technologies are vital tools to manage many of these challenges of the next decade. Clearly, microcomputer technology that is effectively managed can provide a competitive edge to business.

References

Amoroso, D.L. (Fall-Winter, 1989). *Organizational Issues of End-User Computing. Data Base,* 3(4), 49-58.

Amoroso, D.L., & Cheney, P.H. (Spring, 1987). A Report on the State of End-User Computing in Large North American Insurance Firms. *Journal of Information Management,* 8(2) 39-48.

Amoroso, D. L., McFadden, F.R., & White, K.B. (Spring, 1990). Disturbing Realities Concerning Data Policies in Organizations. *Information Resources Management Journal,* 18-27.

Applegate, L.M., Cash, J.I., & Mills, D.Q. (November-December, 1988). Information technology and tomorrow's manager. *Harvard Business Review,* 66(6), 128-136.

Belohlav, J.A., & Raho, L.E. (1987). Perceptions of the organizational information system. *Journal of Information Science, 13*, 247-251.

Benjamin, R.I., Rockart, J.R., Scott Morton, M.S., & Wyman, J. (Spring, 1984). Information technology: A strategic opportunity. *Sloan Management Review,* 25(4) 3-10.

Benson, D.H. (December, 1983). A field study of end user computing: Findings and issues. *MIS Quarterly,* 7(4), 35-45.

Bryce, T. (August, 1983). Information systems - a field in transition. *Journal of Systems Management, 34*(8), 6-13.

Burk, C., & Horton, F.W. (1989). *INFOMAP: Complete guide to Discovering Corporate Information Resource.* Prentice-Hall, New York.

Business Week. (September 24, 1984). How Personal Computers Can Trip Up Executives, 94.

Business Week. (October 14, 1985). Information Power, 108-114.

Curley, K.F., & Pyburn, P.J. (Fall, 1982). Intellectual technologies: The key to improving white collar productivity. *Sloan Management Review, 24*(1), 31-39.

Delone, W.H. (March, 1988). Determinants of success for computer usage in small business. *MIS Quarterly,* 51-61.

Edwards, W.F. (October, 1987). A microcomputer inventory system for the small business. *Journal of Systems Management,* 18-23.

Guimaraes, T. (June, 1986). Personal computing trends and problems: An empirical study. *MIS Quarterly,* 178-187.

Henderson, J.C., & Treacy, M.E. (Winter, 1986). Managing end-user computing for competitive advantage. *Sloan Management Review, 27*(2), 3-14.

Ives, B., & Learmonth, G. (December, 1984). The information system as a competitive weapon. *Communication of ACM, 27*(12), 1193-1201.

Karasik, M.S. (January-February, 1984). Selecting a small business computer. *Harvard Business Review,* 26-30.

Karten, N. (October, 1987). Managing end user computing when the only constant is change. *Journal of Systems Management,* 26-29.

Keen, Peter, G.W. & Woodman, L.A. (September-October, 1984). What to do with all those micros. *Harvard Business Review,* 142-150.

Khosrowpour, M. (1988-89). Office automation as a managerial tool: The underlying importance of education. *Journal of Educational Technology Systems,* 17(1), 79-87.

Khosrowpour, M. (1989). *Microcomputer Systems Management and Applications.* Boyd & Fraser Publishing, Boston, Massachusetts.

King, W.R. (Fall, 1988). Strategic planning for information resources: The evolution of concepts and practice. *Information Resources Management Journal, 1*(1), 1-8.

Kubicki, M. (January, 1985). Information resource management requires data analysis. *Records Management Quarterly, 19*(1), 10- 14.

Lay, P.M. (June, 1985). Beware of the cost/benefit model for IS project evaluation. *Journal of Systems Management, 36*(6), 30- 35.

Lee, D.S. (December, 1986). Usage pattern and sources of assistance for personal computer users. *MIS Quarterly,* 313-325.

Lees, J.D., & Lees, D.D. (January, 1987). Realities of small business information system implementation. *Journal of Systems Management,* 6-13.

Malone, S.C. (April, 1985). Computerizing small business information systems. *Journal of Small Business Management, 23*(2), 10-16.

Manzi, J. (January, 1989). Interview. *Computer Systems News/Business Outlook,* 28.

Mautz, R.K., Merten, A.G., & Serverance, D.G. (June, 1984). Corporate Computer Control Guide. *Financial Executive, III*(6), 24-36.

McFarlan, F.W. (May-June, 1984). Information technology changes the way you compete. *Harvard Business Review, 26*(3), 98-103.

MIS Week. (Monday, March 6, 1989). Intel Chip Promises Supercomputer in PCs, 10(10), 1.

Nolan, R.L. (July-August, 1982). Managing information systems by committee. *Harvard Business Review, 60*(4), 72-79.

Raymond, L. (September, 1983). Decision-aid for small business computer selection. *Journal of Systems Management,* 19-21.

Rockart, J.F., & Scott Morton, M.S. (January-February, 1984). Implications of changes in information technology for corporate strategy. *Interfaces, 14*(1), 84-95.

Saarinen, T., Heikkila, J., & Saaksjarvi, M. (August, 1988). Strategies for managing end user computing. *Journal of Systems Management,* 34-39.

Strassman, P.A. (1985). *Information Payoff: The transformation of work in the electronic age.* The Free Press, New York.

Sullivan, C.H., Jr. (Winter, 1985). Systems planning in the information age. *Sloan Management Review, 26*(2), 3-12.

Thieraf, R.J. (1984). *Effective Management Information System.* Merrill Publishing Company, Columbus, Ohio.

Trauth, E. (July, 1984). Research-oriented perspective on information management. *Journal of Systems Management, 35*(7), 12- 17.

Chapter 2

MAPPING THE CORPORATE MICROCOMPUTER STRATEGY

Lawrence M. Oliva
Sun Microsystems, Inc.

Positioned by both small and large businesses as a critical competitive technology for the 1990s, the microcomputer is poised to transcend the barriers of time, distance, and language and link together various information related technologies into unified information networks. Driven by demand from end-users, the number of microcomputer workstations in offices worldwide will increase to a projected 46 million systems by the end of the 20th century (see Figure 1) (Dreyfuss, 1988). Much as the telephone has become a basic business tool, so will the microcomputer in many different forms and styles. Today, the cost of an inexpensive microcomputer is about the same as providing an employee a dedicated telephone in 1972, the year that phones became cheap enough to eliminate sharing them (Nolan, 1984). The microcomputer will not replace the telephone, but supplement its functionality, much as the telephone did to

Previously published in Information Technology Resources Utilization and Management: Issues and Trends © Idea Group Publishing

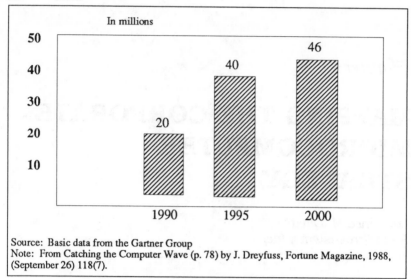

Source: Basic data from the Gartner Group
Note: From Catching the Computer Wave (p. 78) by J. Dreyfuss, Fortune Magazine, 1988, (September 26) 118(7).

Figure 1:   Increase of PCs in the Workplace

telegraph technology.

Determining which strategies can harness this new wave of computing is difficult and involves considerable thought and trust in the future of technology and in the belief that people will continue to accept changes in the way they work and live. Visions of microcomputers for the year 2000 that will have speech capabilities, understand longhand writing, search out specific pieces of information, and have processing capabilities of 20 to 50 times that of today's computers have been received from the founders of the microcomputer industry (Bulkeley, 1989). Are these visions simply creative thinking? Perhaps, but considering that in 1967 the *Wall Street Journal* predicted that there would be 220,000 computers in the United States by the year 2000 (Miller, 1989) and there are 45 million in 1989, it is conceivable that many of the aforementioned features will be standard equipment in microcomputers at the start of the 21st century. As Nelson (1989) stated in a recent newspaper article about the reaction of people to a statement by Alexander Graham Bell predicting that in 100 years people would be able call anyone in the world, "Of course they would have put him away."

This chapter discusses how the focus of the microcomputer is rapidly turning away from fascination with the electronics technology contained in the system to the applications and capabilities it can perform for business. As microcomputers become as common as telephones, the challenge to both non-profit and profit-driven organizations is to understand how to use the integrated automation and communications possibilities now available to even the smallest group or department. Understanding this challenge involves the combination of technology, business, and human behavior, all of which have proven to be dynamic and unpredictable at any given time. The successful managers of the 1990s and 21st century will be those who can obtain the greatest degree of productivity and acceptance from both users and customers of services and products made possible through microcomputer technology.

The next section of this chapter presents an overview of the challenges affecting business. This is followed by discussion of the competitive advantages of microcomputers, the microcomputer as an information bridge, the human element, and multinational competition. To round out the chapter, future trends and emerging technologies are presented and research opportunities discussed. The final section summarizes the main thoughts in the chapter.

Challenges

Merging microcomputers into the corporate strategy is by assumption a dynamic group effort. As corporate goals change, so must the technology supporting them. The information resources organization must understand and balance the forces of change, cost, and effectivity against the corporate forces of market opportunity, profitability, and expanding market share. When balanced, the corporation can exert tremendous competitive pressures throughout its industry, such as the case with the automated reservations systems of American and United Airlines. When not in balance, tremendous financial losses are possible, such as the $170 million loss incurred by Federal Express with its "Zapmail" fax service, or the $200 million loss suffered by Times Mirror and Knight-Ridder in their bids to develop electronic networks for consumer use.

The breakthroughs in electronic technology have not only created opportunities, but also management challenges. The vast number of options, products, applications, and vendors available since the introduction of the microcomputer during the mid-1970s makes the selection of microcomputer technology a much more difficult task compared with the relatively stable minicomputer and mainframe markets. Microcomputer product life spans are now described in months, rather than years, with pricing and features constantly being changed to adjust to performance increases, component costs, and competitors product introductions.

Constantly introducing new technology into the corporate environment is difficult, with issues con-

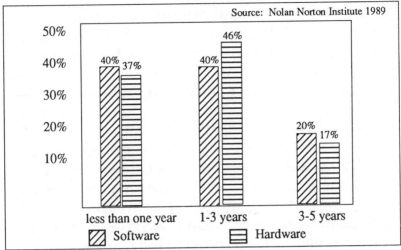

Source: Nolan Norton Institute 1989

Figure 2: Expected Return on End-User Computer Investment

cerning in-house technical support, ergonomic, environmental and human acceptance to change being raised. Managers are increasingly finding software releases lagging three to five years behind the hardware introductions, prompting a concern with whether to buy advanced hardware at premium prices for use in the future or adequate hardware at discounted prices to use now. Today's information resource manager has to make a decision to invest in new technology primarily because of the competitive advantages to be gained, the productivity increases possible, or the replacement of completely obsolete equipment that is vital to the support of the corporation.

Once a guidepost to executive decision making, the financial accounting community has yet to define policies which are applicable to information resource managers seeking to invest in microcomputer technology. The accounting profession has not yet universally agreed on how to depreciate technology that becomes technically obsolete in 12 to 18 months, yet is completely functional. Accounting professionals are confronted with the problem of creating a consistent financial depreciation schedule for both expensive mainframes, which typically have a five-year life span, and inexpensive microcomputers, which may be obsolete in one year. Traditional accounting practices do not consider the economic advantages of using technology to become more productive; they usually consider the amount of labor involved in producing a product. In the information resources environment, where intangible information is gathered, processed, and transmitted, these accounting practices offer little direction to the manager seeking to make a decision concerning technology. Several different accounting associations are working to establish practical guidelines to be used by industry and government (see Figure 2).

Along with technical issues, the business environment has also changed. International trade is now not only a possibility, but a requirement to succeed in

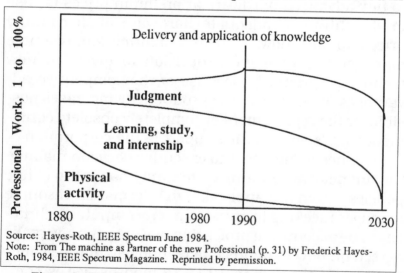

Source: Hayes-Roth, IEEE Spectrum June 1984.
Note: From The machine as Partner of the new Professional (p. 31) by Frederick Hayes-Roth, 1984, IEEE Spectrum Magazine. Reprinted by permission.

Figure 3: The Emergence of Knowledge as a Primary Industry

most markets. Electronic technology, linked with business decisions to reduce the number of suppliers to a select few, have created the "dedicated" customer, one which is linked to a primary manufacturer for the instantaneous transfer of sales, order status, and billing information. While selection as a qualified vendor has solidified business relationships between manufacturer and the selected supplier, this new environment has created even higher levels of competition between suppliers capable of competing at increasingly sophisticated levels of communications, and those who do not. Suppliers who don't compete on even a modest scale using microcomputers are finding fewer contracts and customers available.

"Float time," once the province of financial institutions seeking to maximize business profit, is now a competitive weapon to companies that are able to decrease the time between the receipt of information and the response to near zero, due to the development of national and global information networks in the 1970s and 1980s. For example, premium charges are paid for immediate delivery of stock market prices and is at a premium compared with information delayed 15 minutes. In that market, 15 minutes float time makes a difference to competitors. The microcomputer's ability to link into these local, national, and international networks has made possible direct connection with vast amounts of information located anywhere in the world at any hour of the day, bypassing the time delays of dictation, transcription, and editing and permitting the distribution of information hundreds of times faster than printing, mailing, or personal communications.

The ability to disperse information, rather than

hold it privately, marks the future destiny of a company. Notes Peter Drucker, "The productivity of knowledge has already become the key to productivity, competitive strength, and economic achievement. Knowledge has already become the primary industry, the industry that supplies the economy the essential and central resources of production" (Drucker, 1980). (See Figure 3.) Notes John Naisbitt (1982), "In an information economy, then, value is increased, not by labor, but by knowledge. Marx's labor theory of value, born at the beginning of the industrial economy, must be replaced with a new knowledge theory of value." Microcomputers are being called upon to develop and apply that new theory of value.

The emergence and acceptance of EDI (electronic data interface) protocols for the delivery of information is just one of the factors driving the exchange of computer-to-computer information. McKesson Corporation uses EDI to permit 12,000 independent pharmacists using handheld computers to place orders 24 hours a day, with deliveries made daily. Sales have climbed fivefold, from $1 billion in 1978 to $5 billion in 1987 due to the use of software packages, provided by McKesson, that "locks in" its customers.

EDI produced these benefits for McKesson:

1. reduced order lead times;
2. higher service levels;
3. fewer out-of-stock situations;
4. improved communications about deals;
5. lower inventory costs;
6. better accuracy in ordering, shipping, and

receiving;
7. a reduced labor cost (Peters, 1987).

The pharmacists also benefit through lower inventory levels, consistent pricing, and access to difficult to obtain drugs, which McKesson specializes in.

Corporations of all sizes are beginning to apply their expertise and resources towards exploiting this trend. For example, a greeting card manufacturer might provide a microcomputer to each distributor to track inventories and reorder points, and to keep a record of frequent purchasers, in order to inform them of the arrival of special cards they often buy. This saves the distributor time tracking inventories, permits just-in-time deliveries when stocks run low, and provides the distributor with a cost-effective system to retain loyal customers. A manufacturer of professional-grade hand tools for automobile repair shops might consider installing a microcomputer with superior graphics capabilities along with special training software to allow the mechanics to study for professional certification degrees, or to compare their repair methods with recommended methods. In addition, a connection to an electronic mail system with experts available to answer complex problems would be very valuable in training new mechanics and in repairing an automobile never repaired before in the shop.

The business environment has also changed, with a smaller labor pool of potential employees and increasingly sophisticated customers and suppliers. *Fortune* magazine predicts that the work force growth will slow down from 2.4% per year to 1.2% per year in the 1990s, and that the number of jobs will grow slightly faster than the labor force (Dreyfuss, 1988).

This change will require greater reliance on automated systems to increase productivity and reduce training costs for new employees. As the competition from overseas increases, American companies are increasingly adopting competitive policies such as just-in-time manufacturing; TQL (total quality level), which establishes a defect rate per million items produced; and speed, which establishes a short time-to-market approach for new products. All of these strategies depend on current, accurate information received, consolidated, and distributed to and from multiple sources to succeed—an application at which microcomputers can excel.

Competitive Advantages and Microcomputers

When information resource technology leads to competitive advantage, other organizations must

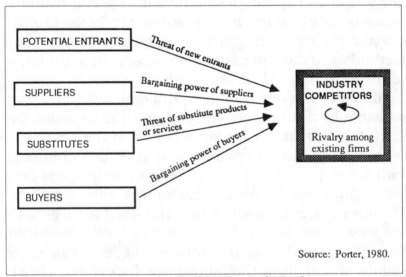

Figure 4: Competitive Forces in Business

react and determine their strategies. In large corporations, business planning groups often map out strategies that include technical support from the information resources organization. In smaller businesses, the owners may talk among themselves or hire a consultant who specializes in the use of technology which they have. Increasingly, the question is asked: Where does the microcomputer strategy fit? A growing consensus is forming to indicate the microcomputer is an integral and integrated part of the overall structure of a competitive business strategy.

The challenge for the 1990s is to determine which type of microcomputer technology in combination with traditional information resource systems should be deployed to achieve a competitive advantage.

The use of information technology to establish entry barriers to competitors is well documented, especially in the airline and hospital supply businesses. As an increasingly large number of industries begin to mature and consolidate during the next 20 years, competition will become fierce for even small gains in marketshare. Products, dedicated to specific markets, locations, and even customers, will require considerable support and service from the manufacturer, no matter where the customer may be. In addition, companies will rely upon the skill levels of employees distributed around the world, rather than in a single location. Portable (and soon, mobile) microcomputers, used for customer service and formed into global networks for the exchange of information, will prove to be a critical support factor as markets expand from a local to a world economy.

The ability to leverage corporate resources via

microcomputers is becoming clear even in today's competitive climate. For example, the distributors for Pepperidge Farms, the largest premium baker in the United States, use handheld computers for ordering products. The handheld computers directly transfer orders to a main computer system where the orders are billed, sorted, and transferred to the appropriate production plant in five minutes. Prior to the use of handheld computers, the processing of orders took a week. Pepperidge Farms is now able to accept orders until 3:00 pm, bake the breads starting at 7:00 pm, and begin deliveries at 11:00 that evening. By the end of 1989, all 2500 of the distributors will have handheld computers, providing Pepperidge Farms with a strong competitive advantage in its industry, which prides itself on freshness. A primary benefit from the conversion has been to boost marketshare by 3.5% and revenues by 25% since 1985 (Forsythe, 1989) in an industry that has remained flat for several years.

Frito-Lay, the snack food distributor, also uses handheld computers to link its sales force first to 200 distribution centers, and then to the corporate mainframes in Dallas, Texas. Frito-Lay claims this approach saves its salespeople 3 to 5 hours per week of drudgery and permits Frito-Lay to monitor market trends within 48 hours of data entry. In the past, managers had to wait up to three weeks to find out which products were selling. A benefit to Frito-Lay has been a decrease in the number of stale products returned to warehouses to an all time low.

In the videotape distribution industry, which duplicates and distributes video-tapes for home viewing, Rank Video Services America has gained an advantage over competitors by downloading order status information directly into a customer's microcomputer each day. Because of competitive pressures to provide the latest video releases to the viewing public, Rank's customers now know exactly when to expect their orders, rather then just waiting for them to arrive (Altman, 1989).

Providing a microcomputer with a specialized database can also create a barrier to entry. For example, if a microcomputer is used by an engineering organization to search for special parts, and the manufacturer of those parts has provided a database for only his parts—not competitors—then users of the system will order his parts. Sometimes competitors protest the use of information systems as an unfair advantage and obtain legal rulings restricting their use. As an example, from the time of their implementation, the reservation systems operated by United and American Airlines presented the flights for the two airlines first and all other airlines' flights next, reducing the probability a travel agent would look through dozens of listings from competitors. During the late 1980s, competing airlines obtained a court ruling requiring United and American to randomly distribute schedules for all airlines, so that the two airlines do not obtain a competitive advantage.

Countless other examples of the advantages microcomputers can provide for a company or organization exist. Interestingly, the microcomputer provides the classic competitive advantage environment Porter (1980) defined years before the IBM personal computer was developed and when home computers were sold as kits, to be assembled by hobbyists. Porter defined five competitive forces in business: suppliers, buyers, substitutes, potential entrants, and industry competitors (see Figure 4). Several key traits specific to microcomputer capabilities and applications exists in each of these forces.

All of the above forces are driven by information related technologies (i.e., computer systems, fax, and telephone systems). Information must be sent or received to obtain a result from any of these activities. People are a critical part of each activity; they must communicate with a customer to place an order, receive an order, or make a change. Microcomputers automate some of the routine activities so that people can make decisions and set goals to obtain an advantage in the marketplace for their organization.

Information technology can be used to decrease or increase the entrance barriers for potential entrants, or raise the investment levels needed by current competitors. Every time a microcomputer is linked into a network used for competitive advantage, a competitor must also install a system just to retain a minimal level of competitiveness. Unique products or services offered through the convenient use of information-resource-based systems can prevent or delay the selection of possible substitutes or alternatives by customers considering a change. Many times, customers will pay a premium price in exchange for access to information systems such as the Dow Jones financial database, which charges up to $100 per hour depending on the database being searched. Networked computer systems linking the five competitive forces in business together create a powerful synergy compared to individual, isolated systems.

Porter developed his concepts based upon the capabilities provided by mini computer and mainframe computer systems. However, with the emergence of the microcomputer, organizations can now develop tactical strategies not possible with larger computers, such as mobile sales offices, on-site financial accounting and order approvals, and telecommuting.

Information Bridge

An information bridge exists when computer compatibility and accuracy is reached between all parties involved in the sending and receiving of data, and the need for mailing or generating paper documents is greatly reduced or eliminated. As a integrated part of information resources, microcomputers are able to bridge the communication gap between mainframe or minicomputer, and voice and data communications. Microcomputers are able to transmit and receive fax formats, store voice and electronic mail messages, and communicate with computer systems from different vendors. As a part of the corporate information resource strategy, this flexibility can create low cost customer-supplier-manufacturer electronic mail or fax networks, with microcomputers being the distribution and transmission point for messages to different departments, locations, or even to outside organizations. Existing mainframes and minicomputers systems can act as file servers for data archive and management functions, although in a large corporation existing systems would also handle some of the communications activities.

The Human Element

People will always play a critical role in the

strategic use of microcomputers for a very simple reason: people use the systems to do their jobs. By understanding the role microcomputers can play in increasing personal productivity and how the use of technology helps the company, people play a critical role in creating the competitive information advantage pertaining to a sales, support, or manufacturing situation. For example, portable or laptop computer technology has significantly increased the productivity of sales representatives who can now enter a order directly from the customers office during a sales call. Efficiency is increased, leading to larger commissions for the sales representative. The company also benefits by reducing the amount of clerical staff needed to process orders.

The human factor is often overlooked in developing strategies that use computers. Although people are usually able to adapt to new technology—given time and training—they often object to constant change, which is often the case within microcomputer user organizations supported by information resource departments. Installing weekly upgrades to a user's operating system may not be the best thing to do, if the cost is greater resistance to technology use by the users. Also overlooked by microcomputer strategists are the social and organizational issues related to the use of technology. For example, it is reported that fewer than 10% of senior executives use microcomputers. Only slightly higher numbers are reported for physicians, attorneys, and senior government officials. Although changes in user interface screens, database access criteria, and communications abilities will have to be made to increase the attractiveness of microcomputers for these individuals, changes in culture and status will be the driving force in ultimate acceptance.

Management control is another area affected by the introduction of the microcomputer into the workplace. With microcomputers, people who were not considered managerial are now managing information. For example, blue-collar workers have become computer operators at automated factories. For organizations linked together with electronic mail capabilities, there are no barriers to sending messages to anyone else connected to the network. Managers can no longer control the flow of information through formal channels due to the speed and distribution abilities of the computer. Zuboff, (1988, p. 82) an associate professor at the Harvard Business School achieves that the role of the manager will have to be redefined in the 1990s: "Since managers are no longer the guardians of the knowledge base, we do not need the command-control type of executive." It will be interesting to see the changes in society

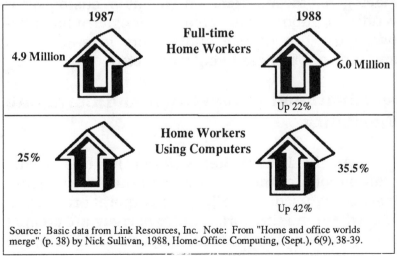

Source: Basic data from Link Resources, Inc. Note: From "Home and office worlds merge" (p. 38) by Nick Sullivan, 1988, Home-Office Computing, (Sept.), 6(9), 38-39.

Figure 6: 1988 Survey of Home Workers Using Computers

produced by the first generation of children who have microcomputers in the classrooms as they advance in their careers and begin to influence corporate and governmental decisions.

Another human factor impacting the decision to switch to suppliers who provide and support an integrated computer system concerns the training of users of the system. Should a customer or vendor currently use a dedicated system, terminal, or network provided by a manufacturer, it is likely that processes and procedures to use that technology have become a critical part of the business. As the company increases its dependence upon the computer access and applications, the chances of changing to a different system significantly decrease. The costs of change—switching from one vendor to another, retraining costs, purchasing of new equipment, preparing new manuals and procedures, and ending a longtime business relationship—all work against displacing one customer or vendor with another. Placing microcomputers on-site at a customer or vendor location usually creates a longterm bond between the two parties and results in substantial amounts of business being transacted.

Multinational Competition and Corporate Flexibility

As the United States moves towards a true multinational economy, microcomputers are increasingly being used as the lever of corporate resources located around the world. Entry barriers are created and maintained in several respects, according to Porter (1980). Of critical importance to the use of microcomputers in business is the ability to share information, programming costs, or know-how, without regard to location or time zone.   Microcomputers permit the corporation to share data throughout the organization, leveraging and balancing resources as needed to accommodate peak needs and temporary shortfalls.   For example, a large manufacturer of computer systems has facilities located in the United States, Europe, and Hong Kong.   Because of the various time zones, work started during the day in the United States is sent via communications networks to Europe for processing or additional work by European experts in the evening hours, sent to Hong Kong from Europe at the end of the European work day via a private satellite channel, and then back to the United States at the end of the Asian work day.   Essentially, three business days are completed in one 24-hour time span.   Competitors seeking to enter the computer manufacturing industry will have to have similar facilities, or work three times harder, to remain competitive.   The ability to share data around the world and gain immediate input from several experts is by itself a great advantage.

Microcomputers also provide the corporation considerable flexibility in adapting to national economic or market conditions compared to investments in larger, more expensive systems.   Being relatively portable, microcomputers can be moved within the corporation's facilities to accommodate the needs of specific projects or products requiring immediate computer support.   As commodity items, microcomputers are also easily purchased and installed, compared with larger, dedicated systems.   Trained users are also in plentiful supply with an estimated 30 million people in the world fluent in the operation of

microcomputers, compared to the specialized training programs required to operate larger, more sophisticated systems.

Because of the rapid changes that can affect a
multinational organization, corporations are par-
ticulary wary of becoming dedicated to a single
process, procedure, or even product. As consumer
preferences become more sophisticated and technology creates expectations of receiving improvements
at continuously decreasing costs, remaining locked
into a single process is becoming ever more costly.
Microcomputers provide the flexibility needed to
reconfigure an assembly line; establish a temporary
or permanent sales office; directly reach consumers
before or after their purchases; and develop, test, and
deliver services in a competitive market.

During extremely time-critical corporate emer-
gencies, such as initiating a nationwide recall alert
for a medical or food product, dozens of microcomputers can be acquired, installed, and programmed in a
few hours to assist employees in disseminating consumer or safety information, compared to perhaps
days for larger and less flexible systems. During
seasonal shopping times, such as the Christmas
holidays when large service requests are placed on
customer order, billing, and shipping staffs for timely
information, the expansion of information resource
systems can be handled in a flexible manner, perhaps through the rental of microcomputers, rather
then through long-term investments in dedicated
systems. Even large, long-term business activities,
such as defending the corporation against a mul-
tiyear litigation effort, can be assisted through the
use of microcomputers due to their portability and

availability.

With a growing trend toward "groupware" (software that helps manage group activities), networking of different computer systems has become even more critical to information resource strategies. Groupware keeps track of deadlines, appointments, meetings, and electronic mail. Especially important for international projects because of geographic distances and time zones, groupware can be used to manage teams temporarily formed to complete specific assignments. Microcomputers play an important role in linking all of the members together through electronic mail, and by being a general purpose computer platform for financial, word processing, and computer graphics applications.

Without transparent networking, concepts such as groupware, electronic mail, and EDI transfers will not be successful. Fortunately, consensus on a limited number of communication protocols is rapidly defining network standards for microcomputers, mini computer/mainframe systems, and fax communications. Moving away from proprietary standards and towards internationally neutral protocols, vendors and users are now adhering to OSI (open systems interconnect) software standards and common hardware components such as Ethernet, twisted-pair, fiber optics, and stranded wire. Users are now able to purchase network components from independent vendors and connect systems together at a fraction of the cost required in the early 1980s (Oliva, 1989).

From a practical standpoint, the default nature of microcomputer networks (stand-alone systems linked together) can also provide some redundancy to total network or system failures, should a unexpected maintenance problem or catastrophic disaster occur. Having data distributed throughout several computers reduces the overall impact of the situation compared to having all of the information stored in one machine, as is the case with a mini or mainframe computer.

Future Trends

Several trends that have developed during the late 1980s, because of changes in the work force, in society, and in business since the emergence of the microcomputer, are providing direction to the competitive strategies of the 1990s:

1. the trend toward integrated supplier-customer relationships
2. the trend toward fewer middle managers, with greater responsibility and involvement for each worker
3. the trend toward telecommuting rather than physical commuting
4. the trend toward using global communications to participate as part of a world economy.

Microcomputers can, and will, play increasingly critical roles in each of these areas as a part of the corporate information resources strategy. For example, automatic reorder points for material inventories from manufacturer computer system to supplier computer system through electronic communication networks is a reality at many factories throughout Japan and the United States. Manufacturers are reducing the number of suppliers they have and are increasing the involvement and quality levels required of their selected suppliers. Many times daily status information must be communicated between the two parties. The General Electric Plastics Group in Albany, New York, has built its strategic advantage around the "service/responsiveness added" concept, of which electronic linkages form an important part. Customers had requested electronic data interchange capabilities to enter their orders electronically and check order status, shipping, invoicing and billing information. General Electric believes that without providing this capability, they would have forfeited hundreds of millions of dollars in sales per year (Peters, 1987).

In another example, P-I-E Nationwide, a Jacksonville, Florida, trucking firm, developed Shipmaster software for IBM compatible microcomputers along with communications software to link P-I-E to national carriers in order to place orders and determine order shipping status electronically.

The trend toward an information-based society is becoming clear as projections now point in the direction of having one microcomputer available for every three workers by 1990 (Manzi, 1989) versus one for every five in 1990 (Dreyfuss, 1988). Company payrolls are predicted to include more than 50% white-collar workers by 1990 (Khosrowpour, 1988-89).

Microcomputers are increasingly becoming the intelligent terminal connected to the corporate mainframe, able to mix the data located in the larger system with independently formulated data, and then transmit the completed solution to other systems in the network. Just how much information will be available to examine was described by Dr. Robert Hilliard, a broadcasting specialist for the Federal Communications Commission in 1970. He said, "At the rate at which knowledge is growing, by the time the child born today graduates from college, the amount of knowledge in the world will be four times as great. By the time that same child is fifty years old, it will be 32 times as great, and 97 percent of everything known in the world will have been learned since the time he was born" (Toffler, 1970, pp.157-158).

As traffic congestion continues to choke large cities in the U.S. and as the potential labor pool shrinks, companies are experimenting with telecommuting (using telephone lines to link one computer to another computer) as an alternative to mandatory employee attendance at a central office (see Figure 6). Although not for everyone, or all the time—some workers still have to come to the office for occasional meetings—telecommuting creates significant opportunities and savings for both the employee and employer. The employee enjoys a substantial cost savings by not going into the office every day, along with some personal schedule flexibility and greater productivity due to fewer work interruptions. Typically, a fair amount of responsibility is given to each worker to plan their day and complete work assignments.

For the employer, an entire new work force is now possible via telecommuting without the need to acquire facilities for them to work in. For example, women or men with young children can stay at home and care for them while working at a microcomputer. People with physical handicaps preventing them from easily commuting to work can also work at home with a microcomputer. Retired business people can again contribute their knowledge and experience to the workplace, without the stress of commuting to the office everyday. If projections about the size of the labor force are proven correct, all of these possible worker populations, plus others, will be required to fill the workplace. It is estimated that in California by the year 2000, the primary work force of 25 to 34 year olds will decrease by 9% (Philp, 1989). With a shrinking labor pool, employers will have to look beyond their traditional hiring criteria to fill their employment needs. Another advantage to employers is that tele-commuting does not require employee proximity to the employer's office. A company in New York can have workers in Montana or Texas using microcom-puters perform the work, and then transmit the completed product or information back to the New York headquarters.

Global communications already are common among the worlds largest corporations, which have developed several private networks at tremendous expense over the past 40 years, linking their offices around the world together. Technology has now dropped the cost of global computing within the range of the average microcomputer user. For example, during the civil unrest in mainland China in 1989, students in the United States used microcomputers to transmit information and news reports to microcom-puters in China through normal direct-dial telephone lines and packet switched networks. Due to the early adoption of communication standards in the micro-computer development process, communications are almost automatic to either other microcomputers, fax machines, or larger computers. Connection into commercial networks and time-share services are also simple and accurate. Recent announcements concerning add-in processor boards for fax receipt and reproduction, and voice mail capability have only served to increase the flexibility and adaptability microcomputers can provide to users.

Emerging Technologies

The technology stage has been set for at least three major trends in microcomputer technology to carry through the 1990s and into the next century. First, the trend towards portable computers for both general purpose and specialized applications is quickly growing in terms of user acceptance and the number of manufacturers producing these machines. Compaq Computer, IBM, NEC, Toshiba, Radio Shack, Sanyo and other vendors introduced 10 laptop-style computers weighing under 10 pounds (most under 5 pounds) between 1988 and 1989. Apple Computer is rumored to have a portable MacIntosh computer under development for introduction in 1990. Several new companies are seeking to market even smaller microcomputers known as "notebooks." These microcomputers are intended for "professionals who use their systems across the traditional desktop, portable and laptop environments, [and are not...] a downsized version of any one machine,", according to H.L. Sparks (1989, p. 72), vice president of sales and marketing for Dynabook Technologies Corporation in California, the manufacturer of a $5,000 notebook size computer.

Handheld computers, typically used for inventory control purposes, are also a rapidly emerging area of microcomputer technology. About the same size as a man's fist, these computers are used as data capture and input devices using bar-code readers, credit-card readers, and voice recognition systems. The hand-helds can also radio their information to larger computer systems, creating a flexible network of low cost, accurate input devices. At least two of the most popular handhelds are capable of running MS-DOS software, with several others working to implement this capability (Pope, 1988). Interestingly, the hand-held computer vendors view the laptop computer vendors as their future competition. As laptops get cheaper and less bulky, they may merge into the handheld market. The second trend, toward more powerful microcomputers, has been established through the introduction of extremely fast micropro-cessors such as the 68030, 68040, SPARC, 88000, and i860 devices from several vendors. Many of devices operate at 33 megahertz or faster, which permits significant increases in their processing power. The SPARC chip, for example, has been measured at over 12 million instructions per second (MIPS) and costs about $200. Breakthroughs in disk drive manufacturing technology have resulted in a one gigabyte disk drive costing about $5000. In 1983, a 525-megabyte disk drive occupied three times the amount of space, was five times the weight, and had a price five times greater. Breakthroughs in inte-grated circuit design have dropped the cost of high speed modems (9600 baud) from over $5000 to under $1000 in five years.

Monitor technology will also change signifi-cantly in the next several years, due to the introduc-tion of high capacity (4 megabit) DRAM chips in 1989 and the manufacturing technology advances of gas plasma and phosphorous displays. Manufacturers are already predicting wall-size (8 by 10 feet) displays with only a few inches of depth to contain the electronics and optical lenses. Of course, costs are expected to remain high for leading edge technology. Color displays are expected to be introduced for use in laptops in the early 1990s, due to breakthroughs in battery and integrated circuit technology. The breakthroughs in batteries are needed because color monitors consume much greater amounts of power than monochromatic displays.

Changes are planned to increase the recording capacity of floppy disks and to reduce their size even further. Several Japanese vendors are working on floppy disks with a recording capacity of 100 megabytes in a standard 3 1/2 inch form factor (about 100 times the capacity of today's disks) and 50 megabytes of data on a 2-inch floppy. Already on the market as a data storage device is a 2.3 gigabyte eight millimeter tape cartridge system produced by Exabyte Corporation, which sells for about $4000.

There will be changes in memory device capacity (increasing from 1 megabit to 16 megabits); speed of long distance data communications systems (increasing from 9600 baud to 1.5 megabits); short-distance data communications (increasing from 10 megabits to 100 megabits with fiber optics); and laser printer resolution (increasing from 300 dots per inch to 1200 dots per inch) between 1990 and 1995. Specialized microcomputers having voice response and artificial intelligence abilities may become more prevalent as practical application software is created for general use.

The third trend has software integration between packages created by different vendors quickly becoming a reality through various user interface systems such as X-window, GEM, Motif, Open Windows, DEC Windows, and New Wave. These interface packages, being introduced in mid 1989, seek to unify data transfer and communications between systems from different vendors. A user will conceptually be able to cut information from a information window on a video screen, and paste it into another window on the same screen. Today, users are able to do this on systems from a single vendor such as Hewlett Packard or Sun Microsystems. Although still in the development stages, the flexibility to exchange data between systems from different venders will be available to users in the early 1990s. An example of this is the 1989 introduction of the Apple MacIntosh "Super-Drive," a floppy disk drive that permits the user to read and write diskettes in MS-DOS, OS/2 and MacIntosh formats.

Research Opportunities

Because of the extent of change existing in the microcomputer business world, tremendous opportunities for research exists for those able to understand the mix of social, political, and business issues affected by microcomputers.

In the social areas of education and employment, for example, only a very limited amount of research has been done concerning the first generation of children to have computers installed in their classrooms. A recent survey of elementary and high schools in the United States by Johns Hopkins University found 2.3 million computers installed, about one for every 20 students. There has been a tenfold increase in the number of computers available to students below the college level since 1983. Fifty percent of the elementary schools using microcomputers in their educational programs reported computers had increased enthusiasm for the subjects being taught; 35% reported computers had increased enthusiasm for the school; and about 30% reported computers offered greater opportunities for independent work (Berger, 1989).

Did exposure to microcomputers give children an advantage over those not exposed to computers? Did the children increase their grade point averages in college? Have these children made contributions to business and society sooner than their peers who did not have computers in their elementary classrooms? A multitude of questions needs research and practical answers to establish exactly what impact microcomputers have made on children's education during the past 10 years; and a population is now available for study by researchers.

In the area of politics, research is lacking on the effect of microcomputers on different levels of society. Has the introduction of microcomputers created different strata of society—the computer literate and the noncomputer literate? This may lead to permanent economic handicaps and career growth to those not computer fluent. Will competency with computers be used as a discrimination criteria? Will the lack of computer literary become a bonafide handicap, such as a medical or physical problem?

How will society solve the problem of retraining employees who find their jobs suddenly altered or obsolete by new technology? Where do they go? What will they do? Is it in the best interest of business or society to retrain these people to make them computer literate or to relegate them forever to being technology illiterate? Hopefully the answer is to retrain them and permit them to reenter the job market once again. For example, Apple Computer has created interactive video training microcomputer environments that integrate computer graphics with text and sound to actually show students how products work or how they can be repaired.

From a business perspective, will corporations be judged as progressive organizations if they do not provide or subsidize employees' access to microcomputers? Will corporate raiders evaluate the percentage of installed microcomputers from a competitive advantage viewpoint and not an asset viewpoint? Will corporations be forced to donate obsolete microcomputers to local schools as a condition of business in the community? Should state and federal governments require corporations to provide computer training classes to all employees who want them, similar to English as a second language classes now being conducted?

There is a growing reluctance among pregnant workers to using video display monitors due to the fear of birth defects. Employers have usually accommodated requests by these workers to move into positions not requiring the use of video monitors until the baby's birth; but what happens when a business does not have the freedom to do this? As sophisticated imaging systems (which use video monitors to display information) are developed and introduced in the future, paper records will gradually disappear. How will employers deal with the fear of video terminals or other electronic technology in the workplace as employees learn more about the various invisible signals emitted by computers? All these questions open important areas of research for the future of microcomputers.

Summary

The microcomputer has overcome the fear, uncertainty, and doubt originally surrounding its introduction and has forever changed the shape and manner of computing. As a critical element in the information resource strategic plan, the microcomputer has created opportunities for strategic advantage and personal productivity heretofore available only through mini computers or mainframe computers, or not available at all, as with many computer graphics, desktop publishing, or engineering packages. Users of microcomputers have established new levels of personal involvement in the technology, as well as in the introduction of these systems into the business environment, oftentimes ignoring or bypassing established corporate policies to be able to use their system at work.

As competition increases on a worldwide basis, microcomputers are creating new ways of bridging the differences in distance, time zones, cultures, and languages to create opportunities not possible before, and to share knowledge between people no matter where they are. The human side of microcomputing is changing ever so slowly to adapt to the constant breakthroughs in technology, which has permitted people to be more productive. The increasing availability of computers in classrooms is helping to introduce children to the microcomputer so they can become comfortable with the technology and its potential.

The introduction and acceptance of the microcomputer has been compared to the introduction of the steam engine, the telephone, and the airplane. It is perhaps all of these combined with the radio, television and space ship. As the world society becomes ever more integrated and dependent on information technology, the question will be asked: "How did society ever progress this far without the microcomputer?"

References

Altman, J. (1989). Rank Video gets the movies out via manufacturing software. *MIS Week* (July 24), *10*(29), 11.

Berger, J. (1989). Classroom computers prevalent. *San Jose Mercury News* (August 27), p. 8F.

Bulkeley, W.M. (1989). Computer gurus cast their eyes toward tomorrow's hot machines. *The Wall Street Journal Centennial Edition* (June 23), p. A15.

Dreyfuss, J. (1988). Catching the computer wave. *Fortune Magazine* (September 26), *118*(7), 78-82.

Drucker, P. (1980). Quoted in a speech by N.B. Hannay, vice president, Research and Patents, Bell Laboratories, at Northwestern University (March 5), Evanston, IL.

Forsythe, J. (1989). Systems give Pepperidge Farms freshness. *Information Week* (March 20), 29-31.

Hayes-Roth, frederick. (1984) The machine as partner of the new professional. IEEE Spectrum (June), 21(6), 28-31.

Khosrowpour, M. (1988-1989). Office automation as a managerial tool: The underlying importance of education. *Journal of Educational Technology Systems, 17*(1), 79-87.

Manzi, J. (1989). Interview. *Computer Systems News/Business Outlook* (January), 28.

Miller, M.W. (1989). A brave new world: Streams of 1s and 0s. *The Wall Street Journal Centennial Edition* (June 23), p. A15.

Naisbitt, J. (1982). *Megatrends.* New York: Warner Books, Inc.

Nelson, T. (1989). Interview. *The Wall Street Journal Centennial Edition* (June 23), A15.

Nolan, R.L. (1984). The PC phenomenon and strategic guidelines. *Letter to Management - Stage by Stage* (Spring) 4(1), 1.

Nolan Norton Institute, (1989). The shape of things. MIS Week (July 24), 10(29), 25.

Oliva, L.M., (1989). Why standards are so important to CIM. *Conference Proceedings from Autofact '89, Society of Manufacturing Engineers*, Dearborn, MI.

Peters, T. (1987). *Thriving On Chaos: Handbook FOR a Management Revolution.* New York: Knopf.

Philp, T. (1989). Jobs will overmatch workers, study says. *San Jose Mercury News* (May 17), p. F-1.

Pope, G.T. (1988). The booming market For handheld computers. *Information Week* (October 17), 37-40.

Porter, M.E. (1980). *Competitive strategy.* New York: The Free Press.

Sparks, H.L. (1989). Interview. *Computer Systems News* (July 31), 72.

Sullivan, Nick. (1988). Home and office worlds merge. *Home-Office Computing* (Sept.), 6(9), 38-39.

Toffler, A. (1970). *Future shock.* New York: Random House.

Zuboff, S. (1988). Interview. *Fortune Magazine,* (September 26), 82.

Part II
Managing
Microcomputer
Technology

The constant evolution of the information technology has made it necessary for managers to update their management strategies to deal with the new and future business challenge. Darold Klauk (A Methodology for Microcomputer Planning and Deployment) argues that the present state of mismanagement of microcomputer technology in some organizations today does not necessarily point to management incompetency. He presents a model to assist managers in their daily tasks by understanding the complexity of issues, including planning, costing, utility, benefits, and life-expectancies of equipment. For small businesses, Elia Chepaitis (Critical Success Factors in the Integration of Microcomputer Technology into Expanding Organizations: Five Case Studies) outlines the Critical Success Factors (CSF) approach to management. It is a method of integrating a micro-based information system (MBIS) that discusses effective information resource management through information sharing. In recent years, desktop publishing has created a new challenge for organization management. Wallace Wood and Robert Behling (Managing the Introduction of Information Systems Techology: The Case of Desktop Publishing as an Organization-Wide Resource) outline how establishing organizational standards, such as budgeting and operating procedures, can lead to a smooth operation and control of this growing new technology.

Chapter 3

A METHODOLOGY FOR MICROCOMPUTER PLANNING AND DEPLOYMENT

Darold R. Klauk
The Consulting Team, Inc.

Frequently, business managers are required to make hasty and difficult decisions regarding the purchase and deployment of microcomputers. All too often these decisions are based on scant knowledge of the subject. Symptoms exist within many organizations indicating many of today's microcomputer environments are not properly managed. This is primarily due to the many managers who are unprepared to manage microcomputers, or micro-manage, a term from Geis & Kuhn (1987). Yet, some managers are prepared; some think they are prepared; still others readily admit they're not. Because of the broad and profound impact microcomputers are having on organizations, this environment should no longer remain unmanaged. Managers should begin to realize they must not only get more directly involved in the oversight process but must also begin to understand and use microcomputers. The world of information technology is one of constant change; even those managers who think they are in control of this environment today must continually assess their strategies. Managers will not always be able to rely on past strategies to resolve future business problems.

This lack of managing does not necessarily imply management incompetency. The issues are more complex and challenging today comapred to managing computer technologies during the '60s and '70s. Today, many managers simply do not have the necessary command of the technologies to manage effectively. This is due to the: (1) rapid rate of changes in information technologies, (2) decentralization of authority and responsibility to the department level, and (3) rise in microcomputer proficiency among staff, that is, end user computing. Indeed, today's office environment has changed radically. The influx of microcomputers has caused social and organizational upheavals and, as such, presents new and serious challenges to managers. Toffler, (1985) in his third of four summary viewpoints on organizational change and planning, states: "there is a planning need for multi-dimensional models that interrelate forces— technological, social, political, even cultural, along with the economic." (p. 18) Business managers must begin to recognize the need to understand the complexity and importance of the issues of microcomputers. These include planning, costing, utility, benefits, and life-expectancies as they impact an organization's workforce, its financial posture, and, therefore, the fate of the enterprise.

Curiously, in spite of huge corporate-wide outlays for microcomputers (in many cases, millions of dollars annually), few organizations require purchasing justifications and, likely even less do follow-up cost/benefit studies. Moreover, few organizations inventory their microcomputers and components nor do they consider these items depreciable. Because of this, would it not be appropriate to have some methodology that assesses the microcomputer purchasing and allocation practices within your organization? For example, are you, and your organization as a whole, making the most of the microcomputer investment? Are your users provided with the most appropriate computing tools? Is it time to start discarding the older model PC/XTs? Should your organization stop buying the nest-generation model ATs and start buying the latest model 80386/80486s? In short, is there a strategy in place within your firm to enable you, as a business manager, to make well-founded decisions regarding the placement of the right microcomputers in the hands of the right users at the right times? In many instances, the answer is no. Management, however, continues to approve requests for new microcomputers thereby continuing a commitment to invest. Indeed, the overall investment can be overwhelming in size and startling in scope as human resource factors are included in the microcomputer-expense equation.

The rationale for a course of action to continue purchasing microcomputers without detailed analyses seems to be that the industry, as a whole, has determined microcomputers to be the "productivity tools of choice" as well as "commodity" purchase items. While a general philosophy that microcomputers play a significant role in the realization of organizational goals is sound, further thought should be given to why they are needed; where they are needed; and who specifically needs them; ergo, the need for a management methodology. Organizations originally began purchasing microcomputers simply to fill a void, which was (and still is) the inability of mainframe DP Centers to meet users' needs. Because of this, users have demanded local computerization. With advances in DOS-based microcomputers now into a third generation (i.e., 32-bit technologies), the initial attitude of buying simply to computerize is no longer valid. Managers should start buying to optimize. They should be taking advantage of the capabilities of newer microcomputers by buying for the power users and redeploying existing and usable microcomputers to others in the organization with lesser needs. The challenge for managers, then, is to systematically and cost-effectively plan for and deploy its microcomputers—a challenging task indeed. Do you have such a plan of action?

Chapter Focus

There is ample information in print regarding the processes of strategic business planning and information systems/technology planning. There is considerably less concerning microcomputer planning, specifically, as it relates to hardware purchases and subsequent deployment. This chapter addresses this last planning activity through the development of the Microcomputer Planning and Deployment Methodology (MPDM) for, in this case, IBM-compatible, DOS-based microcomputers. (The MPDM, however, is easily adaptable to other manufacturers' computer products as well.) Described within are three generic paradigms: the Planning Model, Acquisition and Deployment Model, and Costing Model. From these, managers may apply organization-specific microcomputer "profiles" to produce customized models which, collectively, comprise a multi-year, microcomputer management plan.

The Planning Model is the essence of the MPDM and will be discussed at length. Business managers can use the Planning Model as a generic, yet sufficiently detailed, approach to realizing optimal, long-term microcomputer purchases and deployment. The Acquisition and Deployment Model is developed from the Planning Model and specifies, in summary form, the numbers and types of microcomputers to be acquired annually during the term of the plan. The Costing Model is the final step in this three-step process and is developed using the Acquisition and Deployment Model summary information, to present annual cost projections. Structured for ease in preparation and modification, these models provide summary information in appropriate formats for management analysis.

For this chapter, "customized" Planning, Acquisition and Deployment, and Costing Models are developed and based on the current microcomputer environment within the State of South Carolina. This microcomputer "profile" (used later by example) has been extracted from data collected from a recent survey. By applying the suggested concept and models toward the development of a five-year microcomputer plan for your organization, you will indeed find yourself managing your microcomputer environment.

Addressing Your Interests

During the Eighties, many managers dealt lightly with the use and management of microcomputers; others developed workable strategies. However, these strategies will likely have to undergo change or be scrapped in the Nineties. Therefore, managers should begin to look for new tools and methods to manage their microcomputer environments. Not new, but necessary, is management's commitment to "planning," a first step toward the realization of the difficult and complex challenge of managing information technologies. A key point here is that the commitment to plan should not begin with a specific microcomputer plan but with a long-range strategic business plan. The business plan should then be followed and supplemented by a long-range strategic information systems plan consistent with the business plan. Once these major tasks have been addressed, work should begin on the development of a plan to manage microcomputers. Figure 1 presents a conceptual perspective of such a plan and its relationship to other strategic plans within an organization.

The methodology presented is useful separately by a unit manager(s) or, ideally, used by all managers within an organization. An enterprise's strategic technology planning flow is depicted in Figure 1A. Step 1 suggests a downward flow of corporate "direction". The models developed from this planning methodology would then be summarized upward through the management levels (Step 2 in Figure 1A) arriving at one consolidated, integrated view of the microcomputer plan for the enterprise.

All levels of management should benefit from acceptance and participation in the general planning concept and, specifically in this context, information technology planning. In his work on information system [microcomputer] planning, Martin (1988) identifies some of the major benefits available to the various levels of management through the planning process. He suggests that executive management benefits from planning through (a) the assessment and adaptation of a strategic business plan over a five-

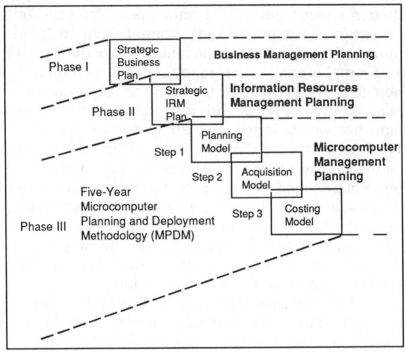

**Figure 1: Relationship of the MPDM to Other Enterprise
Strategic Plans**

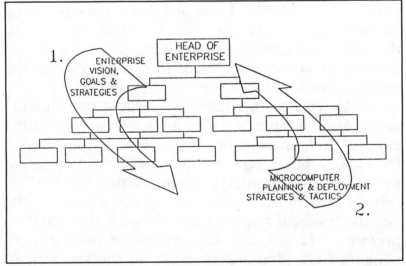

Figure 1A: Enterprise-wide Strategic Technology-planning Flow

year period; and (b) by approaching a planning effort logically to arrive at a business solution that permits an early return on the Information Systems investment. Functional and Operational management should benefit from planning by (a) assessing computing goals and problems logically and (b) realizing that top management is involved in this process. Martin suggests Information Systems managers can benefit through (a) effective communication; (b) top management support and interest; and (c) better planning of the systems needed to meet specific business goals.

The Impact of Microcomputers

The Microcomputer Revolution

Imagine an office with only a typewriter and an adding machine. There is no desktop computer, no color monitor, and no high-speed printer. Further imagine an office where the only link to the world of computers is through rigidly-defined software using single-function, monochrome terminals connected to the Data Processing (DP) Center's centrally-controlled main computer. Support for all users of these technologies rests entirely on the DP Center staff—by default.

Today, offices are populated with an assortment of multi-functional, high-performance microcomputer-based products. These include computer printers, scanners, and facsimile devices, to name a few. Most users of these products have non-technical backgrounds but, regardless, are able to produce work products which once were the sole responsibility of the DP Center. Moreover, office workers are now able to support other office workers to resolve technical problems— no longer is there complete reliance on the DP Center.

Unforeseen and uncontrolled growth. In the late '70s, advances in Very Large-Scale Integration (VLSI) technology facilitated the introduction of microcomputers into offices. As a result of this infusion, offices were, in a word, revolutionized. Offices changed physically, functionally, socially and organizationally. According to Geis & Kuhn (1987) in a simple, yet profound, statement: "the real personal computer revolution is more organizational than numerical, more managerial than mathematical, more behavioral than analytical." (pref. v) Unfortunately, management in the Eighties underestimated the magnitude of this revolution and, therefore, were not able to foresee problems. Thus, many managers now struggle to keep afloat as the new wave of microcomputer technologies and users carries momentum into the Nineties.

Not unique, are organizations encountering problems managing their microcomputer environments. Operationally, symptoms include the proliferation of different brands; the absence, in most cases, of a microcomputer inventory; an inadequate or non-existent user training program; and redundant or unsynchronized data bases, to cite a few. With microcomputers influencing all levels of organizations in some manner, no area is untouched. On the administrative side, a lack of managing permeates in the planning, acquisition, and deployment activities inherent in a microcomputer environment.

Smaller, faster, and cheaper solutions. PC WEEK (1990) published a series of articles as background information on Intel Corporation's family of X86 microprocessors specifically regarding their introduction of the 80486 processor. By way of history, the following summary is presented to emphasize the tremendous advances in technological design and performance from the late '70s.

• 1978: the 8086 chip technology was introduced with a 16-bit architecture, a microprocessor clock speed of 8MHZ, 1Mbyte of memory-address space and packed with 29,000 transistors. This was followed in 1979 with a 16/8-bit version, the 8088.

• 1984:   the 80286 was introduced with full 16-bit architecture, clock speeds of 10MHZ and 12MHZ, 16Mbyte memory-address space, packing 130,000 transistors.

• 1985:   the 32-bit 80386 technology was introduced and could accommodate a 4 gigabyte memory-address space, run at 16, 20, 25 or 33MHZ, with 275,000 transistors on a single chip. A 80386SX version was introduced with a 32/16-bit architecture.

• 1989:   the 80486 chip was also based on 32-bit architecture; processor speeds of 25MHZ and 33MHZ; on-board co-processor; 8Kbytes of internal cache memory; on-board memory management; 4 gigabytes of addressable memory space; on-chip multiprocessor support; and 1.2 million transistors on a chip.

• In the very near future: the next generation of Intel X86 family of processors, the 80586, is expected to enhance on-board functionality of the 80486 and be packed with 4-5 million transistors.

Of significance are the astonishing advances in hardware chip technology— but not at the risk of jeopardizing software compatibility, at least upward. House (1990) set the tone for future releases of the Intel X86 family of processors by stating: "one of the things a lot of users don't understand is that the 386 represents an architectural platform that we're going to live with forever." (p. S/14) This represents a profound statement of technological direction for all involved in the microcomputer industry. Because of the anticipated long-life of the 80386 architecture: (a) software developers benefit from a stable architecture; (b) users benefit having software developers focus on these products; and (c) managers are able to plan knowing the stability of awareness of the key element (software compatibility) in their future business/technical equation.

Microcomputers eased their way into offices, in part, because of manufacturers' abilities to package microcomputers with small "footprints." Because of this, microcomputers and microcomputer-based accessory products (e.g., printers and scanners) were able to be desktop-mounted as opposed to backroom-hidden. These products consumed little office space thereby making their acceptance more appealing. These products also enabled end users in the business units to produce reports faster than, and independently from, the DP Center. Microcomputers also appealed to management as the cost to computerize declined significantly from the traditional mainframe and minicomputer offerings. As an example of the overall advances in the microcomputer industry, the IBM PC was introduced in 1981 at a retail price of $1,595 - $2,000 for a 16K-64K RAM, 16-bit processor with a single floppy-diskette and monochrome monitor. Today, a "clone" 80386 microcomputer (a full 32-bit; 33MHZ processor), 65MB of hard drive, 4MB of

RAM, and a Super-VGA monitor can be purchased in the $3,500 price range— a higher sticker price from that in 1981 but, unquestionably, greater value for the dollar.

Growth in the numbers of installed microcomputers, seemingly exponential to many managers during the Eighties, is now a major management issue for the Nineties. Indeed, the numbers suggest that management should be concerned. March (1990) indicated, from the results of a recent IDC Corporation report, 456,000 units were shipped worldwide by U. S. firms in 1980. This number climbed to 9,138,000 during 1985 with estimates of 15,000,000 units in 1990. These numbers translate to $1.7 billion in sales in 1980, $20 billion in 1985 and an estimated $43 billion in 1990. Sales of microcomputer software to businesses also soared, jumping from $176.5 million in 1982 to a projected $4.8 billion by 1990.

Most in the industry would agree the primary reason for the influx of microcomputers into our offices in the Eighties was the business applicability of the spreadsheet, a truly practicable software package filling a much-needed demand to automate specific numerical- and computational-intensive office tasks (typically, the budgeting process). The spreadsheet virtually, and, in some cases, literally, transformed the microcomputer from the home toy to the office necessity. Word Processing software certainly did its share to enhance microcomputer acceptance in the office as did multi-functional software products such as Data Base Management Systems, Graphics, Project Managers, and Desktop Publishing.

The People Revolution

For the past several years, the office workforce has been moving from total dependence on the DP

Center to increasing independence. Office workers are now "rolling up their sleeves" to deliver on management expectations of increased worker productivity using microcomputer-based office tools. Persistent, however, is the DP Center's aloof attitude toward non-DP microcomputer users; instilling a new focus in these users. Of significance, is that users have become their own problem-solvers. This is particularly evident in their knowledge of application software products used to achieve departmental missions. For instance, users have become proficient in spreadsheet template development, multi-functional word processing, and data base application programming.

Because of this hands-on experience, office workers are now able to communicate with the DP Center staff, using once-cryptic, unfamiliar jargon. With newly-acquired skills, users now speak the "technical lingo" and are often able to deal directly with software manufacturers for problem resolution, thereby strengthening their independence from the internal DP staff. This freedom has not come without a price, however; an issue to be discussed later.

Today's office workers are armed with (a) an ability to understand the technical jargon and (b) the inspiration of knowing they are able to produce work that, in the past, has been the sole purview of the DP Center. As a result, users now feel they "have a voice" and, to a certain extent, provide input to department planning and budgeting cycles. Oliva & Khosrowpour (1989) indicate that "users have played increasingly important roles in defining the future directions of microcomputer technology and directing how management should deploy this technology in the organization". (p. 3) This is relatively new territory for users, that is, participatory management. Naisbitt, (1984) in the second edition of his book, Megatrends, feels that people want a share in the decision-making process if their lives are affected by that decision— which in this context has application in the world of microcomputers. He goes on to project a change in the very core of our value system, particularly in corporations with a trend toward greater employee rights and worker participation in this type of work ethic.

Thompson (1985) stated that: "The first wave [of the computer revolution] focused on the use of information technology to replace people; now we are more concerned with supporting people. We are moving from the automation of structured tasks of the first 10 to 15 years of the computer revolution into the support of unstructured tasks, the support of managerial activity." (p. 3)

The Management Evolution

Traditionally, business managers resolved their business-related issues with additional staff and dollars. Today, however, managers must begin to realize a need to assess the advantages of incorporating information technologies to help solve business problems. With the complexity of their decision-making processes increasing, managers simply must play a more active role in their microcomputer environment. The time has come for managers to come to grips with the enterprise-wide impact of microcomputers; no longer are the major issues simply task automation and high-speed computations. Perry (1987) succinctly postulates in his opening statement that: "the one item that will not exist in the office of the future is the manager who cannot operate his or her own workstation". (p. 1) His work is specifically targeted toward those managers who are ready to use microcomputers. Diebold (1985) suggests that the question for the future should be: can we afford not to have a computer on every desk?

While the direct use of microcomputers by all managers within an organization is unrealistic in the near-term, use by all managers should be a long-term goal of the organization. Reiterated throughout the industry, is the attitude that the initial endorsement and continued support of an internal program dedicated to the use of microcomputers by managers must start at the top— with the heads of organizations. Behaviors and attitudes toward microcomputer use by lower-level managers (and staff) will be greatly influenced through top-level sponsorship and use.

Contributing to the realization of this goal will be the infusion of future generations of managers who have had exposure to microcomputers as early as grammar school. As they infiltrate management ranks, they will not be asking why they should be using microcomputers at work; they will be asking what else can be done using microcomputers— and not only at work but also on the road and at home! McNurlin & Sprague (1989) expand on this by introducing the need for "logical offices" to accommodate managers and staff who have more than one microcomputer and who are required to be away from the office frequently because of travel. Opportunistic managers realize the advantages of hands-on use of microcomputers. Accepted are the headaches (literally, to some) that are an integral part of using microcomputers; recognized are the advantages which far outweigh the disadvantages.

Other key microcomputer management skills required in the '90s include the ability to be creative and imaginative, as well as a risk-taker. Geis & Kuhn indicated that "creative and innovative management, almost by definition, defies up-front quantification and early verification." (p. 97) Creativity and innovation should be fostered, they go on to say. They developed the concept of promoting creativity and innovation through four principles. Paraphrasing, these principles include: (1) emphasizing the risk in the risk-reward ratio; (2) providing an environment fostering freedom and flexibility; (3) facilitating creative personalities; and (4) implementing some basic creativity-generating techniques amplified using microcomputers.

While full-scale use of microcomputers by business managers is a sound objective, today's managers still must rely on a microcomputer support staff. This staff should not only be performing the routine tasks of text and data entry, but also the more complex and time consuming tasks of data base programming and spreadsheet template development. Managers should, for the most part, be utilizers of the information generated for and presented to them until "manager-friendly" software becomes available and cost-effective— sometime later this decade.

Individually, today's managers are faced with this task of assessing their current and future roles within their organizations but also determining their personal desires to commit to understand and use microcomputers. Peer competition will undoubtedly heighten in the future. A hurdle to overcome by many of today's managers is their attitude toward peer and sub-ordinate ranking. Managers must "get into the trenches" with others and begin to realize the importance of knowing as much or more about microcomputers. Moreover, as the computer knowledge and skills of department staff increase, wouldn't it be personally prudent and organizationally beneficial, as the manager, to keep abreast?

Are You Managing Your Microcomputers?

Being Aware of the Issues

Let there be no doubt: despite a lack of adequate managing, microcomputers and end user computing are essential to an organization's well-being as are people and capital. Moreover, the linking of microcomputers is the next logical step. LANs (Local Area Networks), however, present an additional set of issues which are beyond the scope of this particular work. Staying competitive, by itself, should be sufficient motivation to firms to continue its investment in these areas. Since firms can no longer exist without microcomputers, isn't it time to understand how to exist with them and to assess what makes the microcomputer environment difficult to manage? In short, just what are the issues facing managers?

Table 1 identifies seven major areas of concern promulgated by difficulties in managing microcomputer environments. These areas are not mutually exclusive; that is, each has the potential to affect another. As examples, misuse of applications software can potentially result in unreliable data bases across the enterprise; unplanned microcomputer system, software, and component purchases will impact the firm's technical support and user training programs.

In the first area, Costs, managers should be concerned about the (1) initial/one-time, (2) follow-on, and (3) hidden microcomputer costs. Initial costs are typically proposed to management as one-time

A. Costs • Initial • Follow-on • Hidden **B. Support** • Technical • Applications **C. Authority and Control** • Central Management Function • I/S vs. Business Department **D. Technical Limitations** • Functional Obsolescence • Memory Restrictions	**E. Organizational Autonomy** • Interdepartmental Competition • Individuality vs. Teamwork **F. Utilization** • Training • Abuse • Management Expectations • Matching Needs to Performance **G. Data Integrity** • Updating • Archiving/Retrieving • Auditing

Table 1: Management Issues Involving Microcomputers

hardware expenditures. Presented in this manner, management is not forewarned of additional microcomputer expenditures making the budget-management process difficult. Follow-on costs include user application software, networking hardware, utility software, and expansion memory, to name a few. Hidden costs include items such as contracted maintenance, ad hoc repairs, formal user training, and microcomputer-related seminars and travel. Keen & Woodman (1984) note that a $3,000 investment in a microcomputer represents a small risk whereas a $15 million investment in 5,000 microcomputers clearly is a risk. Their example indicates that the initial cost of a single microcomputer can easily triple or quadruple when additional costs are realized. Without an enterprise-wide microcomputer plan, it is difficult to control and budget for these types of expenditures. An essential element of such a plan is the development of a detailed inventory of microcomputers (including related technologies) and their utilization levels. More on this subject later.

The Support issue reveals management concerns on two major fronts: technical and applications. First, the ability to be able to provide adequate technical support fades due to the proliferation of different brands of microcomputers and related hardware and software. An internal support technical group should be expected to be proficient in a limited number of products—not the universe of said. A second concern lies in applications development. Because of decentralization and departmentalization, end user computing (EUC) resulted in individual, local application development and continues to thrive.

While beneficial, EUC does introduce problems for managers. One of these is the lack of formal programming skills of those users who develop their own applications. Application programs developed by non-technical users, in many cases, suffer in responsiveness, computational performance, and user-friendliness. Also lacking is system and user documentation, which is not normally done by the technically unskilled, untrained end user, potentially making future program modifications difficult.

Machrone (1990) talks about discussions emanating from a recent forum of MIS executives. It was noted at this forum that "all of our attendees admitted that end-user computing was essentially out of control, that departments controlled their own budgets, and therefore their own selections." Machrone recaps the group's views on purchasing microcomputers: "they [MIS executives] really had no idea how many PCs they had or what brands." (p. 69). Business managers will experience these problems unless they begin using a planning methodology to help them manage their microcomputer acquisitions and users.

Authority and Control are additional concerns for business managers. As one example, who in the organization should be responsible to plan for and approve microcomputer purchases? In the past, technology purchases were handled by a central group, typically, the DP Center. This group was solely responsible for determining those technologies needed by the entire organization and when they were needed. Having such control, the areas of responsibility for technical support were well-defined. However, with the advent of decentralization, the microcomputer, and EUC, "control" has gained new meaning. This issue also raised personal and departmental conflicts regarding authority, responsibility, and the alignment and synchronization of work-efforts among departments within the organization.

Technical Limitations potentially presents problems for managers because they are the catalysts toward end user demand for more powerful and faster microcomputers. These limitations surface from end users as (a) functional obsolescence and (b) lack of computing power. Either, or both, limitations strain company budgets and frustrate managers. These restrictions are real and should be viewed, in one sense, as positive signs that users are likely making optimum use of their microcomputers. The key to optimum use is to instill creativity of this nature to other office staff. One way to accomplish this is through microcomputer recycling thereby potentially rejuvenating those users seemingly "stuck" with older microcomputers. It is here where a systematic approach to microcomputer deployment is essential and is the essence of the Microcomputer Planning and Deployment Methodology addresses.

Still another potential problem, Organizational Autonomy, can result from a lack of upper-management commitments to direction-setting for an organization. Without such commitments and directions, departments function autonomously competing with sister departments for enterprise resources. A sense of urgency results to purchase "before the money runs out." But surely, this is not the proper course of action. These department managers, unaware of organizational policies and guidelines for microcomputer purchases, likely make decisions befitting their particular needs. A formal, documented and coordinated plan of action with enterprise-wide acceptance, would discourage departmental autonomy— for the sake of organizational goals and strategies.

Utilization issues arise as microcomputers are purchased and assigned to office workers. High expectations emanate from managers for immediate increases in worker productivity. Little thought may have gone into the need for formal/informal user training. Moreover, formal training may be appropriate for some but not for others. It simply does not make good business sense to invest significant amounts of money in microcomputer hardware and software unless users' skill levels are equally enhanced. Utilization issues also address individual computer resource needs. A potential problem occurs as assigned microcomputers do not match users' needs or skills. Without continual attention to individual utilization requirements, many users outgrow their computer resources while others have more resources than are necessary for the tasks they perform.

Similarly, it does not make good business sense to permit high-salaried managers to devote excessive amounts of their normal business hours developing spreadsheets or data base programs; these are programmer and business analyst tasks. Hands-on use by these professionals does not necessarily mean full-time use! Managers should manage and should be "second-hand utilizers" of microcomputers. That is, managers should be the true end users of microcomputers by analyzing and taking action on the information produced by staff using microcomputers. However, this is not suggesting managers should be discouraged from hands-on use of microcomputers. To the contrary, managers must exhibit creativity, experimentation and risk (as noted earlier) but are cautioned to monitor their business-hours use of microcomputers and adjust as appropriate.

Lastly, management issues of Data Integrity surface from a lack of formal procedures for data entry, updating, archiving/retrieving, and auditing. For example, the misuse of application software can directly affect the integrity of information— especially across departments because of unplanned and uncoordinated data base updating practices. This can result in bad management decisions through the use of bad data. For spreadsheets, periodic and automatic auditing is necessary to help improve the accuracy of calculations and validity of resultant business decisions. Moreover, outdated data can result from improper archiving and retrieving practices involving inconsistent data sets/files/structures.

Sumner & Klepper (1987) conducted an end user computing survey looking at different management strategies for EUC. Among other results, the survey indicated that fewer than 20 percent of the users surveyed had developed controls, back-up and recovery methods, and data security procedures.

Are You Asking the Right (or Any) Questions?

Some of the more timely and critical technical questions which ought to be asked within organizations include the following:

• When should 80386s and 80486s be purchased?

• What should be done with the older microcomputers: the PCs, XTs, and ATs?

• When should laser printers begin replacing matrix printers?

• Should all users have color monitors? If not, which users should have color monitors? If yes, what monitor resolution(s) and graphics standards should be adopted?

• Which graphics, spreadsheet, data base, word processors, utilities, etc. packages should be purchased? Are other divisions/departments already using any of these?

These acquisition-related questions should provoke interest from managers to consider other microcomputer issues. Thought should also be given to the more enterprise-wide issues of microcomputer management. Highly recommended is the establishment of a central planning and approval point to formulate policies and strategies regarding the following issues. Managers, at various levels, should be considering how to find answers to the following:

• Should technical standards and guidelines be established for the organization? If so, who decides what these should be?

• At what point in time, and with which technologies, should the firm's microcomputer users be linked to each other into a Local Area Network?

• What is (should be) the role of the DP Center regarding departmental and end user computing? Should mainframe applications be "downsized" to LANs?

• Is there a need for a centrally-operated Information Center or should support staff be dispersed and directly assigned to the departments?

• Is it appropriate to pursue a hardware volume-discount purchasing contract?

• Is there a need for software site-licenses?

• Who should monitor the overall microcomputing activities as these affect the organization as a whole?

Being able, or at least being organized properly, to begin to answer these and similar questions is essential if an organization is truly committed to managing its microcomputers and other information technologies. Specifically, this chapter addresses the commitment to manage microcomputers for the sake of the enterprise. A survey conducted by the American Management Association with the results published in 1988 on End User/Departmental Computing identified a key issue of this phenomenon, as it impacts the organization as a whole. Identified earlier as Organizational Autonomy, their report states: "There is a real danger that while each department may be doing its own computing tasks well, the enterprise as a whole may suffer from lack of coordination and missed opportunities." The report goes on to suggest the need for a central, senior management authority, a Chief Information Officer (CIO) or similarly titled position, as the function within the organization to "marshall the company's information resources to support its strategic and operational goals." (p. 8)

Gerrity & Rockart (1986) identify five elements that should be addressed by management to proactively and strategically manage end user computing. Three of these are directly applicable to this discussion. In addition to the requirement for centralized policies, they suggest: (1) developing a statement of direction on end user computing; (2) looking at the enterprise's goals by taking a broader view of computing; and (3) coordinating end user support under one manager or management function.

The Microcomputer Planning and Deployment Methodology: Describing the Three-Step Process

The Planning Model

The Planning Model is the essence and first step of the Microcomputer Planning and Deployment Methodology (MPDM). The MPDM represents a logical and systematic approach to enable business managers to address problems related to the planning, costing and deployment of microcomputers. Marchand (1990) states that the pace of "Information technology is changing so quickly that if you don't have an ongoing planning process you aren't going to be able to keep up with the shifts and changes that you have to adapt to in a marketplace just to be able to deploy the technology adequately." (p. 41)

Further emphasis on the need for technology planning is shown by Applegate, Cash & Mills (1988) as they point out that "new technology is more powerful, more diverse, and increasingly entwined with the organization's critical business processes. Continuing to merely react to new technology and the organizational change it triggers could throw a business into a tailspin." (p. 128)

Several techniques were incorporated to arrive at the generic Planning Model (Table 6). This microcomputer acquisition and deployment scheme aids in determining the unique timing of the decision-points for microcomputer "purchasing, recycling and discarding" of various models over time. The recommendations specified in the generic Planning Model regarding these events should not be viewed as fixed. The model presented should be analyzed carefully as it is applied to your particular organization. For instance, your organization likely will have its own goals regarding the timing of the phasing out of the XT and AT models and the purchase of the SX and 80386 technologies. Similarly, you may have your own projections regarding the timeframes for "desktop" readiness of the 80486 and 80586 microcomputers.

Other considerations should include: (a) your current microcomputer inventory; (b) your user types;

(c) the "value" of your existing microcomputers; (d) the extent of standardization within your organization; and (e) the business and information systems goals of your organization. (As an aid to the reader, Figure 2 presents the recommended sequence of activities in the development of this three-step process. These activities culminate in the generation of planning and costing summaries for short- and long-term management and financial analyses and forecasting.)

The second step of this methodology, the Acquisition and Deployment Model, entails the transformation of the generic Planning Model information into specific numbers and types of microcomputers projected to be purchased, recycled, and discarded annually, over a five-year timeframe. The third step of this planning process, the Costing Model, enables manag-

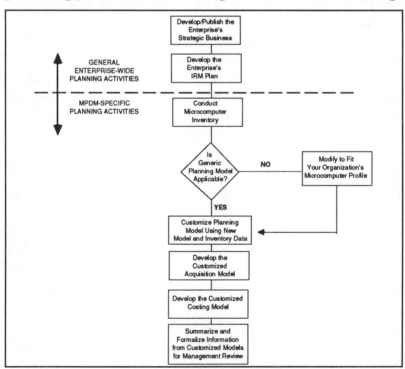

Figure 2: MPDM Activity Flow

ers to develop and summarize a multi-year budgeting plan using the conclusions and data developed through steps 1 and 2.

The Acquisition and Deployment, and Costing Models represent the implementation of a customized Planning Model. This is demonstrated by example using the general microcomputer profile information of the State of South Carolina. The purpose of this example is to demonstrate that (a) the theory behind the Planning Model has practical applicability; and (b) a methodology and related guidelines are now available to managers. By adopting the approaches presented and adjusting the details to fit your organization, you will find yourself managing microcomputers!

By design, the Planning Model of the MPDM is a subset of an Information Systems Plan and, therefore, should be in concert with, and supportive of, that plan. This model is not a singular solution and does not purport to be a precise methodology. To the contrary, it has been designed as a flexible and adjustable paradigm with the intent to accommodate (a) the changing world of information technologies; (b) a changing workforce; and (c) the unique and changing profiles of organizations. Several important considerations are described in the next section and summarized in Table 2 to aid in the understanding of the construction of the Planning Model.

Development Considerations

The direction of the enterprise. Figure 1 depicts the sequence and relationship of the various strategic plans recommended for development within organizations. The Strategic Business Plan (phase 1 in the organization's overall information technology planning process) should contain the identification of a clear vision and course of action over a finite period of time. From this, all managers in the organization are made aware of the programs and their priorities. Business managers should, therefore, be better positioned to develop related plans that, in effect, are subsets of the Strategic Business Plan (SBP) as shown in Figure 4.

Along with establishing specific business goals and strategies, the SBP should reflect the position of the head of the enterprise regarding the role information resources/technologies are to play toward the realization of the stated goals. For example, one of the goals of an insurance company might be "to institute a new service program to reduce claimant problem resolution time by twenty percent within a two-year period— concentrating on the optimum use of high-performance microcomputers." This statement indicates a clear direction in a specific business area and emphasizes the exploration and use of particular technologies to help accomplish the goal over a specific timeframe.

An enterprise-wide Information Resource Management plan (phase 2 of the overall planning process) should be developed and be aligned with the SBP to be effective. Similarly, the components of the Microcomputer Planning and Deployment Methodology, the Planning, Acquisition and Deployment, and Costing Models should align themselves with the IRM and, one of its components, the Information Systems plan, as depicted in Figure 3. Martin (1988) discusses the relationship of business planning and information systems planning and suggests that information systems professionals be involved in the creation of the business plan to ensure that the desirable information systems come into existence. Similarly, microcomputer managers and end users should be involved in the development of the firm's strategic

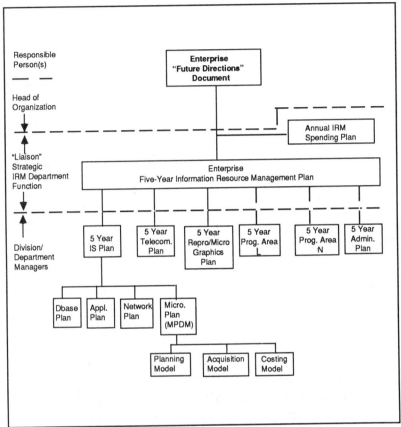

Figure 3:Ingredients of an Enterprise IRM Long-Range Plan

microcomputer plan to help ensure its realization.

The organization's IRM plan should be promoted as the "common denominator" spanning all
other operating units of the organization. Enterprise-
wide goals and strategies emanating from the SBP
should be passed down the management chain.
Recommended, is a "liaison" IRM planning/facilitat-
ing function or department with the responsibility,
among others, to integrate the intent of the head of the
corporation (regarding enterprise directions) with the
individual unit five-year plans. This function could

1. The directions and goals of the enterprise

2. Advances and timing of new microcomputer technologies

3. Enterprises current microcomputer inventory

4. Types of end users

5. Value of enterprise's microcomputers

6. Hardware standardization and compatibility

Table 2: AAS Development Considerations

very well be the CIO position/function being promoted by many in the industry.

The Information Systems (I/S) Plan, along with those of the other operating units, should identify its own particular set of goals. These goals, however, must reflect those activities necessary to support the realization of the organization's overall goals. An I/S plan is typically composed of several parts such as a data base plan, a network plan, and an applications plan. I/S plans should also now include a microcomputer plan.

New technology introductions. The Planning Model has been designed to adapt to and take advantage of future product introductions. New products and technologies appear on the market at such a fast rate that management and users are, typically, unaware of the latest technical discoveries and product announcements. This process of keeping up with these advances is indeed a difficult one, even for staff assigned that job responsibility. However, keeping the model up-to-date is critical to its value as a management tool.

The current Planning Model is structured to accommodate existing (and generically labeled) IBM-compatible models such as the XT, AT, 80386SX, 80386, and 80486 and the yet-to-be-announced 586. These are products available today— although the 80486 fits only into two unique niches (i.e., LAN Server and very high-end desktop) at this time. Regardless, the 80486 will soon become a microcomputer applicable to the masses of desktop users with the 80586 soon becoming a cost-effective system/LAN solution.

A continual assessment of the availability of new technologies is essential to maintaining the validity of the Planning Model. Business managers have a need-to-know what technologies will be available; when; and where to deploy these newer technologies within the organization.

Knowing what is installed. Loosely defined, a plan is a systematic approach to future activity; knowing the starting point of the activity is essential. One of the objectives of this microcomputer planning methodology is to be able to determine the optimum use of existing and future microcomputers through the proper deployment among end users. As such, an inventory is necessary to identify the users assigned to the various models of microcomputers. The inventory process also should include information regarding the utilization of these microcomputers. That is, the inventory should include (a) the identification of the application software running on the various models and (b) notation as to whether the computers are currently meeting users' needs. If users' needs are not met, a determination should be made and annotated as to the cause(s), i.e., whether there is a surplus, or lack, of computing resources. Lastly, the inventory should account for the dollars invested in microcomputers. Data should be collected for all microcomputer-related products such as software, added memory, network cards, printers, and the like.

Defining user types. Cotterman & Kumar (1989) studied the idea of classifying end users for the purpose of assessing associated risks. Their work focused on the development of the notion of a "user cube" which is a three-dimensional (operation, development and control) profile of end users. According to their theory, end users can be categorized at any point on the three planes according to their roles and relationships to microcomputers and information. This profile "can be used to organize the issues, problems, and risks of end-user computing and to devise strategies for its growth and management." (p. 1319) In their research paper, they identified several authors having done work in this area each arriving at a somewhat different conclusion to end user classification.

While recognizing the potential applicability of the "cube" approach in future works, this chapter hypothesizes a subset of said approach by grouping users into two main categories: Intensive and Occasional. Table 3 classifies these users suggesting that an "intensive" user can be described with terms such as full-function, power, or innovative. These types of users may possess one or all of these work ethic characteristics. An intensive user is one who uses application software, such as word processing, spreadsheet, data base, statistics, or desktop publishing, each in a full-function manner and requiring a high-performance computer. Intensive users also exhibit creativity and innovation. The intensive user likely ͻs a job description indicating responsibilities for the

User Type	Characteristics	Applications Use (non-inclusive)
Intensive	Full-function Computer-resource hungry Innovative; Creative Supports managers	Word processing; Spreadsheet design; Desktop publishing; Data base design; CAD; Statistical modeling
Occasional	Limited function Computer-resource sated Repetitive-task oriented Supports intensive users	Text input; Spreadsheet data input; File management maintenance

Table 3: User Profiles

design and development of spreadsheet templates; the design and creation of data base structures; the utilization of multiple fonts and page formats to create comprehensive reports; or the creation of models using statistical analysis techniques. These types of users, referred to by some as "business analysts," oftentimes push the technologies to their limits.

Intensive users typically organize, summarize and present information to management for review. An example of a high-end, intensive user with all three work ethics is one who creates an annual, multiple-dimension, multiple-budget spreadsheet template to be used throughout the company and combines and summarizes the completed spreadsheets from the multiple sources into a single spreadsheet for executive management review.

"Occasional" users, on the other hand, can typically be described using terms such as limited-function, computer-resource sated, or repetitive-task oriented. They likely have supportive, yet important, roles such as data or text entry and are usually the users of templates, or data base programs previously developed by intensive users. Users of this type typically use a limited set of the available software features and functions and perform similar tasks on a daily basis. Occasional users, typically, are not expected to be innovative; usually do memos; and assist in generating reports and documents, and provide general support in the management of small sets of user data-files.

Cost as it relates to acquisition. During the development of a customized Planning Model, the impact of both cost and value- two related, yet separate factors should be considered. Costs address the commitment of a specific amount of funds in the purchasing cycle; value, on the other hand, takes into account a number of other factors as these may apply to the deployment phase of the model and will be

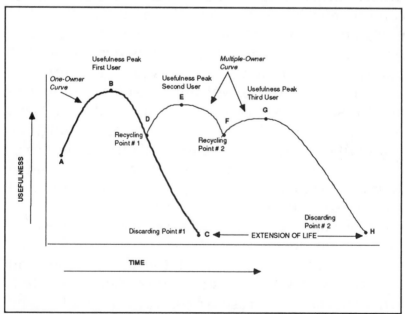

Figure 4: One-owner vs. Multiple-owner "Life Extension" Curves

discussed later.

Microcomputer acquisition planning might entail one or all of the following four traditional cost issues, listed in Table 4. These are the Basic Purchase Price, Price/Performance Ratio, Useful-Life Costs, and Cost-Benefit Analysis. A proposed Basic Purchase Price should be compared with competitive product offerings. These offerings can be retail or discounted prices. The Price/Performance Ratio is an indicator of the capabilities and performance of a product relative to its "sticker price." Unfortunately, no standards exist that can be used as guidelines in the development and use of this ratio; buyers must simply "do their homework."

Useful-Life Costs are defined in terms of Pro-rated Costs/Year and Incremental Costs. Microcomputer system acquisition costs might be viewed from the perspective of cost comparisons of offerings of different lines of products. For instance, the cost/year of a 80386SX with VGA color, considering its projected useful-life, can be shown to be less than the cost/year of a similarly-configured AT, a system with a shorter anticipated useful life—in spite of the higher cost of the 80386SX. Incremental Costs are identified as the differential costs among various system configurations. Buyers assess their choices through a process of identifying a baseline system, defined here to be the AT model, and then determine the cost to purchase the next higher level system(s). The task, then, is to decide if the incremental (differential) cost is worth the additional monetary investment.

To demonstrate the Pro-rated versus Incremental Costing methods, using the AT, a 80286-based processor with 640K of RAM, 40MB of hard disk, and a monochrome VGA monitor as the baseline, the incremental cost percentages reveal that a 80386SX system with a color VGA monitor is only 27% more ($2,600 - $3,000) than a similarly configured AT. In addition, the SX has a projected life expectancy three years longer than the AT. From this, the cost of an SX (about $400 above the AT) ends up being less than $100/year (i.e., its Pro-rated Cost) assuming a useful life of five years for the SX. Even more dramatically, the SX, with its longer useful life of five years vis-a-vis the AT, will cost less per year than the AT. For comparison, the incremental cost to purchase a similarly-configured 80386 amounts to an 89% greater cost than the baseline AT. From this analysis, the recommendation for 1990 and 1991 is to purchase SXs, with 40MB hard disks, and VGA color monitors for all but the high-end intensive users, who should be given full, 32-bit 80386 systems.

Cost (Acquisition-related)	Value (Deployment-related)

1. Basic Purchase Price
  a. Beware of lowest cost
  b. Available spending capital
	1. Usefulness
	  a. Life-extension
	  b. Meeting user needs
	  c. Meeting enterprise needs

2. Price/Performance Ratio
  a. Sticker price vs. capabilities
	2. "Blue Book"
	  a. Tradeable
	  b. Sellable

3. Useful-Life Costs
  a. Pro-rated costs/year
  b. Incremental costs
	3. Personal Acceptance
	  a. User "comfort level"
	  b. Compatibility with other users'
	    microcomputers

4. Cost-Benefit Analysis
  a. Cost reductions
  b. Cost avoidances
  c. Revenue generations
  d. Qualitative benefits	

Table 4: Cost/Value Relationships to Acquisition/Deployment

Cost-Benefit Analysis is yet another purchase-assessment method and the most comprehensive. This process involves the identification of the qualitative and quantitative benefits (and disadvantages) relating to the purchase and life-cycle of microcomputers. The process involves the analysis of the collected information to arrive at a qualified buy/no-buy decision. Included in this analysis should be in-depth research into possible cost reductions, cost avoidances, and revenue generations. In most cases, "quantity purchases" necessitate the need for the cost-benefit analysis approach.

Value as it relates to deployment. Another view of Table 4 addresses the issues relating to microcomputer deployment vis-a-vis value. Microcomputers can have organizational value in three ways: (1) Usefulness, (2) Blue Book, and (3) Personal Acceptance. These values impact a firm's investment in its microcomputers in more than just the initial dollars expended. As such, the imminent analysis and conclusions to discard or recycle microcomputers should consider value in addition to cost. These value factors collectively influence the extent of the life of microcomputers as described in the following paragraphs.

Figure 4 is a graphical view of how the useful life of a hypothetical microcomputer can be extended through the process of recycling. The graph depicts the difference, in Time on the X-axis and Usefulness on the Y-axis, between the "one-owner" curve (ABC) and the "multiple-owner" curve (DEFGH). At point A, the microcomputer is purchased and assigned to a user. Its usefulness will increase for that user until point B, when the user has reached the limit of the microcomputer's functionality. This results in a decline in its usefulness to that user until point C, when the microcomputer is discarded.

The second curve, DEFGH, depicts the "extension" in the life of this microcomputer through the process of recycling to other users at points D and F. At these points, increases in usefulness occur until point H, the final demise of the microcomputer. The extension in the life of this imaginary microcomputer is shown as the "difference in time" between point H and C on the X-axis timeline. Obviously, specific times can not be attached to this graph. This concept suggests that planning for microcomputer recycling is beneficial to an organization. Of significance to managers is the potential impact of this process when applied to the hundreds and thousands of microcomputers installed in larger organizations. (For clarification, the figure is not suggesting that two "recycles" occur per microcomputer. This figure is for illustration purposes only; actual recycle decision points are organization-specific.)

Another value for consideration is Blue Book or asset value. For example, older microcomputers may have enough equity to be used as trade-ins on other, newer microcomputers. Outside buyers may be in need of these "cast-off" microcomputers. Likely, older microcomputers have some value to some organization. For large corporations, the final cost projections of a long-range planning and acquisition strategy can be reduced significantly by pursuing this activity.

The third value, Personal Acceptance, addresses users' "comfort levels" with particular microcomputers. Some users simply do not wish to have their personal computing environment altered. On paper, managers may conclude selected users are ripe for a computer replacement but users may see no limitations to the performance of their tasks using their existing microcomputers and would consider change detrimental. At times it will be prudent for managers to consider the personal side of these issues regarding microcomputer recycling. Managers should be sensitive to this and factor it into their broader buy-recycle-discard strategies.

Microcomputer Standardization and Compatibility. While standardization touches many facets of information technologies (applications, operating systems, networking, etc.), the Planning Model focuses on the standardization of the core element of departmental/EUC, which is the microcomputer hardware itself. Since organizations commit to buying particular brands and models, the impact of these decisions spreads to other IT disciplines (specifically, applications software) as has already been discussed and listed in Table 1.

Microcomputer standardization significantly influences the development and implementation of the Planning Model by helping managers cope with the many issues relating to when to "buy vs. recycle vs. discard." Standardization is an important part of this strategy-building process as it enables better management and technical control of acquisitions and allocations. Standardizing simply reduces the scope and complexity of the issues to be addressed.

In this context, standardization is defined as: having identical equipment available to different users with similar needs. Hardware standardization forces compatibilities in software, media, peripherals and end user computing by enabling users to efficiently move from one workstation to another. The intended goal is to initiate such changes without losses in worker productivity because of differences in keyboards, software, menuing systems, or other functional differences. Critical, however, is a recognition that microcomputer models/brands must meet the needs of the users. Once accomplished, standardization of particular components and configurations is achievable and desirable and reduces the number of different vendor brands and configurations to a manageable number.

As noted earlier and for comparison purposes, a normalized baseline microcomputer system is defined to consist of an AT (80286-based processor) model with 640K of RAM, a 40MB hard drive, and a monochrome VGA monitor. The cost for this baseline configuration is set at $2300, a typically obtainable, discounted corporate price. A key strategy of the Planning Model is the adoption of the 80386 technologies thereby addressing the needs of the masses for the early to mid-1990s.

Industry hardware and software manufacturers are aggressively developing products to take advantage of the powerful features of the 80386 architecture such as virtual-mode, advanced memory management, and gigabytes of addressability—all of which are necessary to produce the speed and performance required in the latest multitasking operating system environment. Table 5 lists six rationale for the adop-

---

1. Application software is consuming more RAM
2. Graphic environments will be predominant and also consume more RAM
3. Price/performance ratios are rising for newest products
4. Near-term technical and functional limitations of XT and AT technologies
5. Growth in user demand to accommodate required functionality
6. Enterprise stategy to "buy for the power user"

Table 5: Hardware Standardization Issues

tion of these 80386 technologies as the hardware "standard" within organizations.

The Generic Planning Model:
A Five-Year Strategy

Strategy characteristics. Work began in 1989 within the State of South Carolina on the subject of future microcomputer acquisitions as these are (and will be) influenced by graphical user interface (GUI) environments. From this initial work, the Microcomputer Planning and Deployment Methodology was developed to address additional issues relating to the planning, acquiring and costing of microcomputers. The Planning Model, the first step in this process, addresses the deployment of microcomputers within organizations. The model, shown in Table 6, is built around trends which project: (a) users' demands for advanced functionality and increased power will continue; (b) organizations will continue to buy software to meet those demands; (c) this new software will require more hardware computing resources than are currently installed; and (d) newer, more advanced hardware will be purchased to accommodate the more functional software. From these projections, it would not make good business sense to purchase software for today's end users if the microcomputers themselves have insufficient hardware to support the software or if additional dollars are needed to upgrade older hardware technologies to maintain software compatibility. The Planning Model takes these issues into account.

A key question to ask at this point is: why replace existing hardware that runs existing software satisfactorily? The answer lies in the expectation of end users' demands for increases in computing resources and functionality. Managers can anticipate replacement microcomputers will be needed within a three - four year period of the original purchase. Managers should take advantage of this situation by purchasing for the "power user" and then recycling the microcomputer from the power user to a user doing work requiring less computing resources. Such is a basic strategy of the Planning Model.

Table 6 depicts a generic, five-year strategy for the management of microcomputer acquisitions and their deployment. Since it covers the 1990-1995 timeframe, current microcomputer models can be mapped into the strategy except the 80586 (the next generation of the X86 family of Intel Corporation's microprocessors) which is expected to be introduced in 1991. This generic strategy was developed using three of the "development considerations," described earlier and listed in Table 2. Specifically, those that apply here are (1) the timing of new technology introductions; (2) estimated and relative microcomputer

Year Model	1991	1992	1993	1994	1995
XT	Start Phase-out	Continue Phase-out	Continue Phase-out	End Phase-out	N/A
AT	Recycle (Occasional user)	Recycle Occasional user)	Recycle (Occasional user)	Start Phase-out	Continue Phase-out
386SX	Buy (Intensive user)	Buy Intensive user)	Buy/ Recycle	Recycle (Occasional user)	Recycle (Occasional user)
386	Buy (Intensive user)	Buy (Intensive user)	Buy (Intensive user)	Buy/ Recycle	Recycle (Occasional user)
486	Buy (File Server)	Buy (File Server & intensive user)	Buy (Intensive user)	Buy (Intensive user)	Buy (Intensive user)
586	N/A (File Server)	Buy (File Server & intensive user)	Buy (Intensive user)	Buy (Intensive user)	Buy Intensive user)

Table 6: Generic Planning Model

values and life-expectancies; and (3) microcomputer hardware standardization. Also influencing the model is the information gathered from the cyclical nature of microcomputer use and introductions.

Building the generic planning model. The generic model was developed using the following general guidelines and assumptions. An assessment of these should be made regarding their potential impact as a customized Planning Model is developed to fit your organization. A generic model can be easily developed for specific industries such as manufacturing, banking, and engineering, to name a few. (The following conclusions and assumptions are included to demonstrate the development process of the various models and do not necessarily represent the official position of the State of South Carolina, at this time.)

1- the XT's useful life has been exhausted and should be discarded by 1994. Peterson & K-Turkel (1990) describe their views on the evolution of the X86 family of computers by suggesting the XT "won't run many of the new, souped-up programs." (p. G-5)

2- the AT is on the down-turn regarding its useful life (relative to user needs and better price/performance ratios of newer technologies) and should be recycled downward to XT users; replaced by SXs and 80386s; then totally discarded by 1996. Discussing the 80286, the views of Peterson & K-Turkel can be summed up with the following: 80286s may appear as good deals through sales, but not so if you want to keep up with the latest programs on into 1992.

3- the 80386SXs are one of the microcomputers of choice at this time and should remain in the "buy" status until 1993 when partial recycling should begin downward to AT users and replaced with 80486s and 80586s. SXs are gaining a larger share of the planned purchases according to a recent PC Week survey indicating the SX is expected to capture 39% of the market share over the next twelve months. The 80386 is expected to garner 37% of the microcomputer market.

4- the 80386 is currently on the early up-slope of its useful life and should be a microcomputer of choice until 1994 when partial recycling should begin and be replaced with 80486 and 80586 microcomputers. Methvin (1990) discusses the debate over the 80286 versus the 80386. He states that 80386 software is here and the price gap is closing when looked at over the long-term. He goes on to suggest that "it is unreasonable to expect any company to discard its installed 8086 and 80286 PCs. But it's not unreasonable to stop buying them when it's clearly a bad investment." (p. 23). The Planning Model recommends that no more XTs and ATs be purchased and that users be given newer technologies, when and where warranted.

5- the 80486 is the newest product of this family of microcomputers and, at this time, is recommended for purchase for users with very unique computing needs, such as CAD, statistics, heavy-duty graphics, and simulation modeling. The niche for the 80486 today is a multi-user central system and a Local Area Network server. The 80486 should be a cost-effective solution for the "desktop" users by 1993. Lovejoy (1990), in an interview with an IDC Corporation representative, stated: "When you look at 80486 shipments, you're not looking at hefty shipments until 1992." (p. S/28).

6- the 80586 is predicted (by many in the industry) to be an advanced version of the 80486 and not a new architecture; is projected to be introduced in 1991; but will not be a cost-effective desktop solution until 1994.

7- laptops and portables are not included in this model since they represent a relatively small portion of the masses of DOS users within organizations and usually perform functions that require microcomputers of this type. Therefore, these products are not conducive to recycling to the masses, at this time. This picture will likely change as new technologies and the workforce continue to change. The Planning Model assumes negligible growth in this area relative to the growth rate of the other DOS-based microcomputers and, therefore, are not factored into the model. In time, it is likely these models will be included in the generic model.

8- Apple MACs are not primarily DOS-based and, like laptops and portables, fit into a niche within organizations fulfilling specific application functions. For these reasons, MACs are not included in the model. This situation too will likely change over time as MACs continue to provide increasing support for the DOS world. Also, the generic Planning Model could be modified to fit those organizations with large populations of Apple products.

9-microcomputer networking (LANs), although strategic to many organizations, has not been included as it raises issues beyond the scope of this work— although consideration has been given to future file server acquisitions. Over the next few years, LANs, using 80486 and 80586 technologies as file servers, will be challenging the traditional mainframe architecture in organizations and, therefore, will become more of an enterprise, I/S and microcomputer management planning issue.

A basic assumption made in the construction of the generic model is that a microcomputer has a useful life (to more than one user, typically) of about ten years from the time of marketplace availability. Glitman (1990) recently interviewed David House, president of Intel Corporation's Microcomputer Component Group. House described the microprocessor life-cycle as starting at the top in volumes shipped and, over the span of about ten years, becoming a low volume product. He, of course, was speaking from the chip manufacturer's perspective. However, there is a direct correlation between the volumes of chips shipped and the commercial system demand for microcomputers. From this, it is proposed that microcomputers be discarded after a ten-year life— a consideration in the development of the Planning Model.

The demand for newer microcomputers will vary according to individual worker skills, worker creativity, industry type, and management philosophies regarding the role of technologies in their businesses. What is not known at this time, obviously, is the future useful life of newer technologies. The useful life of these products will be a function of the (a) extent to which new technologies advance over time and (b) software that will be written to optimize the ever-increasing capabilities and speeds of these newer technologies. In short, because the microcomputer industry has had a brief history, relatively speaking, there is a limited amount of facts and trends useful in the construction of this first Planning Model. Information of this type will become available over the next few years thereby incorporating even more substance to the development of future generic strategies. Until such time, it is suggested this initial version of the Planning Model be used as the tool to plan, budget for, and acquire your organization's microcomputers in a more effective manner.

The Microcomputer Planning and Deployment Methodology: Customizing the Models

Developing a Customized Five-Year Planning Model

This "customized" planning model worksheet (Table 7), included as an example, uses the microcomputer "profile" data collected from a survey conducted in the State of South Carolina in 1990. The survey was conducted to (a) get a first-time count of the number of microcomputers installed; (b) evaluate the aware-

Model	1991	1992	1993	1994	1995	Totals
8086 8088 XT	4264 27%	2843 18%	1422 9%	0 0%	N/A	
80286 AT	4579 29%	4579 29%	4579 29%	3434 22%	2289 15%	
80386SX	1500 9.5%	2054 13%	2528 16%	2528 16%	2528 16%	
80386	948 6%	1579 10%	1894 12%	2549 16%	2549 16.1%	
80486	79 .5%	315 2%	631 4%	1901 12%	2269 14%	
80586	N/A	N/A	316 2%	958 6%	1736 10.9%	
Others	2842 18%	———————————————▶				
MACs	1579 10%	———————————————▶				
Totals*	15,791	15,791	15,791	15,791	15,791	

* assumes a no-growth EUC environment for demonstration purposed

Table 7: Customized Planning Model Worksheet

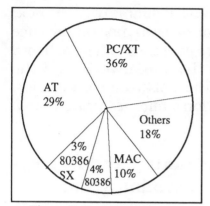

Figure 5: Installed Microcomputers by Model (1990)

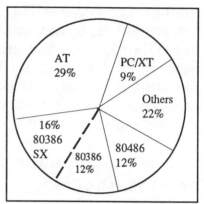

Figure 6: A Projected Move to
80386 Technologies (1993)

ness and attitudes of employees regarding specific statewide information technology programs, standards, and services available to the microcomputer users; and (c) develop a DOS-based application data base that other users may reference prior to embarking on their own software development projects, i.e., an applications directory is available to help reduce the extent of the NIH (not invented here) syndrome.

With a survey response rate of 81% (147 mailed; 119 completed returned), the results reveal a total of 15,791 microcomputers (administrative use only) installed in South Carolina State Government. This represents a 4.7:1 ratio of employees to microcomputers. The breakdown of microcomputers by model is shown in Figure 5 and indicates PC/XTs comprise 36% of the total number of microcomputers installed; ATs 29%; 80386SXs 3%; 80386 4%; Others 18%; and MACs 10%. From the customized Planning Model, a projection can be developed indicating the change in the model's profile as the 80386 technologies become the microcomputer of choice (Figure 6) during the early 1990s.

In general, the Planning Model addresses (1) the numbers of microcomputers currently installed by model type and (2) their percentages of total microcomputers. The model can be developed by working through the matrix on a year-by-year basis (the "implementation" of the example plan began in 1990 and assumes a no-growth scenario through 1995) and by incorporating other information and strategies, such as annual model/product phase-out rates and points of total elimination. The customized Planning Model produces information which indicates the total numbers of microcomputers by type projected for acquisition and deployment annually to the year 1995. Also included is the percentage of these microcomputer types to the total number of microcomputers planned for acquisition.

The "givens" for the example include the objectives to phase-out: (1) all XTs by 1994; (2) all ATs by 1996; and (3) all SXs by 1998. The rationale for this elimination algorithm is due to: (a) the realization of the life expectancies of the various models and (b) a sensitivity to the total costs necessary to replace these products.

Developing Customized Five-Year Acquisition and Deployment, and Costing Models

Through extrapolation, the Planning Model can be summarized further to produce the number of microcomputers planned for purchase annually, by model (shown in the Acquisition and Deployment Model Worksheet, Table 8). Figure 7 graphically depicts specific acquisition and deployment hardware trends by microcomputer model over the span of the five-year plan. This graph should be updated annu-

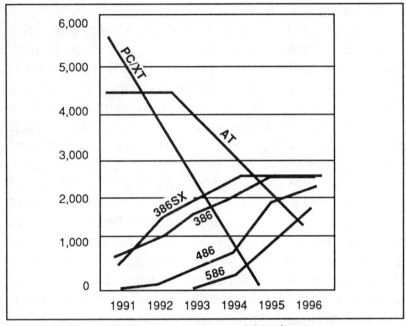

**Figure 7: Microcomputer Acquisition/Deployment
Trends during the Five-Year Plan**

ally as new data is available. The chart is helpful in
trend analyses and the development of budget projections as the latter stages of the five-year plan unfold.
Using the summary data from the Planning Model, it
is now possible to develop cost projections for this five-
year plan.

The final step in this three-step process involves
the development of the financial projections for the
five-year period 1991-1995 as shown in the Costing
Model Worksheet, Table 9). This is done by multiply-
ing the estimated costs of specific microcomputer
types (using pre-defined system configurations discussed earlier or those established to fit your organization) by the projected numbers of units each year by
type.

The costing assumptions made for this example
are based on 80286, 80386SX, and 80386 systems

configured with 1-2 MBs of memory, a 40MB hard drive, a floppy drive, serial and parallel ports, a keyboard and a VGA color monitor. This "standard" configuration is used as it represents one that is functionally useful and available across several system lines. However, the 80486 single-user systems available today typically include a minimum of 65MBs of hard disk with 4MBs of memory; multiuser 80486 systems go far beyond these capacities; 80586 systems are yet to be introduced. Even within specific processor models there exists a wide range of processor speeds and performance from which the buyer can choose and which result in specific system costs. Again, the purpose of this standard configuration is for comparison. The pre-defined costs are $2,600 for the AT; $3,000 for the SX, $4,400 for the 80386, $6,500 for the single-user 80486, and an anticipated 1993 (single-user) cost of $6,500 for the 80586, which has yet to be introduced but is projected to be "desktop" available in 1993. For planning purposes, each of these system costs will be reduced 15% annually. These costing and availability assumptions are based on (a) the microcomputer pricing history; (b) 1990 costs as a baseline; (c) typical volume-purchase discounts; (d) mail-order pricing; and (e) the history of the introduction points of the X86 family of microprocessors.

The Microcomputer Planning and Deployment Methodology: Putting It into Perspective

Observations ...

As shown in Table 9, a significant financial commitment will be required to realize the projections of the example models. Figure 8 presents another

Model	1991	1992	1993	1994	1995	Totals
8086 8088 XT	-1421	-1421	-1421	-1422	N/A	-5685
80286 AT	0	0	0	-1145	-1145	-2290
80386SX	+1026	+554	+474	0	0	+2054
80386	+316	+631	+315	+653	0	+1917
80486	+79	+236	+316	+1270	+367	+2268
80586	N/A	N/A	+316	+642	+778	+1736
Others MACs	N/A	N/A	N/A	N/A	N/A	N/A
(1)	+1421	+1421	+1421	+2567	+1145	+7975
(2)	-1421	-1421	-1421	-2567	-1145	-7975

(1)No. of microcomputers to be acquired   (2) No.of microcomputers needing replacement

Table 8: Customized Acquisition and Deployment Model Worksheet

Model	1991	1992	1993	1994	1995	Totals
8086 8088 XT						
80286 AT						
80386SX	$2550 1026 2,616,300	$2165 554 1,199,410	$1840 474 872,160			$4,687,870
80386	$3740 316 1,181,840	$3179 631 2,005,949	$2702 315 851,130	$2296 653 1,499,288		$5,538,207
80486	$5400 79 426,600	$4696 236 1,108,256	$3992 316 1.261,472	$3392 1270 4,307,840	$2883 367 1,058,061	$8,162,229
80586	0	0	$4696 316 1,483,936	$3992 642 2,452,864	$3392 778 2,638,976	$6,685,776
Others MACs	NOT INCLUDED IN THIS CUSTOMIZED MODEL					
Totals*	4,224,740	4,313,615	4,468,698	8,369,992	3,697,037	$25,074,082

Table 9: Customized Costing Model Worksheet

view of the costing projections produced from the customized model: costs per microcomputer type per year. From this, upper management is made aware of the trends evolving for the duration of the plan. The annual sub-totals to implement the customized models as scheduled are as follows:

```
1991   $4,224,740
1992   $4,313,615
1993   $4,468,698
1994   $8,369,992
1995   $3,697,037
```

Grand Total $25,074,082

As startling as these totals appear, investing in and supporting the microcomputer environments in larger organizations does indeed involve tremendous costs. One of the benefits of using this methodology is that it brings this fact to life. Not to be forgotten is that these dollar totals do not include the costs for microcomputer software, training, repairs, accessories and so on. Truly, microcomputer environments are consuming larger slices of organizations' capital assets. Because of the anticipated similarity in the magnitude of the figures as your organization develops its customized models, several observations are appropriate regarding the basic strategy used and the resultant costing figures.

Regarding the planning model

(a) Upon analysis, the objective to eliminate all XTs by 1994 is not unreasonable. Introduced in 1983, the XT's "life" has now spanned seven years. Users have already begun replacing this product. This process should continue to be used through the next three

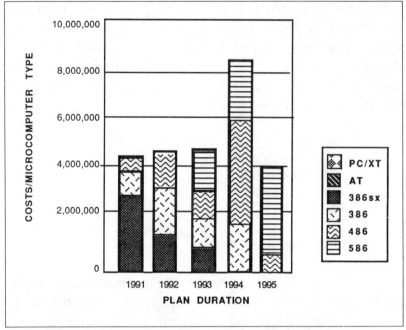

Figure 8: Management Report on Cost Projections

years culminating in an XT total life span of 10 years.

(b) Because of (1) the excellent price/performance ratios of the 80386SX and 80386 technologies; (2) the increase in users' microcomputer knowledge and skills; and (3) a rise in the creative uses of microcomputers to solve business problems, many users have already been requesting (and needing) replacements of their ATs with SXs and 80386s.

(c) The determination as to the specific buy-recycle-discard decision points defined in the generic strategy is subjective and, therefore, changeable. This is precisely the purpose of the generic matrix; it was designed to be a starting point and a guide to a particular strategy that fits the make-up of your organization.

Regarding the acquisition and costing models

(a) The "models" have been developed for demonstration purposes only; the microcomputer data is real. The data was extracted from a recent survey conducted in the State of South Carolina. The customized Planning, Acquisition and Deployment, and Costing Models were built from this summary data but do not, at this time, necessarily reflect the State of South Carolina's official stance regarding statewide microcomputer strategies. These statewide strategies are incorporating this planning methodology which is in the formulation stage, as of this writing.

(b) The development process assumed a "no growth" company scenario for the duratio of the five-year plan, for demonstration purposes. Actual growth figures must be factored into the generic and customized modes, as appropriate to your organization.

(c) The costs for the various microcomputer types are those that can be realized through either large-company volume discount contracts or mail-order catalogues and should be acceptable for planning and costing purposes. The advantages and disadvantages of buying through these markets are demonstrable but beyond the scope of this work.

(d) The stated costs pertain to a basic 640K processor, keyboard, 40MB of hard disk, and a color VGA monitor. Of course, the basic processor now "comes standard with," in most products, serial and parallel ports, expansion slots, battery back-up, and clock.

(e) Not factored into the annual Costing Model figures are the dollars potentially realized through microcomputer trade-in's and/or the reselling to outside parties. Also not included in the final numbers of this five-year costing model are costs for expanded memory, input and output devices (printers, scanners, mice, plotters, etc.) software, training, repairs, and maintenance.

(f) A most difficult task is to quantify the qualitative benefits realized through the use of microcomputers— in particular those gains realized through the use of the "latest and more powerful and functional" technologies. This has been, and will continue to be, an industry-wide issue. It is becoming apparent that newer microcomputers now perform functions not possible using earlier generations of microcomputers. Organizations are simply becoming more dependent upon microcomputers, as their very life-blood. Viewed from this perspective, moving toward the newest products as quickly as feasible (and warranted) seems to make good business sense.

A major hurdle to overcome will be the reluctance of senior management to commit to the projected financial burden. However, when the projected costs from the Costing Model are compared with the company's actuals from previous years, some similarity should be anticipated, thereby validating the systematic and consolidated planning approach. This realization may also introduce the elements of chagrin and surprise in management. They may be chagrinned because the planned annual sub-totals appear enormous; surprised when it becomes known the projected costs are not out-of-line with previous actuals.

Monger (1988) in his work on developing an Information Technology Management Framework as it relates to information technology planning and investing, suggests that management achieve a balance between a number of forces including a balance between (a) a firm's future competitive needs and the technology's capacity to fulfill those needs; and (b) between the rate of technological change and management's willingness to invest in technologies.

The reality is that long-term planning is desirable and, yet, difficult to accept and implement (especially over the long term). It is one thing to develop a long-range strategy sanctioned by senior management; it is another to get the financial commitment to implement the plan— for the long haul. Therefore, it is dichotomous for business managers to plan and budget for the long-term and, yet, be held short-term, profit-and-loss accountable.

Organizational Utility of the MPDM

As a long-range planning tool. Monger further describes the need to present a single perspective to senior management regarding the management of information technologies. He suggests in his Framework paradigm the need for management to look upon the use and acquisition of information technologies [microcomputers] for the good of the enterprise and as a coordinated, organizational activity. Briefly, these premises suggest that microcomputers (1) produce quality products and services; (2) they must be managed for the good of the enterprise; and (3) they are the key tool to the continuous improvement of systems.

From this and the works of other information technology planners, it should be clear that an organization should be managing its microcomputers (and all other information technologies) and managing them in an orderly and well-structured manner. The capital asset value of microcomputers and related technologies continues to capture a larger slice of the total value of capital assets of organizations. Surely, as the company's financials are clearly affected, this should be sufficient motivation to begin to more effectively manage its microcomputer environment.

For better management of order and control. It is essential to establish some form of central, functional control if there is indeed to be a genuine commitment to manage one's microcomputer environment. This control function could be one person; a department; a part of an information technology support department; or a review or advisory committee. A key to the success of this approach is the recognition by department managers and staff of the existence of a single control point. However, whatever the form or structure, the provinciality of goals from the various departments must somehow be in concert with the overall business goals of the enterprise as defined in its Strategic Business Plan.

A brief discussion about the use of the word control is important at this point. If not used or presented in the right context, the implementation of the microcomputer control function could be impeded because of negative perceptions from those outside the control function itself. Nadel (1987) begins his work by defining the word control. He feels the standard definition of control, (i.e., to check; to regulate) should be extended to include checking and regulating data accuracy as well as microcomputer purchases and user training. He goes on to point out that these are legitimate activities to be under control "because they directly affect the use of microcomputers and the welfare of the company." (p. 2) The point is that some form of control is necessary but caution should be exercised regarding its promotion and implementation. What is required is a delicate balancing of absolute control and no control; that is to say, a moderate approach consisting of both freedoms and mandates.

Henderson & Treacy (1986) studied the relationship of end user computing strategies, in this context, vis-a-vis control. Their findings indicate a need for managers to adopt an "evolving management strategy," one which assumes this EUC infrastructure is dynamic. They add that managers must change their EUC strategies to fit the shifting importance of the following four issues: support infrastructure, technological infrastructure, data infrastructure and evaluation/justification planning. In short, they are suggesting that EUC managers be flexible and adaptive in their "control" of their EUC environments.

To better understand the overall microcomputer environment. By-products of this systematic and consolidated planning process are a further awareness of the microcomputer needs of the organization's staff, and current and future technologies. Earlier it was recommended that during the process of taking a microcomputer inventory, other assessments be included such as (a) the extent to which existing software and hardware meets users' needs and (b) the level of creativity and innovation exhibited by users.

Knowing this, management can properly plan for and deploy higher performance microcomputers to those users with needs requiring such levels of computing horsepower. This is key to the customized buy-recycle-discard Planning Model. In fact, without this information, one would be attempting to implement the model without foundation and would thus be defeating the purpose of customizing this plan "to place the right microcomputers in the hands of the right users at the right times."

The data from the inventory process also produces projections regarding user training needs. In addition to knowing who has what technology, an assessment can be made as to particular end users' needs for initial and/or follow-on training. From this information, an enterprise-wide education and training plan can be developed to take advantage of economies-of-scale regarding training costs.

The information about end users also can be helpful in the development of other types of enterprise-wide support programs. Recently, the industry has seen the emergence of terms and functions such as Business Analysts (i.e., applications support staff assigned to specific business units), End User Computing, Information Resource Centers, and User Support Groups. These are necessary in organizations using microcomputers but may be implemented in one form or another depending on the make-up of the organization. These support activities have been found to be useful management tools as they tend to (a) directly promote end user utilization of microcomputers and (b) indirectly enable information to be presented to management in a more timely, comprehensible, and accurate manner. The planning process presented also forces organizations to become more familiar with microcomputer technologies per se. Through the inventory process and the development of the customized Planning Model, an organization cannot help but delve further into the issues of microcomputer capabilities, problems, and availabilities.

To help contain related microcomputer expenditures. Earlier, a discussion focused on the initial, follow-on and hidden costs inherent in the purchase and use of microcomputers. A recommended activity also identified earlier was to standardize on technologies, where feasible. As end user needs become known, through the inventory process as one example, and as standards are established, a microcomputer technical and support infrastructure can be established. Through this planning process and the requirement of individual department managers to develop their specific microcomputer plans in sync with enterprise goals, upper management will be better positioned to consolidate the information about the microcomputer needs of the enterprise and thus be in a better position to forecast related expenditures.

Moreover, volume-discount hardware and software contracts may be negotiated with vendors since purchasing volumes are now determinable over the long term using this planning methodology. Vendors are more able to customize purchase and maintenance contracts that are based on customers' plans that are well thought-out.

Selling the Plan

Management resistance and reluctance. All too often, the information technology planning function does not receive the attention attributed to the operational units. In many cases, this planning function is hidden in the organizational structure or is simply non-existent. Those business managers operating in these environments and wanting to do information technology planning are faced with the additional challenge of convincing management of the merits of technology planning.

In all environments, however, including those in which planning is an integral part of the business, management will, and obviously should, interrogate the results of the customized models when presented. Using the results of the five-year example as a yardstick for your specific microcomputer plan, it is evident that a significant financial commitment will be required from senior management to implement a similar plan for your organization. The plan presents to management long-term projections but also requires an immediate, large, and up-front financial commitment. Because of this, management likely will elicit comments regarding the plan's: (a) projected costs, (b) aggressiveness, and (c) uncertainly and complexity.

In response, managers should produce supportive information indicating past microcomputer expenditures are not too different from the plan's projections. The difference is that the planning approach permits management to forecast these expenditures rather than to react on an ad hoc basis. Moreover, the cyclical nature of the use and introductions of these products will cause a cost stabilization in microcomputer acquisitions until the next major technical and functional change in microcomputers is introduced in the industry, which is likely to occur late in this decade. At that time, user replacement requests and planning cost projections will again begin to rise (reflecting the "new and novel" products) until the unit costs become practicable and cost-effective for desktop use.

To some, the plan may simply be termed "too uncertain and complex" since it contains a number of variables and assumptions. However, any plan, by definition, contains these elements. The task, of course, is to carefully sift through the issues and to systematically arrive at a conclusion regarding the risk factors associated with the plan and to develop a contingency plan in the process.

And to some upper-level managers, a customized microcomputer plan, similar to that developed in the example, may be considered "too aggressive" and, therefore, inconsistent with the basic philosophy of their organizations. Some companies are technology leaders; others wait for technologies to stabilize before they commit their resources. While understandable, management should view this approach in light of their competition; that is, is your organization meeting its business objectives? If not, your organization's goals and information technology strategies may need review.

The politics of change. Puttre (1990) recently interviewed Alvin Toffler on the subject of decentralization, or as he termed it, "demassification." In the interview, he suggested that MIS managers not resist this movement since it is a very deep social process. Toffler went on to indicate that the primary objective of MIS management should be the effective delivery of information to support the business.

In the world of information systems, demassification is moving MIS and users closer together. It is anticipated by many that this movement will be accelerated as end users continue to display the skills necessary to do their own computing; and as LANs, using 80486 and 80586 technologies, begin to replace mainframes. This latter event is already happening in the industry but on a selective basis. In the past, MIS had a monopoly on its customer base as the only information producer in the organization. Over time, however, the consumer and the producer of information are becoming the same agent. In effect, the shift toward decentralization implies a shift in management authority and responsibility. What was once the sole responsibility of MIS has been gradually transferred to the departmental manager.

Conversely, however, unit managers must not look upon their newly acquired authority as a means to their end. With these new information-generating powers, the tendency may be to become autonomous and to compete with other units for corporate resources. These managers may be reluctant to commit their budgeted dollars to a plan that includes the potential deployment of microcomputers from within their departments to other departments "for the sake of the enterprise." Assurances must be given from the outset of the plan's acceptance, that departments will not be drained of their computer-horsepower and/or their computers as the plan is implemented.

Conclusions

There is substantial evidence available to suggest that planning for the optimum use of information resources should be a vital organizational function. This view of the resources inter-related with the delivery of timely and quality information, services, and products is known as Information Resource Management (IRM). It should follow, then, that organizations should begin to realize the need for a plan to use and manage its microcomputers. While still in its infancy because of the nature and brief history of microcomputers, the Microcomputer Planning and Deployment Methodology presented in this chapter represents a step in the right direction for business managers to begin to turn, what has been, a seemingly unmanageable and uncontrollable situation into one that can indeed be managed.

Applegate, Cash & Mills (1988) conclude their work on the relationship and impact of information technology and managers with the following: "it [information technology] will require thoughtful planning and responsible management. But as never before, it will tax the creative powers of the business leaders who must decide when to use it— and to what end." (p. 136)

Somewhat predictable in the world of microcomputers is their cyclical nature. Trends are evolving in prices, capabilities, and the ways users employ microcomputers. As the current rendition of microcomputer technologies matures and as more historical information becomes available, the methodology described within will draw closer to the real events— until the next major evolution in microcomputers. Toward the turn of the century one should anticipate significant changes in our workplaces and our workforces, with vastly different and powerful microcomputer-based products. Organizations will be finding new and unique uses for these products resulting in the start of another microcomputer cycle consisting of unique management issues and concerns. In light of this ever-changing environment, the most appropriate methodology organizations could pursue, as a guide in their continued use and reliance on microcomputers, is the development and use of a strategic, multi-year microcomputer plan, specifically, the

Microcomputer Planning and Deployment Plan.

References

Applegate, Linda M., Cash, James I, Jr. & Mills, D. Quinn. (1988). Information Technology and Tomorrow's Manager. Harvard Business Review, 66(6), 128-136.

Berge, Noel, Ingle, Marcus D., & Hamilton, Marcia. (1986). Microcomputers in Development. West Hartford, CT: Kumarian Press.

Cotterman, William W. & Kumar, Kuldeep. (1989). The Communications of the ACM, 32(11), 1319.

Diebold, John. (1985). AMACOM, American Management Associations, Managing Information. The Challenge and the Opportunity, p. 37.

Drude, Ted. (1990, May). Overhaul The 286. Computer Shopper. pp. 133-134.

Geis, George T. & Kuhn, Robert L. (1987). Micromanaging, Transforming Business Leaders with Personal Computers. Englewood Cliffs, New Jersey: Prentice-Hall, Inc.

Gerrity, Thomas P. & Rockart, John F. (1986). End-User Computing: Are you a leader or a laggard?. Sloan Management Review, Summer 1986, pp. 3-14.

Glitman, Russell. (1990, June 4). Intel Executives Put the 486 Processor into Perspective. PC Week, pp. S/14 - S/17.

Greenberg, Eric Rolfe, Project Director. (1988). The AMA Report on End-User and Departmental Computing. An AMA Research Report with the Cooperation of The Microcomputer Managers Association, AMACOM Briefings and Surveys. Bohl, Don Lee (Ed.). Skagen, Anne E. (Asso. Ed.). DeBow, Yvette (Staff Writer). Introduction by Hoffman, Gerald M. Ph.D. AMA Publications Division. p. 8.

Henderson, John C. & Treacy, Michael E. (1986). Managing End-User Computing for Competitive Advantage. Sloan Management Review, 27(2),3-14.

Keen, Peter, G. W. & Woodman, Lynda A. (1984). What To Do With All Those Micros. Harvard Business Review, 62(5), 142-150.

Lovejoy, Paula. (1990, June 4). Power, Flexibility Seen Luring Unix Users to Intel Platform. PC Week. Interview with Nancy McSharry, IDC representative. p. S/28.

Machrone, Bill. (1990, June 26). Who Calls The Shots? PC Magazine, p. 69.

March, Richard. (1989/1990, January 1). Explosive PC Decade end on Cautious Note. PC Week, p. 10.

Marchand, Donald. A. (Spring, 1990). The Expert's Opinion. Interviewed by Khosrowpour, Mehdi. Information Resources Management Journal, 3(2), 41.

Martin, James. Strategic Information Planning Methodologies. (1988). reprint, Englewood Cliffs, New Jersey: Prentice-Hall Inc.

McNurlin, Barbara C. & Sprague, Ralph H., Jr. (1989). Information Systems Management in Practice, Second Edition. Englewood Cliffs, New Jersey: Prentice-Hall. pp. 324-325.

Methvin, Dave. (1990, April 30). Despite the Debate, the Future Belongs to the 386. PC Week, p. 23.

Monger, Rod F. (1988). Mastering Technology, A Management Framework for Getting

Results. New York: The Free Press, A Division of Macmillan, Inc., London: Collier Macmillan Publishers.

Naisbitt, John, (1984, second ed.). Megatrends, Ten New Directions Transforming Our Lives. New York: Warner Books.

Nadel, Robert B., CPA, JD, MBA, (1987). Avoiding Microcomputer Headaches, How to Control the Acquisition, Use, and Security Risks of Microcomputers. New York: McGraw-Hill Book Company, p. 2.

Oliva, Larry & Khosrowpour, Mehdi. (Spring, 1989). Microcomputers: Strategic Tools for the 1990s. Journal of Microcomputer Systems Management, 1(1), 3.

Perry, William E. CQA. (1987). Management Workstations: Strategies for Office Productivity. Blue Ridge Summit, PA: TAB Professional and Reference Books, Division of Tab Books, Inc.

Peterson, Franklynn & K-Turkel, Judi. (1990, January 21). Computer revolution far from over. The State, p. G-5.

Puttre, Michael. (1990, May 7). Decentralization trend mirrors societal changes. MIS Week, p. 1. Referencing Toffler, Alvin. The Third Wave. (1980).

Rideout, Kathrine. (1990, May 7). Micros Based on 386SX Processor Now Dominate Planned Purchases. PC Week, p. 142.

State of South Carolina, Department of Education, Committee on Computer Hardware and Software Acquisitions. (1989). Information Technology Guidelines, A Position Paper To Provide Assistance in the Area of Information Technology Planning Within the South Carolina. (Research paper). Columbia, SC: Author.

State of South Carolina, Budget and Control Board, Division of Research and Statistical Services, Office of Information Technology Policy and Management. (1990). Microcomputer Survey. Columbia, SC: Author.

Sumner, Mary R. & Klepper, Robert, Dr. (1987). The Impact of Information Systems on End User Computing. Journal of Systems Management. 38(10), 12-17.

Toffler, Alvin. (1985). The Adaptive Corporation. New York, NY: McGraw-Hill Book Company, p. 18.

National Research Council, Commission on Engineering and Technical Systems, Board on Telecommunications and Computer Applications. McDonough, Francis A., Chairman. (1985). Thompson, John, Contributing Author. Managing Microcomputers in Large Organizations. Washington, DC: National Academy Press, p. 3.

Zachmann, William. (1989/1990, December/January). Explosive PC Decade Ends on Cautious Note. PC WEEK. Source: International Data Corporation, p. 10.

Chapter 4

CRITICAL SUCCESS FACTORS IN THE INTEGRATION OF MICROCOMPUTER TECHNOLOGY INTO EXPANDING ORGANIZATIONS: FIVE CASE STUDIES

Elia V. Chepaitis
Fairfield University

The Critical Success Factors (CSFs) approach was designed to meet senior managers' information needs, by identifying key indicators in the health of a business (Rockart, 1979). This method is of significant value in the integration of Microcomputer-based Information Systems (MBIS) for the small owner- or partner-managed business. Typically, CSFs for a small enterprise might include: the retention and equitable remuneration of partners, uninterrupted operation, increased market share, or superior client service.

The achievement of CSFs requires appropriate systems design and implementation strategies. After conversion to a MBIS, CSFs are dependent upon, and in turn support, effective Information Resource Management (IRM), the optimization of organizational resource handling through information sharing and enhancement.

Although curricula often neglect small businesses, these enterprises offer ideal cases to evaluate the impact of management strategies, technological maturity, and environmental change upon the MBIS integration.

This chapter contrasts three small and expanding organizations which successfully converted to an MBIS and two large enterprises who failed, and identifies contributory factors in all five outcomes. CSFs were ill-defined and not measured formally in any organization, but they were well-articulated and communicated informally in all the enterprises.

Background

In the 1980s, five expanding service organizations adopted MBIS under relatively favorable conditions in southern New England: a group law practice, a court recorder firm, a large orthopedic practice, a small-city municipal department, and the financial control division of a major international bank. Each organization had reached a developmental plateau, and could not improve upon the quantity or the quality of operations without upgrading their information systems. Organizational expandability and improved financial, service, and personnel management depended also upon effective systems upgrades.

The structure of all the enterprises, both private and public, was typical, dependent upon and shaped by the information available and its utilization (Brussaard, 1988). Each organization acknowledged that an MBIS was desirable to exploit existing opportunities. However, the urgency to computerize, expand, and improve information resources also stemmed from a perceived threat that haphazard record keep-

---

- Poor Financial Management
- Excessive Caseloads
- Expanding Services
- Overcrowded Site
- Need To Attract Additional Professionals
- Spiraling Staffing Levels
- Neglected Strategic Objectives
- Emergent Alliances and Regulators
- Poor Information Access
- Lack of Data Integrity
- Operational Bottlenecks

Figure 1: Motivations for MBISs.

ing and knowledge handling could become chaotic under certain conditions and work-loads (Fig. 1).

All the managers identified CSFs for information management which closely corresponded to those formally developed for large scale Information Centers by Brancheau, Vogel, and Wetherbe (1985).

All five organizations experienced and expected seminal, ongoing business changes. As a result, designs for improved IRM reflected numerous internal and environmental factors, as well as the desire for flexibility to better manage change:

1. the mission, culture and purpose of the organization

2. responsivity to business and professional change: opportunities for competitive advantage

3. available MBISs: technological imperfections and maturity, and profession-tested packages

4. market imperfections: the quality of vendor competition, intra-professional communications, and system support

5. strategic, tactical, and operational management objectives: including product/service improvement at all levels

6. client needs and expectations

7. environmental conditions: external information, changing regulations, intra-enterprise alliances, uncontrollable increases in caseloads and paperwork, pricing constraints

8. existing information resource management (Fig. 2)

Technological considerations were imbedded in non-technical but information-intensive factors

Every organization was relatively munificent and progressive; each hoped that an MBIS would improve resource management, the quality of services and competitiveness. Moreover, the enterprises hoped that technological conversion itself would serve strategic purposes. All hoped to help the organization to construct a holistic view of weaknesses and strengths. In other words, systems analysis was intended to

Organization
Competitive Advantage
Technology
Market
Management Objectives
Client Base
Externalities
Existing IRM

Figure 2: Internal and environmental factors weighed in IRM design

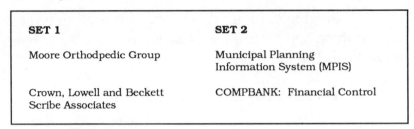

SET 1	SET 2
Moore Orthodpedic Group	Municipal Planning Information System (MPIS)
Crown, Lowell and Beckett Scribe Associates	COMPBANK: Financial Control

Figure 3: Subjects for case studies: In two sets

serve as a diagnostic, to identify weak links not only in information resources and applications, but also in structure and in non-informational tasks. Strategic managers looked upon the integration project as an ideal occasion for brainstorming and creative thinking which had been neglected, a project which would assist managers to assess important and pressing challenges and to redesign operations.

The five organizations can be profitably divided into two sets: three owner-managed group offices (physicians, lawyers, and court recorders) and two departments, one within a city administration and one in an international bank (Fig 3).

In the first set, the integration of MBISs by the small businesses purposefully introduced non-technological changes (NTCs) which were occasionally as significant as the introduction of new technologies; in turn NTCs enhanced the viability and effectiveness of the information system (Fig. 4).

Also in the first set, CSFs, components identified as vital to the expected value of the MBIS, were tailored meticulously to suit the organization and its market, and reflected personalities, preferences, existing technologies and industry standards. Some system features were frankly experimental, but owner-managers often did not want to computerize without creative provisions and offered cogent arguments for

Staff	Professionals
elimination of backlogs	analysis of productivity patterns
specialized activities	freedom from clerical functions
work area redesign	appropriate division of labor
improved ratio of staff to professionals	global view of enterprise
improved morale systematized training	information base for strategic service expansion: scope and scale

Figure 4: Set 1—Desired non-technical change through MBIS integration

reducing future uncertainties by playing with planned risk.

In addition, the isolation and identification of CSFs, however informally, provided a valuable occasion for improvements in organizational communication, cohesion, feedback and control. The exercise enabled the owner-partners to formulate cogent arguments and seek consensus on managerial goals and objectives, including NTCs.

The participants were able to tap into the dynamics inherent in these successful and expanding enterprises to bring energy and expertise to IRM design (Shank, Boynton & Zmud, 1985; Smith & Medley, 1987).

In the owner-managed business, of the three components of IRM—information, resources, and management, management is typically dominant (Owen, 1989). Set 1's three organizations conformed to this pattern, and management initiatives and prioritization often dominated the pace and direction of systems analysis, design and implementation. The entrepreneurial qualities of these dynamic owner-managers were decidedly first-rate. They possessed distinctive competence in a lucrative field, a strategic awareness of market opportunities, drive, and a capacity for learning as well as leading. Their leadership styles ranged from authoritarian to highly democratic, and were logical in the context of business culture and origins.

The integration of MBISs in the second set, the departments, contrasted markedly with the experience of the first group. First, the conversion was more remote from managers and staff, although closely supported by systems professionals. Second, the systems failed egregiously in seminal areas, and third, NTCs were minimal and often detrimental for both the organizational unit and the parent. The failure to identify and to commit to appropriate CSFs was one element in the poor performance of the second set.

This chapter will concentrate on the first set, that is, the successful small-business adaptations, and will exploit the experience and failures of the small-city department and the financial controllers to highlight germane differences between the conversions.

Owner-managed small businesses do not always possess absolute advantages over larger public and corporate enterprises for MBIS integration, but these three organizations did exploit the vision, commitment, and accountability which are often decisive assets in cohesive group practices. The identification and dedication to operational, tactical, and strategic CSFs were a key elements in their success (Fig. 5).

Operational		Tactical	Strategic
receivables	**I**	reports	financial projections
correspondence	**M**	efficient division of	projections:new site
scheduling	**P**	professionals' time	attract new partners
inventory	**R**	expansion and control	maximize opportunity
product/	**O**		
service	**V**	staff hour reduction	new services/markets
payables	**E**	product/service focus	redesign structure
working		information retrieval	unstructured queries
conditions		employee retention	interface: externals

Figure 5: Critical Success Factors: Set 1

Issues

The IRM Imperative

IRM in the small business environment has become necessary as enterprises of all sizes have computerized and upped the technological ante for entry into most industries and market segments, as markets shrink and also as competition expands.

The leading motives for the introduction of IT include financial reward and reduced dependencies. Deterrents include fears of employee discomfort and dissatisfaction and a loss of supervisory control (Davidsson, 1989). Only if owner/managers expect financial rewards is a sense of personal achievement also a significant motivation (Davidsson, 1989).

On the one hand, Set 1's businesses feared MBIS acquisition and maintenance costs, increased wage-rates for staff, new dependencies, lock-outs, and imminent obsolescence. On the other hand, they understood that the well-designed and competent computerized firm can achieve unprecedented economies of scale and scope, improve product/service, and utilize in-house professional expertise for major strategic advantage.

IRM Development

For the information systems dollar, the owner-managed enterprise can coordinate information technology (IT) and business plans with impressive direction and drive (Holland, 1989).

In Set 1, the three group practices' organic, rather than mechanistic, organizational form was ideal for prioritizing applications, and was highly satisfactory for the evolutionary development of IRM (Nosek, 1989) (Fig. 6).

Within Set 1, the three young owner-managed professional offices—Moore Orthopedic Group, Crown, Lowell, and Beckett, and Scribe Associates, were atypical of most small businesses in two areas: they were neither undercapitalized, nor did they have a narrow service/product focus (Collins, 1987). They did, however, confront dominant issues and exhibit characteristics, needs and behaviours typical of group practices and expanding organizations in their professions.

The law firm and the orthopedists were performing well before computerizing and enjoyed signifi-

---

Dynamism
Focus
Pro-Active Behavior
Economies of Scale and Scope
Market-Targeted Products/Services
Challenging Externalities:
      Regulations
      Alliances
Expanding Demand for Professional Expertise

Figure 6: Set 1—The Owner-Managed enterprise:
Factors facilitating effective IRM

cant competitive advantages. The court recorders founded the firm concurrently with the introduction of an MBIS, and within months also offered superior services, steadily broadening their client base.

The firms were actually expanding physically, and each was planning to move into much more spacious quarters; all three enterprises owned their office buildings within five years. The anticipated relocations served as stimuli to computerize for three reasons: to avoid two major simultaneous or overlapping disruptions in business activities, to design the site for an expandable debugged system, and to coordinate and supplement existing capital and human resources through the MBIS.

Of the three stages of development (foundation, turbulence, and maturity which typify the small business (Carbone, 1985), the second stage, characteristic of Set 1, is the optimal time for introducing or improving an MBIS, because of the receptivity to change. Furthermore, studies have shown that in the small business, manager-owners are likely to use PC's personally (Nickell & Seado, 1986); uneven utilization of the PC's levelled off within a few months in Set 1, but did cause friction during conversion, a short-term problem.

Small business managers also are influenced by a broad range of influences in their decision to convert, by peers, family members, and waves of salesperson/vendors (Malone, 1988). The quality of the influences which affected Set 1 were uneven, and the timing of the contact was disproportionately significant. The plethora of influences caused anxiety and confusion initially, but helped to firm the decision to computerize and to familiarize the owner-managers with MBISs.

Business Change and Expansion

In addition, receptivity to business change and expansion in Set 1 conformed to type, and was also influenced by stages and lifestyle, social and political considerations (Gibb, 1985), leadership and team styles, and, of course, personal preferences for certain market niches.

Levels of satisfaction with MBISs are high among entrepreneurs after conversion (Carbone, 1985), and small businesses typically exploit strategic advantages offered through computerization. They are concerned also, more than their corporate counterparts, with external information and external access (Johnson & Kuehn, 1987), reflecting responsivity to market, business, and policy change.

Among the MBIS features typically undervalued by small businesses, and seldom appearing in CSFs, are security, privacy, and other ethical and supervisory considerations(Pendergraft, 1987). Perhaps because of strong traditions of confidentiality in the medical, legal, and court recorder professions, Set 1 did not conform to Pendergraft's model.

These firms, the orthopedists, the lawyers, and the court stenographers, researched alternative courses of action and their probable utilities, two with the help of consultants, evaluated external uncontrollables, such as changes in co-pay procedures, and informally assigned weights to significant variables. They were concerned about the opportunity costs of the conversion effort and expense, and sought to balance the desire for a timely MBIS integration with an appreciation for the possible value of emergent technologies. In other words, the owner-managers knew the important questions in IRM and MBIS conversion, if not all the answers.

In all, the enterprises successfully created, possessed or purchased vital prerequisites for successful MBIS integrations (Fig. 7). Of seminal importance was the formulation of CSFs, either formally or informally, which required efforts ranging from 3 months to 3 years, which nearly equalled the time subsequently required for a complete conversion to MBISs in each case. Managers closely studied the conversion experiences of their peers and competitors, and conscientiously perused periodical literature for case studies and recommendations.

Critical Success Factors did not focus on technical aspects such as file conversion and subject Data Base Management Systems (DMBSs) since conversion was vendor-facilitated and because off-the-shelf profession-specific software included modules for prototyping, queries, and customization. On the other hand, since every business preferred the "black

---

Moore Orthopedic Group
Crown, Lowell, and Beckett
Scribe Associates

MBIS Conversion Advantages

1. munificence
2. relocation as stimulus
3. effective CSF analysis
4. demonstration effect of peers
5. availability of packed software
6. a buyers' market:
   fierce vendor
   competition and highly
   negotiable terms
7. sufficient leverage to guarantee maintenance
8. cohesion and vision

Figure 7: Set 1's latent and created advantages for MBIS Integration

box" approach, that is, to bypass the need to understand the technical aspects of computerization, the critical importance of available and competent maintenance cannot be overstated. None of the operations could survive significant downtime.

Although in-house expertise was limited, all three groups planned to expand applications, alter configurations, and develop personal areas of expertise in information utilization.

Systems and Market Characteristics

Grouped professionals and departments of large organizations, both groups in Sets 1 and 2, typically confronted six sets of systems and market characteristics in the selection process in the 1980's (Figs. 8 and 8a):

1. mature proprietary systems in a near-perfect market;
2. immature proprietary systems in an imperfect market;
3. failed proprietary systems in an imperfect market;
4. mature open systems in a near-perfect market;
5. immature open systems in an imperfect market; and
6. failed open systems in an imperfect market.

The advantages of securing mature systems in a near-perfect market are affordability, minimum debugging, expandability, multiple peripheral options, upgrades, easy maintenance, and viability: i.e., the vendor is not about to go out of business. Scribe

Associates and Crown, Lowell, and Beckett secured mature systems in a near-perfect market.

The imperfect market is characterized by imperfect information and imperfect competition, leading to an inability to contrast and chose between overtly competitive systems. Typically, this condition stems from the inadequate availability of public ratings and marketing material, and because of an insufficient number of vendors. The imperfect market includes software written in-house or systems produced by vendors enjoying near-monopolies.

Crown, Lowell, and Beckett and also Scribe Associates were able to secure mature systems in a near-perfect market. For them, the ability to be early adopters increased the firm's competitive advantage at a crucial time, while they were well-positioned in a major growth industry.

Open systems will be more characteristic in the

SET 1	**SYSTEM TYPE**	**MARKET TYPE**
Moore Orthopedic Group	Immature Proprietary	Imperfect
Crown,Lowell and Beckett	Mature Proprietary	Near-Perfect
Scribe Associates	Mature Proprietary	Near-Perfect

Figure 8: System and market characteristics in set 1

SET 2		
Municipal Planning Information System (MPIS)	Failed Proprietary	Imperfect
Compbank: Financial Control Division	Immature Open	Near-Perfect

Figure 8a: System and market characteristics in set 2

1990s, as will be the adoption of workstations, but closed systems typically dominated easy-to-use small business applications in the 1980's.

Solutions

Moore Orthopedic Group

The past twenty years have been marked by mergers and acquisitions in health care. Medicare and other entitlement programs have caused combinations, as major medical group practices sought to maximize reimbursements and remain competitive in the struggle for market shares (Mieling, 1989).

Physicians began to market and customize their services, attracting patients through brochures, expanded hours, improved access to care, and one-stop services: X-rays, testing, specialist diagnosis, and rehabilitative therapy (Jensen, 1987). Some groups joined HMOs (Health Maintenance Organizations), offered house calls, or published health care newsletters.

The rapid increase in medical group practices reflected the economies of scale achieved in group production of physician services and group investment in office space and equipment. The American Medical Association conducted survivor analyses of medical practices, and found that solo practices were markedly inefficient and marginal, and that the market favored large, multispecialty groups, especially in the Northeast (Marder, 1985). IT, from appointment scheduling to desktop publishing, is vital at every level of service and management for most practitioners.

Significant generational differences exist in

medical practices, and older doctors are less likely to combine, bureaucratize, and market(Jensen, 1987).

Dr. Moore is an internationally known orthopod who has delivered numerous well-received papers on microscopic surgery. He resisted computerization but was inundated by advice from his colleagues at the hospital on systems selection. He ran a prosperous solo practice until 1985, when his two sons completed their medical education, internships and residencies to join him in a group practice.

Dr. Moore ran a highly profitable organization, and accumulated considerable wealth in the form of portfolio investments, real estate, and rare automobiles. Although he displayed a marked aptitude for automotive engineering, he said that he despised computer systems. "My idea of user-friendliness is when you open the refrigerator door and the light goes on," he told his consultant.

Dr. Moore's administrative style was authoritarian, and his staff worried about the introduction of new technologies and new partners, as well as the impending move to a new site. Dr. Moore found it difficult to find and retain help, and searched for several years for a competent office manager who understood medical practice, accounting, human resources and information technologies, without success.

The Moore Group chose a system from a vendor whose viability was marginal, with little reliable help from trade literature or the medical establishment. One periodical, *Physicians and Computers*, focused on issues and options in computing, but professional associations such as the American Medical Association did not evaluate computer systems. Other trade literature, such as *Medical Economics*, was more likely to contain articles on prenuptial agreements for second marriages, and investment opportunities, than on information technologies.

The proprietary software was reasonably user-friendly, but the performance was poor and the hardware inadequate. Many application modules were under-utilized, and basic features such as word processing were unsatisfactory. The maintenance contracts were inadequate, and debugging involved three years of effort, lock-outs and expensive modifications.

The munificence of the organization enabled the group to survive the lengthy conversion process; from the beginning, the MBIS represented a marked improvement over the archaic filing and reporting system which it replaced. At present, in spite of cost overruns and delays, the organization is pleased with the MBIS and feels that the system is far superior to most of their competitors, a small indication of the quality of medical office systems. In May, 1990 the Moore Orthopedic Group decided to retain but upgrade their hardware, to move to a larger out-of-state vendor who assured local support, and to add significant amounts of memory and storage.

The Moore Group has expanded to include more partners, moved to their new building, and is seeking competitive advantage through several tactics, including specializations in sports medicine, expanded physical therapy, and knee reconstructions. Patient volume continues to increase, and the information system supports decisions regarding emergency coverage, workman's compensation, Medicare, and re-munification systems. On-line access to insurers and hospitals, as well as software upgrades which reflect new regulations and form changes, has been indispensable. The Group could not function without the internal retrieval and transmission of records, for example, from examination cubicles to radiology. The system has significantly reduced backlogs and problems with data integrity and redundancy. The system swiftly paid for itself through improvements in accounts receivables (Fig. 9).

Dr. Moore has become an MBIS aficionado, and is anxious to incorporate optical scanning, more complex imaging systems, laser storage, and optical processors as soon as they are perfected.

The introduction of IT was vital for the expansion of the business and competitiveness, and it also, inadvertently, eased some transitional difficulties and generational differences by rationalizing decisions and enhancing flexibility.

Crown, Lowell, and Beckett

In 1986, the young partners of Crown, Lowell, and Beckett realized that a CBIS was vital to operations. The practice was flourishing, but badly in need of restructuring and control. The partners agreed on the need to bring in word processing and time and billing as soon as possible. They foresaw the addition of another partner to the firm, and were moving to a spacious new building in eighteen months. They wanted a CBIS up and running before the move, and had been favorably impressed with systems chosen by peers in the profession.

Competing firms in the New Haven area were computerizing, and the legal community was quite knowledgeable about the common features of the available packaged software, in large part because of significant coverage of MBISs in trade periodicals

Billing:	justification and refinement interface with word processing improved turn-around for accounts receivable

Patient Care:	accessible reference material and records
	improved appointment system
	coordination of surgery, hospitalization,
	          post-operative care, therapy
	efficient storage and updating of patient
	          records

Staff:	less backlog superior productivity satisfactory training improvements in retention improved projections for inventory and supply

**Physicians/
Managers:**
	information-sharing
	coordinated correspondence, billing,
	          scheduling
	research and publishing facilitated
	support for new specialties
	ongoing analyses for appropriate expansions
	minimal disruption in gradually turning
	business over to younger partners
	minimal disruption during transfer to new site
	          services
	          accounts receivable
	          time management
	strategic planning and projections
	holistic, global view of business
	support and assistance for tax accountant
	telecomputing: record-keeping and reference
	          management of personal asset
	          rental properties
	          luxury used car business
	          portfolio investment
	          cohesion and comity

Figure 9: Moore Orthopedic Group : Critical Success Factors

such as *Legal Economics, Law Office Economics and Management* and *ABA Journal.* The American Bar Association (ABA), unlike the American Medical Association, sponsored periodic evaluations of legal software by a Legal Advisory Technology Council (LTAC) which approved satisfactory packages. These LTAC reviews are widely circulated and cited, contributing to the near-perfection of the market by providing evaluative product information and fostering vendor competition.

The partners decided that Beckett should research and select an appropriate system, beginning with improvements in time and billing. Accounting, real estate management, and word processing were also required.

Beckett accumulated 24 cubic feet of literature on legal systems, including clippings, articles, and compendious vendor brochures, and was unable to evaluate a persistent Lanier salesman's offer for free word processing system for six months, followed by an offer to lease or buy the system and additional applications.

The remaining partners, particularly Crown, periodically quizzed Beckett on his progress and could not empathize with his inability to construct a schedule of selection and implementation. After nine months, Beckett was restive and frustrated: "I can either study computers or practice law," he said. The partners agreed that Beckett should hire a consultant, a professor of computer information systems at a local university, to assist him.

The systems and analysis design project was an educative and non-traumatic experience for the firm. The consultant was contacted at the beginning of July, analysis and design with significant input by two of the partners was completed by August. Vendor proposals were detailed and professional, and included demonstrations, references, and maintenance options. However, the proposals' terms, including cost, were not as negotiable as proposals for medical MBISs.

MANAC software was chosen on the basis of

LTAC reviews, the vendor's proposal, and guaranteed local maintenance. The MBIS was installed and training completed by the end of September. Upon the advice of the consultant, one-third payment was delayed until data conversion was satisfactory and complete.

The partners were very pleased with IRM, and found that, as is typical of computerized law offices, the automation of writing was a key improvement (Perritt, 1989). Time and billing has extremely cost-effective; it replaced a manual system in which many calls and short transactions were unrecorded and not charged.

The quality and quantity of the office's work product improved significantly. Writing, communication, and analysis were facilitated, but reporting and DSS have not replaced owner/partner brainstorming sessions. The CSFs of the organization were supported (Fig. 10).

- word processing for briefs and correspondence
- refined and reliable time and billing
- capture lost charges for short phone calls
- superior storage and retrieval of client files
- flexibility for file updates
- information sharing between partners
- iterative services: wills & contracts
- coordinate correspondence, billing, scheduling
- flexibility and support for long term research needs
- analyses of business to accommodate new partners
- minimal disruption of services, accounts receivable, time management during move to new site
- capacity to access external databases and services

Figure 10: Critical Success Factors: Crown, Lowell, and Beckett

Scribe Associates

Scribe Associates originated because of the existence of state-of-the-art computer-aided transcript (CAT) MBISs. Its founders broke away from their employer, a large, traditional court recording firm which used antiquated mechanical methods of transcription, editing, and reproduction. The Scribes recognized the competitive edge which CAT technology put within the reach of entrepreneurial firms, briefly tried to persuade the traditional firm to modernize, and pooled their capital and expertise to swiftly establish their own firm.

Trade periodicals such as *The National Shorthand Reporter* enhances systems information within the profession. Superior CAT systems are produced by several major vendors, such as AristoCAT, Baron-Data, StenoCAT, XScribe, and Cimarron. Lively intra-professional exchanges reveal the technological bent of the members.

The partners selected Xscribe without a consultant, and worked closely with the vendor to construct an appropriate and expandable system. The group is delighted with computerization. Depositions are captured by the profession's shorthand off-site, stored, transmitted, by modem, transliterated, and formatted at the office electronically. The court reporters have extensive editing, searching, and data communication power and have reduced the turn-around time for depositions from weeks to days.

Using MBIS-based IRM, the partners have reversed the ratio of staff to professionals, turning the ratio on its head, and have recruited new court reporters for the organization. They have purchased two office buildings, and occupy one, and operate an effective electronic office in Stamford which is, physically, essentially a closet. Scribe Associates have an international reputation for peerless service and turn-around time (Fig. 11). Their only significant bottle-neck is the copy machine, which in their former office was the epitome of speed and high tech.

Moore Orthopedic Group experienced the most modest success in MBIS integration, although the system vastly improved resource management at all levels and was considered more than satisfactory. The group law practice and the court recorders adopted turnkey systems in a near-perfect market: with near-perfect information and near-perfect competition. The systems were affordable, expandable, and fine-tuned for applications such as time and billing, reports, and computer-assisted transcripts (CATs). Furthermore, the organizations were assisted by rating systems, expert evaluations, and germane studies in major trade magazines and professional journals.

- purchase state-of-the-art CAT system
- start up business, professionalize service
- reputation for rapid turn-around on briefs
- easy editability and search
- coordinate correspondence, billing, scheduling
- enhanced services
- on-hand reference material
- reduce turn-around time for depositions
- minimize staff support: reverse ratio of staff-professionals from 4-2 to 2-4
- maintain low staffing needs throughout expansion
- recruit new court reporters
- utilize distributed, off-line processing for document transcription overnight
- eliminate duplication and mailing bottlenecks
- minimal disruption of services, accounts receivable,
- time management during move to new site
- capacity for EDI with distributors, suppliers, clients
- responsivity to regulatory or procedural change
- back-up, security and control
- enhanced capacity for strategic business analysis

Figure 11: Scribe Associates: Critical Success Factors

Managers and staff adapted easily to the conversion: power users emerged in the organization, vendors were locally available for satisfactory training and maintenance. The organization anticipated the need for changes in structure, productivity measurements, planning, and control and regarded them favorably. Both young firms found that the CBISs significantly improved competitiveness and accelerated their rate of growth.

A Municipal Planning Information System

In striking contrast to the MBISs installed by the small businesses in Set 1, in the early- and mid-1980s, the technologies available for public administration were poor and untested. Significant gains in productivity and strategic advantage in the public sector were lacking, in contrast with private IRM (Otten, 1989).

The market was markedly imperfect, with no industry leaders in software production, minimal evaluative services in the industry, and a paucity of appropriate trade literature (Chepaitis, 1990). Furthermore, public administrators and staffs were ill-trained and poorly positioned to assist in the design and control of a municipal planning information system (MPIS) (Kraemer & Northrup, 1984 & 1989; Kiel, 1986). Much "computer education in small-city governments is confined to software—specific training, and only 15% of M.P.A. curricula required a course in MIS in 1986 (Kiel, 1986). In addition, little staff training in information systems and record management is budgeted (Brown-John, 1984) (Fig. 12).

Yet, in contrast to other emergent management tools, a substantial increase in MIS investment did

---

- poor IT: unsatisfactory software
- lack of MIS-orientation in Public Administration curriculum
- lack of dynamism, cohesion, and accountability
- poor market information and imperfect competition
- social and political disincentives to effective implementation
- lack of trained staff

Figure 12: Municipal Information Systems: Flawed technologies imperfect markets, and inadequate administrator training, and control.

occur throughout the 1980s (Poister & Gregory, 1989).

Gorr (1986) convincingly cites the failure to distinguish the unique developmental needs in public systems, and advocates prototyping through an Interactive Systems Development Cycle (ISDC), especially for the utility of special events data.

Advances in intelligent mapping (Craig, 1989), imaging, distributed databases, data communications, optical scanning, and voice entry hold promise for municipal IRM, but political turf-building and social barriers to technological innovation may be negating factors in many public administrative cultures. The lack of leadership and long-term planning is significant in contrast to successful small business IRM in Set 1 (McGregor & Daly, 1989).

Examples of successful applications and MPIS projects illustrate the potential which IRM should hold for municipalities. The indispensable utilization of MBISs in police departments exemplifies the utility of case-oriented designs and subject databases in public administration (Danziger & Kraemer, 1984). Los Angeles utilized teams of MIS students to achieve impressive administrative cost savings, form reductions, on-line user manuals, and a menu-driven system (Jackson & Caribbo, 1986).

A small Connecticut city's Municipal Planning Information System (MPIS), based in the Neighborhood Planning Department (NPD), was characterized by the most atypical and uneven development of the five cases.

Funded by a national grant and assisted by a major university, MPIS was touted as a pilot project which would serve as a MBIS prototype for small cities. This MBIS failed primarily because of untested and inadequate software, the lack of local support, the absence of trained and knowledgeable users, arcane hardware, and an egregious lack of leadership, feedback and control.

In the 1950's and 1960's, New Harbor prided itself on its reputation as a model city, and attracted significant federal and private grants each year to test the efficacy of socio-economic engineering programs of the Great Society. By the 1980's, the seventh-poorest city in the country, with $9 million in unspent federal anti-poverty money, New Harbor emerged as a symbol of municipal ineptitude, uncontrollable crime, infant mortality, and drug abuse.

Poor IRM was a central problem in poor planning, misallocated services, the decline of public order, and scandalous mismanagement. The lack of coordination, information, and expertise in decision-making induced the city to experiment with several micro-based prototypes in the early 1980's, including projects for arson prevention, delinquent tax collection, and analyses of multiple-family dwellings.

A team of staff experts, consultants, and city officials developed an information coordination plan in a project co-sponsored by the Ford Foundation and a prestigious university. The city hosted a national conference on municipal information systems and the

American Planning Association published the conference proceedings (Chepaitis, 1990).

Political leaders hoped that the introduction a
state-of-the-art distributed MBIS in 1983 would attract future monies for the conversion from centralized, batch data processing to inter-agency information sharing, and be a political asset. The system,
MPIS, was in the Neighborhood Planning Department,
but did not live up to its marketing or its promise, and
exhibited many shortcomings cited in the literature
on IRM and public administration (Fig 13).

The MBIS was intended to facilitate resource
management initially through ad hoc queries such as
a breakdown by neighborhood of properties by type,
by agency activities, and by the impact of existing

- introduce a state-of-the-art MPIS
- attract external expert and financial assistance
- coordinate operations, tactical management, and policy-
   making at a reasonable cost
- drive structural organization change through inter-agency
   information sharing
- refine IRM to determine and justify allocations and
   socio-economic engineering
- provide for ongoing development of new applications
- guarantee responsivity to change:
   create a subject DBMS
       neighborhood type
       agency activities
       impact of existing programs
- include ad hoc query capability for DSS
- engineer and publicize early successes
- reward power users
- market the system
- train staff
- enhance electability focus on progressive image
- justify increases in budget and personnel

Figure 13: MPIS Critical Success Factors

programs; more sophisticated applications would be constructed through a mature DBMS.

City planners politicized the development process by including a campaign to market MPIS. Marketing strategies were formulated to sell the system through dramatic successes in low-risk applications. Computer-aided analyses of prior decision-making was prepared to overwhelm potential detractors and to guarantee the popularity, not merely the success, of MPIS.

MPIS never functioned satisfactorily, even within the NDP. Fatal hardware deficiencies, software bugs, a lack of expandability or maintenance, and the absence of trained developers and users eroded its usefulness (Fig. 14).

MPIS did not produce structural changes in city administration, nor resource-sharing, collaborative problem-solving, or strategic advantage for the administration, its designers, or the NPD.

Compbank

Compbank, with a global staff of over 60,000, operates in an intensely competitive environment for financial services. Among its client services, ironically, are on-line information retrieval from the communications and entertainment media and shared databases. In the 1980s, Compbank experienced continuous repositioning for strategic advantage, not only because of increased competition but also because of emergent opportunities resulting from deregulation and from enhanced profitability in information services.

Compbank has been an industry leader in internal retrieval and reporting expertise, and founded new service profit centers with alacrity, especially in

- inadequate hardware for expansion
- complex and unfriendly software
- minimal application development
- overdependence on key personnel and failure to retain them
- turf-building: political disincentives for information-sharing
- lack of training and motivation for staff to assist in systems
    maintenance and development
- the diversion of resources to market rather than
    develop the system
- lack of trained staff
- lack of local support
- poor MIS-training and orientation for public administrators,
    especially mayoral appointees
- lack of satisfactory maintenance contracts with the vendors
- poor market information and imperfect competition
- turnover in leadership political instability, scandal, and
    secrecy
- failure to identify CSFs for implementation and optimal
    utililization

Figure 14: MPIS's critical failures

online services, information retrieval, and IRM consulting.

Yet, although the financial services organization was an international leader in selling information
and value-added systems, Compbank's own information system was not satisfactory and after well-publi-
cized disappointments with a centralized mainframes,
Compbank's financial controllers moved to an MBIS.

To optimize profitability and growth, in the mid-
1980s Compbank identified a broad range of CSFs for
their Connecticut-based Financial Control Division,
intending to reduce staff, improve professional autonomy, and enhance client services (Fig. 15).

Compbank sought to achieve these goals simul-
taneously through the introduction of a distributed
information system featuring extensive micro-based
desktop autonomy for financial controllers.

In June, 1988, an in-house poll of controllers in

desktop decision support systems
ad hoc query capabilities
swift application development especially for business
    analysis
compensate for insufficient staff support for managers
friendly menu-driven software for reporting
enhanced control over task- and time-management
enhanced capability for recruitment and training

Figure 15: Compbank's CSFs

ninety countries pinpointed and measured their discontent with the MBIS, especially packaged software, in Compbank's new distributed system.

The controllers complained that applications were not menu-driven, and employees were discouraged by an egregious lack of training and support. Routine reporting was arduous and time-consuming, and controllers complained that they had little time for analysis and decision support. Shortages of staff,

System Factors	**Business Factors**
inability to handle voluminous reporting	declining analytical activity
inability to answer ad hoc queries	increased reporting and clerical demands
reliance on manual systems in some groups	failure to recruit staff
lack of software support	failure to keep up with new products and services
	declining morale
lack of modeling and statistical power	failure to address new accounting and tax policy
	ambiguous measures of productivity

Figure 16: Compbank's critical failures

adaptation to a global environment for banking services, and new business practices overwhelmed the division (Fig. 16). Conversion to an MBIS exacerbated business problems, and a task force was commissioned to assist in the design of a new system.

Set 2's integration of MBIS's failed not only because of poor management and inadequate control, but also because they lacked advantages which the professions in Set 1 enjoyed, such as IT maturity, rigorous technology assessment, and broad and open vendor competition (Fig. 17).

Future Trends and Emerging Technologies

Generic advantages and liabilities can be identified in these cases, advantages which support the critical success factors necessary for the successful integration of MBISs into expanding organizations.

These advantages provide a valuable demonstration effect for the development of appropriate system components for other occupations. System components include not only hardware, software, and

- MBIS maturity
- near-perfect IT markets
- organizational munificence
- ambition and leadership
- positive attitudes toward NTCs
- affordable conversions
- local support
- affordable expandability
- software upgrades
- adequate training
- well-communicated tasks and measurements
- desire to use IT for competitive advantage
- cohesion and communication

Figure 17: Seminal advantages in the integration of MBISs into some expanding small businesses through appropriate CSFs

data, but also people. In the 1990's, the two-pronged effort to maximize human resources continues: increased and ongoing computer training and friendlier software. Increasingly, programmers and vendors attempt, where possible, to create software which is not only end-user friendly (EUF) but also <u>every</u> end-user friendly (EEUF), for a truly democratic technology.

Voice, optical scanners, self-diagnosing systems, and cellular units will enhance not only ease-of-use, but also integrity and portability.

Open systems promise to optimize hardware and software options and flexibility, and workstations promise to deliver mainframe capacities to modest office units, perhaps powered by optical processors and enhanced by nearly limitless site storage and off-site retrieval services. Improved connectivity and the ability to tap into state-of-the-art communications systems will revolutionize data access and ownership.

Security, information overload, and the development of qualitative and evaluative measurements for information at hand remain challenges for the decade.

Conclusion

Microcomputer technology has advanced within the past decade at different paces for many small businesses—largely due to the availability of high-quality menu-driven software, support, and turnkey systems for some office systems. The confluence of technological maturity and business opportunity has acted as a synergid, particularly in dynamic owner-managed businesses in lucrative fields.

A striking development in the introduction of

CBISs into the three owner-managed small businesses was the easy migration to strategic Information Systems (SISs). Moore Orthopedic Associates, Scribe Associates, and Crown, Lowell and Beckett recognized the opportunities for SISs before initiating systems analysis and design.

Strategic Information Systems (SISs) flow from a unique set of goals, critical success factors, and critical assumptions in burgeoning and expanding small businesses.

SISs differ in intent and in applications from the management information systems (MISs) which are the traditional focus of the curriculum; SISs are designed not only to improve basic processes and to satisfy managers' and professionals' information needs, but also to provide competitive advantages or to reposition the organization. Although SISs have been the subject of intensive study and debate, little attention has been paid to small organizations' SISs. Study has focused on large system issues such as decentralization and control, and state-of-the-art technological platforms. Small organizations' competitive strategies, especially the unique perspective and dynamics of the owner-managed, enterprise, require more research. The risks of rising entry barriers, increasing switching costs, alterations in the balance of power within organization, and top-down consensus-building for new strategies—all are topics for future study.

Resource endowments which at first appear distinctive and discrete often resemble those in like organizations, as do the the adoptive paths which are chosen for SIS analysis, design, and implementation.

References

Ahituv, N. and Munro, M.C. (1986). Acquiring a computer: Advice for small business. *International Journal of Management. 3* (2), 61-79.

Anderson, James G. & Jay, Stephen J. (1984). Physician utilization of computers: A network analysis of the diffusion process. *Journal of Organizational Behaviour. 6* (No. 3/4), 21-35.

Brancheau, James C., Vogel, Douglas R., and Wetherbe, James C. (1985). An investigation of the information center from the user's perspective. *Database. 11* (3), 4-17.

Brown-John, C. Lloyd. (1984). Teaching: Public administration or public managers of both? *Optimum. 15* (3), 93-100.

Brussaard, Bas K. (1988). Information resource management in the public sector. *Information and Management. 15* (2), 93-103.

Carbone, T.C. (1985). The stages of success. *Management World. 14* (4), 36-37.

Chepaitis, Elia. (1990). New Haven's Information System: Public Lessons for Private Systems. *Fairfield Business Review.* 38-45.

City of New Haven and the Ford Foundation. (1984). Conference *Summary and Background Materials: Managing Municipal Information Needs.*

Clemons, Eric. (1988). Competition and Cooperation in Information Systems Innovation. *Information and Management. 15* (1) 25-35.

Collins, Stephen H. (1987). Interview: Small business committees chairman. *Journal of Accountancy.* 163 (6), 143-150.

Connor. Denis A. (1988). *Computer Systems Development.* Englewood Cliffs: Prentice Hall.

Craig, Dianne. (1989). Coquitlam maps the future with GIS technology. *ComputerData. 14* (9), 28-29.

Danziger, James N. & Kraemer, Kenneth L. (1984). Computerized data-based systems and productivity among professional workers: The case of detectives. *Public Administration Quarterly. 8*(3), 343-368.

Davidsson, Peter.(1989). Entrepreneurship - and after?: A Study of growth willingness in small firms. *Journal of Business Venturing. 4*(3), 211-226.

Day, Stacey B., M.D. & Brandejs, Jan F. (1982). *Computers for Medical Office and Patient Management.* New York: Van Nostrand.

Freedmand, David. (1987). Are We Expecting Too Much from Strategic IS? *Infosystems, 34* (1) 22-24.

Gaynor, Martin. (1989). Competition within the firm: Theory plus some evidence from medical group practice. *Rand Journal of Economics. 20* (1), 59-76.

Gibb, Allan. (1988). The enterprise culture: Threat or opportunity. *Management Decisions. 26* (4), 5-12.

Gibb, Allan & Scott, Mike. (1985). Strategic awareness, personal commitment and the process of planning in the small business. *Journal of Management Studies. 22* (6), 597-631.

Gorr, Wilpen L. (1986). Use of special-event data in government information systems. *Public Administration Review. 46*, 532-539.

Henderson, John C. and Sifonis, John G. (1988). The Value of Strategic IS Planning: Understanding Consistency, Validity, and IS Markets. *MIS Quarterly. 12* (2), 187-200.

Holland, Robert. (1989). The IRMing of America. *CIO. 2* (6), 61-62.

Huff, Sid L. and Beattie, E. Scott. (1985-86). Strategic Versus Competitive Information Systems. *Business Quarterly, 50* (4), 97-102.

Ibrahim, A.B. & Goodwin, J.R. (1986). Perceived causes of success in small business. *American Journal of Small Business. 11* (2), 41-50.

Jackson, Michael & Caribbo, John.(1986). Productivity Internship. *Bureaucrat 15* (2), 47-48.

Jacobs, Gordon L. (1986). Strategic planning for automation. *Legal Economics. 12* (6), 49-62.

Janulaitis, A. Victor. (1986). Barriers to Developing Competitive Systems. *EDP Analyzer. 24* (10), 13-14.

Jensen, Joyce and Larson, Steve. (1987). Nation's physicians adding health care services, marketing their practices to attract new patients. *Modern Healthcare. 17* (16), 49-50.

Johnson, J. Lynne and Kuehn, Ralph. (1987). The small business owner/ managers search for external information. *Journal of Small Business Management. 25* (3), 53-60.

Kiel, L. Douglas. (1986). Information systems education in masters' programs in public affairs and administration. *Public Administration Review. 46*, 590-594.

Kops, Daniel W., Jr. (1986). *Managing Municipal Information Needs Using Microcomputers.* American Planning Association, Planning Advisory Report Number 393.

Kraemer, Kenneth L.& Northrop, Alana. (1984). Computers in public management education: A curricula proposal for the next ten years. *Public Administration Quarterly. 8* (3), 343-368.

Kraemer, Kenneth L. & Northrop, Alana. (1987). Curriculum recommendations for public management education in computing: An update. *Public Administration Quarterly. 49* (5), 447-453.

Kralewski, John E, Pitt, Laura, and Shatin, Deborah. (1985). Structural characteristics of medica; group practices. *Administrative Science Quarterly. 30* (1), 34-45.

Lawson, Kent. (1987). 4GL Paves the Way for City's Advanced Data Integration. *Data Management, 25* (8), 15-16.

Lemann, Nicholas. (1989). The Unfinished War. *The Atlantic Monthly. 263* (1), 52-68.

Louis, Raymond. (1985). Organizational characteristics and MIS success in the context of small business. *MIS Quarterly. 9*(1), 37-52.

Malone, Stewart C. (1985). Computerizing small business information systems. *Journal of Small Business Management. 23* (2), 10-16.

Marder, William D. and Zuckerman, Stephen. (1985). Competition and medical groups: A survivor analysis. *Journal of Health Economics, 4*(2), 167-176.

McGregor, Eugene B. & Daly, John. (1989). The Strategic Implications of automation in public sector human resource management. *Review of Public Personnel Administration. 10* (1), 29-47.

Mieling, Terence M. Market. (1989). Overview. Topics in Health Care *Financing. 15* (4), 1-8.

Morse, Paul. (1990). Metro to decentralize LIS. *ComputerData, 15*(2), 1-2.

Nickell, Gary S. and Seado, Paul C. (1986). The impact of attitudes and experience on small business computer use. *American Journal of Small Business, 10*(4), 37-48.

Nosek, John T. (1989). Organization Design Strategies to enhance information resource management. *Information and Management, 16*(2), 81-91.

Onove, Allan J. (1985). Future trends in law office technology. *Legal Economics, 11*(3), 54-55.

Otten, Klaus W. (1989). A changing information environment challenges public administration. *Information Management Review, 4*(4), 9-16.

Owen, Darrell E. (1989). IRM Concepts: Building blocks for the 1990s. *Information Management Review, 5*(2), 19-28.

Pendergraft, Norman, Morris, Linda, & Savage, Kathryn. (1987). Small business computer security. *Journal of Small Business Management, 25*(4), 54-60.

Perrit, Henry H., Jr. (1989). Dividing up the lawyer's desk: Deciding what to automate. *Legal Economics, 15*(6), 37-38.

Poister, Theodore H. & Streib, Gregory. (1989). *Public Administration Review, 49*(3), 240-248.

Rockart, John. (1979). Chief executives define their own data needs. *Harvard Business Review, 57*(2), 81-93.

Saxon, Myron. (1988). Evaluating legal computer systems. *Legal Assistant Today, 6*(2), 52-57.

Schaal, Ernest A. (1989). Desktop publishing in the law office. *Legal Economics, 15*(5), 18-20.

Schatz, Robert E. (1985). The business side of a medical practice. *Computers in Healthcare, 6*(8), 64-68.

Schmitz, Homer H. (1989). Information resource management. *Health Care Supervisor, 7*(2), 13-22.

Shank, Michael E. and Boynton, Andrew C., & Zmud, Robert W. (1985). Critical success factor analysis as a methodology for MIS planning. *MIS Quarterly, 9*(2), 121-129.

Smith, Allen N. & Medley, Donald B. (1987). *Information Resource Management.* Cincinnati: South-Western.

Solomon, Morton, M.D. (1985). *Using Computers in the Practice of Medicine.* Englewood Cliffs: Prentice Hall.
Smith, Allen N. & Medley, Donald B. (1987). *Information Resource Management.* Cincinnati: South-Western.

Solomon, Morton, M.D. (1985). *Using Computers in the Practice of Medicine.* Englewood Cliffs: Prentice Hall.

Sinott, Daniel. (1988). 1990s and beyond. *Legal Economics, 14*(8), 35-38.

Stoner, Charles R. (1987). Distinctive competence and competitive advantage. *Journal of Small Business Management, 25*(2), 33-39.

Trauth, Eileen M. (1989).The evolution of information resource management. *Information and Management, 16*(5), 257-268.

Trippi, Robert R. (1989). Strategic Information Systems: Current research issues. *Journal of Information Systems Management, 6*(3), 30-35.

Wiseman, Charles. (1988). Strategic Information Systems: Trends and challenges over the next decade. *Information Management Review, 4*(1), 9-16.

Wiseman, Charles. (1988). *Strategic Information Systems.* New York: Irwin.

Chapter 5

MANAGING THE INTRODUCTION OF INFORMATION SYSTEMS TECHNOLOGY: THE CASE OF DESKTOP PUBLISHING AS AN ORGANIZATION-WIDE RESOURCE

Wallace A. Wood
Bryant College

Robert P. Behling
Bryant College

Effective management of information system technologies in the 1990s will be a combination of information system and management training, detailed planning and organization, and understanding the technical and human needs of the corporation (Grodman, 1988). Key to the successful introduction of any new technology is planning. A comprehensive information systems plan should be based on the organization's overall business plan and should reflect organizational goals. These plans may include modifying and restructuring the organization to take advantage of emerging technologies. Gallagher (1988) identifies four interacting factors contributing to cor-

Previously published in Managing Information Resources in the 1990s © Idea Group Publishing

porate interest in utilizing computer technology: (1) recent advances in computing hardware making possible a new generation of applications, (2) a developing perception that information and knowledge is a corporate asset; (3) easy-to-use software products and an increase in the sophistication of applications; and (4) the utilization of information technology as a competitive weapon.

Introducing New Computer Information Systems

In any business environment, new computer information systems are implemented to increase customer service, improve productivity, or cut costs (McManis & Leibman, 1988). Introducing new systems, then, is often necessary to meet the competition and retain a customer base. At the same time new systems are being developed and introduced, the widespread use of information technology throughout the organization is causing information overload (Berger, 1989). Many organizations face a crisis: they don't believe they can prosper or even survive without continually introducing new information technology, while at the same time they are frustrating their mangers with an ever-changing and often difficult to understand and utilize information system.

Several key issues need to be considered by management if the new system is to have a smooth transition into the organization. Most important in the implementation of the new system besides the actual hardware success is the attitude of the personnel using the system. The organization must recognize the importance the human resource function can play in the process. Other issues that require consideration include the effects of technology introduction on the organizational structure, effects on job responsibilities within the organization, and a change in the way managers perform their tasks (McManis & Leibman, 1988).

Some of the changes that the introduction of computer technology cause include: (1) a change in the relationship between individuals and departments; (2) a change in training needs for system users; and (3) a change in work relationships, managers often become more dependent on high-tech employees. (Denton, 1986)

Managing change is becoming a way of life in modern organizations, including managing and controlling the pace of innovation and change when implementing the use of computer technology (Lucas, 1986). The emergence of this technology brings with it a number of important management concerns: (1) a concern for ergonomics and the associated health and injury risks such as repetitive strain injury and vision problems associated with using keyboards and video display terminals; (2) the development of systems by naive computer specialists, causing management to focus attention on trivial areas at the expense of more important areas; and (3) the focusing of control of an organization into the hands of those who control the information resources (Er, 1987).

Strategy

Technology strategy is itself but one part of an overall business strategy, therefore it must always be conceived and implemented within the context of the overall strategic management of business (Wilson, 1989). Information technology's increased importance means senior executives, information systems personnel, and users must plan and control the introduction and use of information technology (Grindlay, 1986). The primary steps involved in creating and maintaining an effective strategic plan for information systems include: (1) identification of objectives - the IS should support the objectives of the parent organization; (2) establish balanced priorities for investment in technical resources and user applications; (3) establish a reasonable time frame for the planning horizon and the anticipation of the future IS environment; and (4) expect the unexpected, as many external forces will impact the plan (Miller, 1988).

Strategy for implementing information systems has changed significantly over time, as have the hardware and software products available to organizations. In the large central systems of 1960s and 1970s, management focused on transaction oriented systems supporting large administrative units. Economies of scale were often cited as a powerful argument to promote administrative efficiency. Supporting the individual manager with decision support applications has been the focus of the 1980s. These applications are often microcomputer driven, and their use has eroded much of the monopolistic control by MIS over information processing resources. The 1980s has brought a climate of high expectation for new computing technologies, however a new group of technology users has been created with no central control. The outlook for the 1990s is to focus on using information technology to gain a competitive advantage, moving the emphasis away from the individual manager and once more putting the focus on the organization rather than the individual (Gallagher, 1988).

New Technology Risks

Managing information technology resources has significant risk in itself but other business risks come into play as well. Technology risk in a project is influenced by three factors: (1) project size (determined by cost, duration, required integration); (2) technology experience (the less experience, the more surprises) project structure (how well defined are the intended results of the project) (Barton & Boast, 1988).

Gallagher (1988) identifies three sources of risk associated with the development of information systems: (1) the degree to which the organization must undergo any significant structural changes to achieve benefits from the new system; (2) the degree to which the applications require solving significant underlying technological support problems; and (3) the extent to which there is uncertainty surrounding the suitability of the application. These factors must be weighed against the perceived benefits of the application. One often overlooked risk is the organizational change risk which comes about when a business underestimates changes in work process, organizational structure, and other management components that must be adapted to the new technology. One problem often encountered by organizations employing new technology is that essential organizational changes are sometimes ignored or poorly handled. (Barton & Boast, 1988). Knowing your company's strengths and weaknesses is critical for effective decision-making and avoiding user resistance when selecting hardware and developing software (Klatch, 1988). By combining knowledge of the organization with risk evaluation, management is able to reduce the chance for disabling system failures when introducing new technology.

C. Parker (1989) identifies a new type of risk underlying conventional types of IS risk - the risk that the organization may not be using new technology strategically. The issues that lie behind corporate vulnerability include data integrity, volume, and flow of information, as well as the complexity of modern organizations. Managing information systems technology has become a complex and demanding challenge, and the traditional cost and benefits study is no longer enough to justify an IS strategy (Tate, 1988).

Managing Applications

The time has come to move information system technologies to where they matter most: Customer service and support, that is away from the traditional accounting areas (Kolodziej, 1989). While moving toward integrating business functions and information technologies, organizations must also be concerned with allocating limited budget resources among a potentially large number of competing computer products and services functions. They also must plan an information systems strategy that addresses rapid technology change, increased information systems expenditures, enterprise wide impact of IS activities, and competitive advantage gained through the application of information system technology (C. Parker, 1989).

Desktop publishing (electronic publishing) uses a microcomputer system to generate documents comparable to those produced by a professional printer, and is an example of a rapidly expanding technology growing at a tremendous rate (McCarthy, 1988). Management of desktop publishing resources is often outside the control of IS, and presents numerous management challenges. A relatively sophisticated PC configuration is needed and the ability to handle the equipment, as well as skills in page layout and design are required for successful applications (Wolfe and Fields, 1988). Advantages of investing in and using this technology include speed (getting nice looking reports and fast), the ability to control your own jobs, and data security (Peterson and Turkel, 1988). The problem of interconnecting disparate systems, coordinating management, and bridging publishing and information processing disciplines are the main organizational headaches facing management (Winkler, 1988).

Operational concerns include the high cost of hardware and software (especially high quality printing hardware), and training requirements. Estimates of training requirements run from 80 to 200 hours before an individual can use these systems effectively (Peterson and Turkel, 1988). The fact that so many users are willing to forge ahead regardless of the costs and technical obstacles points to a powerful need among business (Nance, 1987).

The simplicity suggested by vendors of desktop publishing systems in their advertising and promotion downplays the complexity required to produce quality documents. It gives the task of determining style and aesthetics to people who are not skilled at making such decisions (Hurst, 1987). Users need to take the time to learn about both electronic publishing and design if they are to be successful using this new technology. Good ideas combined with bad design produce disastrous publications. At the same time it should be recognized that electronic publishing extends the users creativity and is very user seductive.

Establishing Standards

Winkler (1988) states that "In most organizations, electronic publishing is a prime example of technology run amok." and cites as the primary reason for this is that no one is in charge. There is evidence that IS managers in most companies rate the management of desktop publishing as a low priority (Wood, 1988). Establishment of standards for desktop publishing will be difficult for an organization lacking a central department or person charged with this responsibility.

The first step for an organization which recognizes that it has a problem with the proliferation of desktop publishing, after it decides that it wishes to address this problem, is to decide who will be responsible for its management. One approach is to have the in-house communications or printing services department take the initiative in establishing publication standards for the organization (MacGibbon, 1987). This approach would leave the standardization of hardware to the IS department and would result in having each department be responsible for that area in which it has the greatest expertise. This approach also has the added benefit of allowing most organizations to utilize departments that already exist rather than establishing a new position such as a chief publishing officer.

Since desktop publishing is already widespread in many organizations, it is too late to have these organizations establish policies and establish standards for existing applications. At this point, they can only play catch up and establish policies and develop standards for future desktop publishing applications.

Market trends (R. Parker, 1989) indicate that with the advent of word processing packages with many desktop publishing features, more users will have the ability to do low end desktop publishing. This makes it imperative that organizations with an existing base of applications, as well as those just entering the publishing arena, formalize policies and standards.

An organization which has as its goal the management of desktop publishing must first make the decision to give budgetary control of desktop publishing to the department or departments charged with the responsibility for managing it. Once fiscal control is established, organizations can then develop policies as to which departments in the organization will be authorized to utilize desktop publishing systems. Such policies should include guidelines for determining whether a desktop publishing package is needed or will a sophisticated word processing package with page layout capabilities serve just as well. These guidelines should describe the purpose of the desired desktop package and the types of publications to be generated, the skill level of potential users (for example, are they already skilled in word processing?), and how much training the users are prepared to undergo (Lach, 1989).

Questions such as does the department have the personnel resources in the form of people capable of using the desktop system or the budget to provide the extensive training to its personnel to acquire this expertise must be answered before a commitment to desktop publishing is made. Some businesses are recognizing that being a desktop publishing guru is full-time pursuit and that it might be better to hire someone with the expertise rather than training a present employee (Altman, 1988). The policy also needs to address fundamental human resource management questions such as does it make sense to have a $50,000 a year engineer using desktop publishing and spending time figuring out font size.

The policies should also address the standardization of software and hardware. Just as it makes sense for an organization to standardize on a single word processing or spreadsheet package, it also makes sense to standardize on a single desktop publishing package. Standardization on hardware allows the sharing of resources such as expensive printers or type setting devices or the use of a single source for those organizations using outside vendors for printing. Perhaps more importantly, it facilitates the work of the in-house publications office in assisting various departments in their desktop publishing efforts.

To address one of the most important concerns with regards to desktop publishing - the quality of the documents generated - policies need to be developed regarding the role of the in-house publications office. Much of the concern to date with desktop publishing relates to the poor quality of the documents generated. This problem is not going away, and in fact, with low cost color printers on the horizon (Gantz, 1989) it will become even more severe. Since it may prove impossible for the publications office to review every publication because of sheer volume, the policy could be that the publications office would review prior to printing all publications which have an audience external to the organization. Thus the company would address those publications that most directly reflect on its corporate image. This does not imply that publications intended for internal audiences in the company would be ignored for the publications office can provide editing assistance for those offices generating such publications. For those companies just beginning in desktop publishing, it might be wise to initially confine desktop publishing to departments which publish only in-house material.

The publications office should develop guidelines and standards for using desktop publishing and disseminate them to everyone in the organization likely to create documents. Such guidelines and standards could be customized by the publications office to suit the company or they could be adopted from an external source such as those published by DataPro Research Corporation (1986). The publications office should follow up this initial dissemination with periodic updates, seminars, and training sessions. Publications or articles devoted to desktop publishing should be distributed to users. Articles with engaging titles like *The Seven Deadly Sins of Desktop Publishing and How to Avoid Them* (Campbell and Rinaldo, 1989) are non technical and easy for a layman to read, and go a long ways towards educating users of desktop publishing.

Other policies, while difficult to develop, should address time spent on publications. When publications were done using external sources, the time spent on documents was limited by externally imposed deadlines and budget constraints. With desktop publishing, these deadlines have disappeared. This along, with the ease of editing brought about by desktop publishing, increases the tendency of users to spend additional time fiddling with the design with no appreciable improvements in quality.

Regardless of whether a company follows these guidelines or uses some other model for establishing standards, it is important to recognize that there is probably no quick method to bring the management of desktop publishing under control. There also will probably be no immediate reduction in costs for many companies have found that any money saved by desktop publishing was put into increasing the number of pages or adding color to publications (Hirsch, 1988).

In addition, desktop publishing has gotten more expensive with time (Curtis, 1988) and with the continued introduction of new equipment, costs promise to continue to increase. This should be viewed by management as all the more reason to take steps to bring desktop publishing under control.

Conclusions

Technology strategy must be conceived and implemented within the context of the overall business strategy. Making the decision to utilize desktop publishing for internal document generation must include making the commitment to the development of policies and standards to effectively support the desktop publishing activities, or the organization will not receive the full benefit from this new technology.

Budget authority and fiscal responsibility determines the accountability structure for desktop publishing activities. Once financial control is established an overall set of guidelines for evaluating desktop publishing applications can be developed. This should include a means for the formal review of the types of publications to be generated, and the evaluation of the skill level of the potential users and their training requirements. To maximize interdepartmental flexibility, hardware and software standards need to be developed. Document quality control can be established by defining the role of the in-house publications office in the overall use of desktop publishing. Finally, policies regarding user training are needed to create a proper work environment.

References

Altman, R. (1988). Making the Right Desktop Publishing Decisions, *Boston Computer Currents*, vol 3, October , 22-23.

Barton, R. and R. Boast. (1988). How to Manage the Risks of Technology, *Journal of Business Strategy*, Nov/Dec., 4-7.

Berger, P. (1989). Balancing Information System Priorities, *Computer Decisions*, March , 17.

Campbell, A and J. Rinaldo. (1989). The Seven Deadly Sins of Desktop Publishing and How to Avoid Them, *CAPS*, *1*(4), 1-5.

Curtis, G. (1988). The Real Challenge of Electronic Publishing, *PC Report*, 7(2), 25-28.

Denton, D. (1986). Success With High Tech: It's Up to You, *Personnel Administrator*, March , 96-105.

Er, M. (1987). The Impact of Information Technology on Organizations," *Journal of Systems Management*, April, 32.

Gallagher, J. (1988). *Knowledge Systems for Business*, Englewood Cliffs, Prentice-Hall.

Gantz, J. (1989). Ready or Not, Color in Desktop Publishing Looms on Horizon," *INFOWORLD, 11*, November 20, 1989, 51.

Grindlay, A. (1986). Managing Information Technology, *Business Quarterly*, Spring , 19-24.

Grodman, L. (1988). A Strategic Plan for the 1990s," *Computerworld*, December 26.
Guidelines: Possibilities and Perils of Desktop Publishing, *DataPro Research Corporation*, Delran, NJ, 1986.

Hirsch, M. (1988). Is desktop publishing worth the effort? *PC World, vol 6*, May ,218-221.

Hurst, R. (1987). The Perils of Desktop Publishing," *Computerworld*, October 7,35-37.

Klatch, W. (1988). Computer Overkill Can Kill Efficiency, *Small Business Reports*, Dec., 71-73.

Kolodziej, S. (1989). The Smart Integration Manager," *Computerworld*, February 6, 24.

Lach, E. (1989). Choosing the Right Tool: How to Decide Between Desktop Publisher and Word Processor, *INFOWORLD, vol 11*, March 13, 45.

Lucas, H. (1986). Utilizing Information Technology: Guidelines for Managers," *Sloan Management Review*, Fall, 36-47.

MacGibbon, J. Desktop Publishing: A Threat to Communication Standards, *Communication World, vol* 4, November, 30-32.

McCarthy, R. (1988). Stop The Presses! An Update on Desktop Publishing, *Electronic Learning,* March, 24-28.

McManis, G. and M. Leibman. (1988). Upgrading Office Technology, *Personnel Administrator,* October, 33.

Miller, H. (1988). Developing Information Technology Strategies, *Journal of Systems Management,* September , 28-31.

Nance, T. (1987). The Desktop Revolution," *Boston Computer Currents,* December, 40-41.

Parker, C. (1989). *Management Information Systems,* New York, McGraw-Hill, Inc.

Parker, R. (1989). Desktop Publishing Confronts Hard Times, *INFOWORLD, vol 11,* September 18, 52.

Peterson, F. and J. Turkel. (1988). Making Publishing Cents, *Boston Globe,* March 1.

Tate, P. (1988). Risk! The Third Factor, *Datamation,* April 15, 58-64.

Wilson, I. (1989). The Strategic Management of Technology: Corporate Fad or Strategic Necessity? *Long Range Planning,* April, 21-22.

Winkler, C. (1988). Corporate Publishing: Who's in Charge? *Computer Decisions,* April, 48-50.

Wolf, C. and K. Fields. (1988). Desktop Publishing: Professional Looking Documents from the Office Micro, *Journal of Accountancy,* March, 81-87.

Wood, W. (1988). Principal Information Systems Issues," *Journal of Systems Management,* vol 39, November, 39-40.

Part III
Microcomputer Technology and End Users

During the 1980s, as microcomputer applications became more user-friendly, we have seen a huge increase in end-user computing (EUC). With this increase has come a concern for methods of training the end user to keep some standard of operation within an organization and to ensure training is keeping current with technological changes. Karen Nantz (Supporting End-User Application development with the Information Transformation-Analysis-Management Model) presents the TAM model, focusing on information transformation, information analysis, and information management. The model is intended to increase end-user capabilities by briding the gap between the IS department and end users. Jane Mackay and Charles Lamb, Jr. (A Framework for Addressing End User Training Needs) offer another framework, Functional Job Analysis (FJA), intended to assist end users by training them to use software more efficiently.

Chapter 6

SUPPORTING END-USER APPLICATION DEVELOPMENT WITH THE INFORMATION TRANSFORMATION-ANALYSIS-MANAGEMENT MODEL

Karen S. Nantz
Eastern Illinois University

The major trade publications in late 1989 and early 1990 have reminisced about the impact of the microcomputer in the last decade and its implications for the future. It is compared with the printing press, the car, the airplane, and the television in terms of its effect on the world (Glitman, 1990). Naisbitt in *Megatrends* called this evolution the "Information Age" (Naisbitt, 1982). Current estimates are that 50 million personal computers are in use (Glitman, 1990) and that 45% of all capital spending is on information technology (Evans, 1989). Sixty percent of all workers are involved in information processing (Senn, 1990). A clear outgrowth of the increased reliance on computer technology is the rise of end-user computing—the development and use of computer applications without reliance on information systems departments

Previously published in Managing Information Resources in the 1990s © Idea Group Publishing

(McLeod, 1990).

Microcomputer technology has brought us from 64K 8088-based machines to 486-based super performers. It has brought organizations world-wide communications, instantaneous information retrieval, sophisticated decision support systems, and a plethora of applications software to facilitate information processing. The increased sophistication of hardware and software has also brought about an increased sophistication on the part of the end user community.

These three factors—expanded technology, sophisticated applications software, and more knowledgeable end users has brought about what Dennis Hogarth calls the democratization of data processing (Hogarth, 1988). That is, computer processing is not the province of data processing shops anymore. Complex business applications necessary for managing today's organizations are in the hands of the end users. "These end users, not the traditional systems development staff, are now the key forces driving the acquisition and use of computer resources" (Gerrity & Rockart, 1989). This democratization is characterized by perceptions of increased productivity, a decrease in systems development backlogs, and a demand by end users to be involved in the development process. In fact, experts predict that up to 90 percent of all computer-based information processing in the 1990s will be accomplished by end users (O'Brien, 1990).

From an IS department point of view, all this hardware and software capability coupled with increased user involvement has a dark side. We have 486-based technology, but not 486-based workers. Management believes that productivity lags, training isn't keeping up with technological advances, and end users are doing their own thing development-wise without regard for the organization's ability to manage and control data resources. Many analysts believe that end user information processing is out of control. Specifically, organizations are facing three major problems with regard to end-user computing:

1. decreased worker productivity despite increased investments in technology

2. rising costs of training to keep workers "current" and the problem of providing the right training for the user's level in the organization

3. lack of control over information processing within the organization as end users assume more responsibility for application development

The first problem is that organizations are making huge investments in technology that have not brought like increases in productivity. In fact, one estimate is that organizations spend $3000 per user for hardware, software, support, and training, but white-collar productivity is declining at the rate of 1% per year (Evans, 1989). Evans attributes this decrease to organizations that fail to take an organizational perspective on end-user computing. As a result, knowledge and experience in the use of technology remains isolated to individual users (Evans, 1989). The organization, as a whole, is not benefitting.

The second problem facing organizations is the cost of training for end users and the selection of correct training for each user. *Training* magazine estimates that $825 is spent annually per employee on computer training (Schindler, 1988). Yet this training has many times yielded button pushers who have no concept of how to make the software produce usable, reliable information. Organizations need to strike a balance in computer training. Certain minimum requirements are needed for every user, and these skills should be mandated by IS departments. According to Paul Schindler of *PC Week,* training should be required for each PC and each new application delivered to a user (Schindler, 1988). But computer training should also be targeted for different audiences and different levels in the organization (Wilkinson, 1989). Top managers don't necessarily need the same quality and quantity of training as the clerical staff. Operations staff don't need what strategic planners do. What is needed most is training targeted for specific audiences coupled with a good support system provided by the IS department (Spector, 1988).

The third problem faced by organizations is that decentralized end-user computing is not managed by any centralized organizational entity. This problem causes duplicate application development, inadequate or non-existent documentation, no audit trails, and no testing guidelines (Wilkinson, 1989). Yet, when the end user gets stuck or the application breaks down, the IS staff is called in for crisis management. IS staff argue, justifiably, that it is "impossible for a support person to understand the nuances of a user-developed system" (Zarley, 1989). If an employee leaves the organization, no one knows anything about the application, perhaps even that the application exists. The problem is further exacerbated when microcomputers are networked and linked to mainframes or when user-generated applications access organizational databases.

The bottom line is that end users have a micro view of computing and IS staffs have a macro view, but each has an impact on an organization's ability to supply timely, reliable information for decision making. Unless steps are taken to bridge the gap between IS departments and end users, never the twain shall meet.

Information systems managers need to accept that end user computing is a fact of life and that end users will continue to develop applications with or without the blessing of the IS department. Rather than bemoaning the problems caused by end-user computing, IS departments must take a pro-active role in developing a training model to promote productivity, to target skill development to the end user's "need to know," and to establish applications development guidelines.

One model that focuses on developing end-user computing skills is the Transformation-Analysis-Management Model (T-A-M). The T-A-M model, proposed by this author, targets three skill areas for end-user computing: information transformation, information analysis and problem-solving, and information management. Figure 1 shows the three skill areas of the T-A-M model. Every end user needs development in all three skill areas. How much training in each skill area depends on the end user's level in the organization.

The Transformation-Analysis-Management Model for End-User Development

Information Transformation

Information transformation skills are broadly defined as the Input-Processing-Output sequence associated with traditional data processing. That is, data must be captured, processed or transformed into information, and output so that it can be used for decision making. End users must have the ability to get data from one form to another, and, more importantly, to understand the best way to accomplish the task. Specific data capture skills might include keyboarding, voice recognition, MICR and OCR, or data transfer from other sources. Processing can be accomplished with many major software products: word processing, spreadsheets, databases, integrated software, desktop publishing, presentation graphics, and data communications or even the more traditional third-generation programming languages. That is not to say that end users need to be experts in any or all of these products, but they do need to understand how to select the best development tool for the task at hand. For example, Lotus 1-2-3 has database capabilities, but it is not the best software for database management if complex query and report functions are needed. WordPerfect has the ability to perform mathematical functions, but it certainly cannot take the place of a spreadsheet or statistical package. A client swore that Lotus 1-2-3 was an excellent word

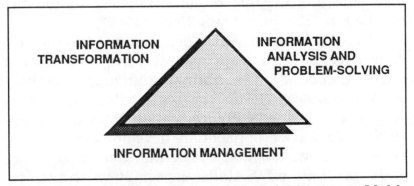

Figure 1: Information-Transformation-Analysis-Management Model

processor, but he failed to mention that it took six months of macro writing to get Lotus to do what any low-end word processor can do. What he saved in software costs was a pittance compared to the time invested in writing Lotus macros to right justify and word wrap.

Output capabilities include the ability to get information in the best form for analysis and decision making. Format possibilities are wide-ranging, including text, graphics in two- or three-dimensional formats, and glitzy multi-media presentations. Here the end user must understand desktop and presentation graphics capabilities beside the standard output devices. Users must also understand how data and information can be transferred from one technology to another and the advantages, disadvantages, and implications of doing so.

End users also need to be taught that some applications are better left to the professionals, despite the fact that they may have the knowledge and the software may have the capabilities. Applications software is not the be all and end all. Senn notes that high-volume transaction processing systems, applications that span organization units, and applications affecting organizational databases should be handled by IS departments (Senn, 1990).

On the other hand, IS departments have to acknowledge that not all applications have to be written in a third-generation programming languages. Ad hoc queries, simple retrievals, and sensitivity analysis can all be accomplished with application software (Senn, 1990). End-user application development has its place in the organization and certainly can take some of the pressure off IS staffs, especially when two- to five-year backlogs are still being experienced (O'Brien,

1990). The point here is that software today is so versatile that there is no clear cut guidelines for which package to choose or even whether IS department or end users should develop the application. By educating users and working with them in application development, IS departments can help users make informed decisions about the information transformation process and guide them in the application development process while lessening the IS development burden.

The level of the end user in the organization will help determine how much training in transformation processing is needed. Users at the strategic level will have less need for specific information transformation training, but they will still need to understand what is possible and how it might be accomplished. Clerical workers and operational managers have a greater need for proficiency in transformation skills. Once the level of the end user and the specific information transformation skills are identified, these skills are the easiest for the IS staff to teach since a variety of commercial training packages are available and software is becoming much more user friendly.

The second part of the T-A-M model is information analysis and problem-solving; that is, using computer technology for decision support. Users need to be taught how to apply computer technology to decision making, including using computer technology to assist in solving semi-structured problems, to support management's judgments, and to improve decision-making effectiveness (Keen and Scott Morton, 1978).

The skills needed in analysis and problem solving have been established in a framework developed by G. Anthony Gorry and Michael S. Scott Morton of

MIT. They developed a grid that relates the structure of the problem being solved by computer technology to the management level of the individual analyzing the problem (Gorry and Scott Morton, 1971).

Gorry and Scott Morton rank problems as structured, semistructured, or unstructured. Management levels are operational control, management control, and strategic planning.

Gorry and Scott Morton state that all three management levels solve structured, semistructured, and unstructured problems but that each level uses different tools to support problem solving and decision making.

Their framework can be used in the T-A-M model to identify computer skills needed for each level of management based on the types of problems typically solved. Operation-level decision makers (lower management) need tools for decisions in inventory control, production scheduling, cash management, accounting, and PERT systems. Management-level decision makers (middle management) need tools for

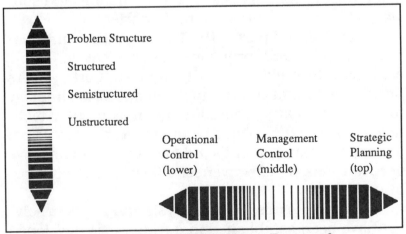

**Figure 2: Gorry and Scott Morton Framework
(simplified version)**

budget analysis, forecasting, budget preparation, and sales and production tools. Strategic planners (top management) need tools for capital budgeting, product planning, research and development, and mergers and acquisitions (Gorry and Scott Morton, 1971).

By targeting the training to the specific management level of the end user and the types of problems being solved, IS departments can make end users managers more productive and informed decision-makers while holding costs down for end-user training.

Information Management

The third part of the T-A-M model is information management—the ability of end users to manage the information they have stored electronically. Information management skills included the ability to physically manage data, to use application development guidelines, and to understand the necessity for control of an organization's information resources. Of the three parts of the T-A-M model, information management skills are conceptually much different from information transformation or information analysis and problem solving. They are the quickest to teach and will probably meet the most resistance since users think they operate in a vacuum and their applications will have no effect on other computing resources.

When microcomputers were a new technology, information management skills involved handling a few floppy disks. Now users have access to gigabytes of storage across different operating systems and networks. Unfortunately, users are still managing their resources like they did when they first learned the technology. Keeping 500 files in a root directory of

a hard disk is a good example of information management skills lagging far behind the technology being
managed.

IS departments can easily establish standards
that will greatly simplify the information management
process and increase worker productivity.

First, all users regardless of level in the organization need guidance on how to manage their own
data and why data management is important. That is
not to say that users need to understand how to
partition and format hard disks or optimize disk
storage, but they do need to know how to logically
name files, to set up and traverse directory and
subdirectory systems, to backup files systematically,
and to purge unneeded files in a timely manner.

Second, application development guidelines
need to be taught to insure system quality. Application developers need to follow the same steps as the IS
staff: designing, programming, testing, and docu-
menting (Evans, 1989). Other topics to teach include
the role of application development in the overall computing strategy for the organization, the role of the IS
department in the application development process,
documentation, data integrity, testing and quality
control, and the Systems Development Life Cycle
(Wilkinson, 1989).   The point here is not to stymie
application development but to make users aware of
the impact of their development projects on the
organization's information resources. It also increases
the probability that users will keep the IS department
informed of applications development since, hopefully, end users will see the IS department as a
partner, not as an adversary.

Third, the IS staff needs a tracking mechanism
for user-developed applications.   Not every Lotus

macro needs to be reported, but any application that has the potential to impact organization computing should be known in the IS department. This tracking also protects the end user from having the IS staff make changes in databases, etc. that could impact an end-user application.

Fourth, the IS staff need to act as application development overseers to facilitate guideline adherence. This overseer function reinforces that IS departments have the responsibility for all information resources in the organization.

Figure 3 shows the relationship between the skill areas of the T-A-M model and the management levels identified by Gorry and Scott Morton. All levels of end users need the same level of information management skills so the line cuts across the center of the figure. Top management has a high need for information analysis and problem solving computer skills with a much lower need for information transformation skills. Middle managers need both transforma-

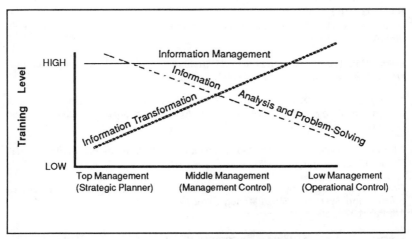

Figure 3: Relationship between the T-A-M Model and the Gorry Scott Morton Framework

tion and analysis and problem solving skills so the lines cross approximately in the middle of the training level for those two skill levels. Lower management needs more information transformation skills and less analysis and problem-solving skills.

As end users become more proficient in automating business tasks, the relationship between end users and IS departments must change. IS departments must become "enablers"; that is, helping end users learn to conform to organizational computing strategies (Zarley, 1989). Part of the IS strategy must be to recognize that not all end users need the same level of computer expertise. By looking at the level of the end user in the organization and the types of problems being solved, IS departments can target training, thus enhancing end user productivity while decreasing training costs. Ultimately, the IS department, the end user, and the organization win as end users become more productive and IS departments re-establish control of information resources.

References

Coffee, Peter. (1989). Software Will Have to Teach as Well as Execute. *PC Week*, 6(8), April 17, 1989, 35.

Evans, Ron. (1989). Reaping the Full Benefits of End-User Computing. *Computerworld*, 23, August 21, 1989, 67, 69, 71.

Gerrity, Thomas P. & Rockart, John F. (1989). End-User Computing: Are You a Leader or a Laggard?. *Management of Information Systems*. Chicago: The Dryden Press, 503-517.

Glitman, Russell. (1990). The '80s Leave a World Defined by PC Explosion. *PC Week*, 6(51), January 1, 1990, 1,11.

Gorry, G. Anthony & Scott Morton, Michael S. A Framework for Management Information Systems. *Sloan Management Review*, 13, Fall 1971, 55-70.

Hogarth, Dennis. (1988). Democratizing Data Access. *CA Magazine*, 121, December, 1988, 55-56.

Kask, Alex. (1988). As Technology Changes. So Does Corporate PC Training. *Computerworld*, 22, October 10, 1988, 52.

Keen, Peter G & Scott Morton, Michael S. (1978). *Decision Support Systems: An Organizational Perspective*. Reading, Mass.: Addison Wesley Publishing Company.

Lucas, Henry C., Jr. (1986). *Information Systems Concepts for Management*. New York: McGraw-Hill Book Company.

Lucas, Henry C., Jr. (1989). *Managing Information Services*. New York: Macmillan Publishing Company.

McLeod, Raymond, Jr. (1989). *Introduction to Information Systems   A Problem-Solving Approach*. Chicago: SRA, Inc.

McLeod, Raymond, Jr. (1990). *Management Information Systems: A Study of Computer-Based Information Systems*. New York: Macmillan Publishing Company.

Naisbitt, John. (1982). *Megatrends*. New York: Warner Books, Inc.

O'Brien, James A. (1990). *Management Information Systems: A Managerial End User Perspective*. Homewood, Illinois: Richard D. Irwin, Inc.

Schindler, Paul. (1988). If You Think Training is Expensive, You Could Try Ignorance. *PC Week*, 5(49), December 5, 1988, 47.

Senn, James A. (1990). *Information Systems in Management*, 4 ed. Dubuque: Wm. C. Brown Publishers

Spector, Gregory. (1988). Few Companies Budget for PC Training. *PC Week*, 6(51), January 2, 1989, 47, 49.

Wilkinson, Stephanie. (1989). Making the Most Out of Users Who Program. *PC Week*, 5(1), January 23, 1989, 48-49.

Zarley, Craig. (1989) When Users Write Their Own Applications. *PC Week*, 6(50), December 18, 1989, 66,69.

Chapter 7

A FRAMEWORK FOR ADDRESSING END USER TRAINING NEEDS

Jane M. Mackay
Texas Christian University

Charles W. Lamb, Jr.
Texas Christian University

The growth of end user computing has been one of the most significant information management developments of the 1980s (Benson, 1983). End user computing (EUC), the use and/or development of information systems by the principal users of the systems' outputs or by their staffs (Wetherbe & Leitheiser, 1985), has diffused rapidly over the past two decades. This diffusion has generated substantial interest within the management information systems (MIS) discipline (Doll & Torkzadeh, 1989; Magal, Carr, & Watson, 1988; Rivard & Huff, 1988).

It has also created an unprecedented need for end user training (Magal et al., 1988). Studies by Mackay (1987), Hughes (1988), and Mykytyn (1988) support the proposition that software products are not easy to learn or use. They maintain that ease of

Previously published in the Journal of Microcomputer Systems Management, Vol. 2, No. 4 ©
Idea Group Publishing

use is highly dependent upon effective end user training.

This paper further develops the proposition that end users need training to use software efficiently and effectively. Specifically, the purpose of this paper is to apply a conceptual job analysis framework called Functional Job Analysis (FJA) to EUC training. FJA, based on a philosophy of hierarchical training from simple to complex, provides an approach which might improve end user training.

The paper is divided into the following five sections: (1) a review of the EUC training literature; (2) an overview of functional job analysis; (3) a description of the steps involved in using FJA to develop EUC; (4) implications for EUC training and (5) defining the research agenda.

A Review of EUC Training Literature

Most of the past research conducted on EUC training can be characterized as exploratory or descriptive (Ein-Dor & Segev, 1988; Nelson & Cheney, 1987; Rivard & Huff, 1988). Sein, Bostrom and Olfman (1987) reported that little research has been conducted in the area even though the contribution of effective training towards the success of EUC has been acknowledged by both practitioners and researchers in MIS.

One important series of experiments focused on the effects of different instructional formats on learning (Carroll, Mack, Lewis, Grischkowsky, & Robertson, 1985; Carroll, Smith-Kerker, Ford, & Mazur-Rimetz, 1988). They reasoned that trainees tend to be overwhelmed by the numerous features available in an application software package and that novice users should only be presented with the full system after they have gained confidence in their ability to use the software (Carroll & Carrithers, 1984). They used the term "training wheels" to refer to the idea of restricting the number of computer software features available to beginners.

Another experimental approach to avoid inundating trainees with information was reported by Carroll et al. (1985). The researchers used a set of instructions designed to encourage "active" learning by the trainees. These software instructions were "guided exploration" cards which consisted of a goal statement, hints, checkpoints, and remedies for that card's topic. Thus, users were presented with the minimal instructions necessary to complete the task.

These guided exploration cards evolved into what Carroll et al. (1988) called the "Minimal Manual." The manual is based on the principle that novice users of application systems need to use a tool that they believe will help them do their own work. The manual specifically trains users in error recognition and correction. Users are expected to approach the learning task with considerable understanding of task relevant concepts and to be motivated to use the tool. The rationale for this approach is that training should make it easier for users to apply the knowledge they already possess in performing job-related tasks (Carroll et. al., 1988).

Although the Minimal Manual was successful in increasing productivity compared to self-instruction manuals, neither method utilized a strategy of training users sequentially from the least complex function to the most complex function. An alternative method of training proposed in this paper entails adopting a hierarchical complexity approach of first training users to master simple commands before attempting the more complex commands (Fine & Wiley, 1971). Users who attempt complex procedures without having learned the simple commands may be less efficient in accomplishing their tasks.

The importance of organizing EUC training from the least complex to the most complex tasks has been documented by Mackay (1987). She concluded that novices should be trained to use simple functions before they attempt to learn more complex functions. The rationale is that an understanding of more complex functions is often dependent upon understanding simple functions that are used in a series of complex key strokes.

Mackay and Lamb (1989) also concluded that EUC training based upon a hierarchical complexity framework makes sense. They proposed a research agenda comparing productivity rates of users trained in a hierarchical format versus others trained using non-hierarchical formats. One method of establishing such a hierarchy is FJA.

An Overview of Functional Job Analysis

The United States Training and Employment Service (USTES) developed FJA for several purposes including developing job summaries, job descriptions, employee specifications, and measuring worker activity levels (McCormick, 1979). This system is widely used in the public sector, and used to a lesser extent in the private sector of the economy (McCormick, 1976; Milkovich & Newman, 1987). FJA may be the strongest single influence on job analysis practice in

DATA	PEOPLE	THINGS
0 synthesizing	0 mentoring	0 setting up
1 coordinating	1 negotiating	1 precision working
2 analyzing	2 instructing	2 operating-controlling
3 compiling	3 supervising	3 driving-operating
4 computing	4 diverting	4 manipulating
5 copying	5 persauding	5 tending
6 comparing	6 speaking-signaling	6 feeding-offbearing
	7 serving	7 handling
	8 taking instructions- helping	

Source: Adapted from U.S. Dept. of Labor, Employment Service, Training and Developing Administration. (1972). *Handbook for Analyzing Jobs.* Washington, D.C.: Government Printing Office: 73.

* Functions arranged from most complex to least complex.

Figure 1: Functions Associated with Data, People, and Things*

the United States (Milkovich & Newman, 1987).

Figure 1 shows the FJA functions associated with data, people, and things. A combination of the highest functions which workers perform in relation to data, people, and things expresses the total level of complexity of the job-worker situation (U.S. Department of Labor, 1972). The USTES has used these worker functions as a basis for describing over thirty thousand job titles in the *Dictionary of Occupational Titles* (U.S. Dept. of Labor, 1977).

Figure 2 provides a description of the six data function scales listed in Figure 1. Data are described as:

...information, knowledge, and conceptions related to data, people, or things resulting from observation, investigation, interpretation, visu-

Level	Definition
0	SYNTHESIZING—Takes off in new directions on the basis of personal intuitions, feelings, and ideas (with or without regard for tradition experience or existing parameters) to conceive new approaches to, or statements of problems and the development of system, operational, or aesthetic solutions or "resolutions" of them, typically outside of existing theoretical, stylistic, or organizational context.
1	COORDINATING—Decides time, place, and sequence of operations of a process, system, or organization, and/or the need for revision of goals, policies (boundary conditions), or procedures on the basis of analysis of data and of performance review of pertinent objectives and requirements. Includes overseeing and/or executing decisions and/or reporting on events.
2	ANALYZING—Examines and evaluates data (about things, data, or people) with reference to the criteria, standards, and/or requirements of a particular discipline, art, technique, or craft to determine interaction effects (consequences) and to consider alternatives.
3	COMPILING—Gathers, collates, or classifies information about data, people, or things, following a schema or system but using discretion in application.
4	COMPUTING—Performs arithmetic operations and makes reports and/or carries out a prescribed action in relation to them.
5	COPYING—Transcribes, enters, and/or posts data, following a schema or plan to assemble or make things and using a variety of work aids.
6	COMPARING—Selects, sorts, or arranges data, people, or things, judging whether their readily observable functional, structural, or compositional characteristics are similar to or different from prescribed standards.

Source: : Adapted from: Fine, S.A., and Wiley, W.W. (1971). *An Introduction to Functional Job Analysis.* Kalamazoo, Michigan: The W. E. Upjohn Institute for Employment Research: 32-33.

Figure 2: Data Functions Described

alization, and mental creation. Data are intangible and include numbers, words, symbols, ideas, concepts, and oral verbalization (U.S. Department of Labor, 1972, p.73).

Fine and Wiley (1971) have noted that involvement with data is inherent in even the simplest job instruction. Data are always present in a task even though the major emphasis might be dealing with things and/or people. Where things are primarily involved, data tend to show up as specifications. Where people are primarily involved, data tend to show up as information about objective events or conditions, information and/or feelings.

Steps Involved in Using FJA to Develop EUC

Figure 3 shows the steps involved in developing a training program based on FJA. In order to put into practice the principle of teaching less complex procedures before teaching more complex procedures, a particular task must first be defined; preparing a departmental budget, for example.

Second, the subunits which comprise the task must be defined. The subunits of budget development include entering budget categories, entering and formatting appropriate amounts and determining budget totals. Each of these subunits may be further subdivided if necessary.

Following the breakdown of the task into subunits, the subunits must be ranked according to complexity from most to least complex. In this example, determining amount totals is the most com-

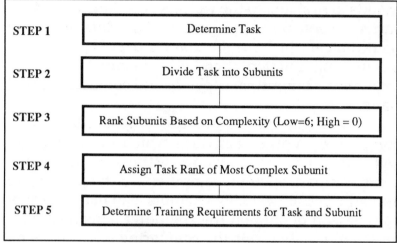

STEP 1	Determine Task
STEP 2	Divide Task into Subunits
STEP 3	Rank Subunits Based on Complexity (Low=6; High = 0)
STEP 4	Assign Task Rank of Most Complex Subunit
STEP 5	Determine Training Requirements for Task and Subunit

Figure 3: Task Evaluation Process

plex, and would be assigned level 4, computing. Entering the budget amounts in the appropriate format and entering the budget categories are both copying, level 5.

Then the overall task must be assigned the highest complexity ranking associated with a subunit of the task. For budget creation, this is the calculation of totals. Based on the FJA hierarchy, the rank of the task would be level 4, computing, equal to the rank of the most complex subunit.

The final step is to determine the training requirements for the task. This includes (1) conceptualizing the layout of the budget information, (2) entering the appropriate budget categories and amounts, (3) formatting amounts, and (4) entering formulas to calculate the appropriate totals. The training program would cover, in order, design, entry and calculation. It is, of course, assumed that appropriate error recovery techniques would be included with each command taught.

Figure 4 shows how business software commands are related to the various FJA data levels for a variety of software applications. FJA data levels are hierarchical which means that if a user is performing a compiling function, then he or she must know how to perform computing, copying, and comparing functions.

As Figure 4 shows, the lowest FJA level - comparing - entails activities which occur prior to software utilization. In each case the user must make some comparison of precomputerized data. Users of spreadsheet software, for example, can make a visual comparison of data on the computer screen without any manipulation. At the comparing level, users do not manipulate software, but make precomputer decisions about procedures to be followed.

Synthesizing is at the top of the hierarchy and is the most complex FJA data level. In spreadsheet software, using conditional 'if statements' to perform syntheses of manipulated data falls into this level. Conceptualization and execution of this procedure is difficult. To synthesize tasks, users need to understand the lower-level tasks that result in synthesizing. To synthesize, users should know how to execute the functions in the levels of coordinating, analyzing, compiling, computing, copying, and comparing.

In developing the training program for the budget task, the appropriate software would be a spreadsheet. Using Lotus 1-2-3 as an example, a training course can be devised that takes the user from the least complex software commands to the most complex commands needed to complete the task. Figure 5 illustrates the sequence in which these commands should be taught to the user. The order is from design to entry to calculation.

Thus, how users perform tasks using software

FJA Data Level	Word Processing	Spreadsheets	Databases
0 Synthesizing	Integrating graphics into text	Using conditional if statements	Relating fields of different files
1 Coordinating	Creating form letters to use with merge	Writing macros	Programming, creating standard input forms
2 Analyzing	Editing texts	Executing selects, what if tables	Performing selects from databases
3 Compiling	Executing mail merge	Moving, copying or sorting	Creating reports in arranged format (sorted)
4 Computing	Printing documents	Performing arithmetic functions	Creating reports without data arranged
5 Copying	Organizing and entering text	Entering data into the spreadsheet cells	Entering data into the database fields
6 Comparing	Determining type of document to be produced	Making visual comparisons of data without the use of software commands	Determining which data are entered into which fields

*FJA data levels are arranged from the most complex to the least complex

Figure 4: Examples of Software Functions Associated with FJA Data Levels

FJA Data Level*	Spreadsheet Definition	Software Commands[+]
4 Computing	Performing arithmetic functions	Enter formulas Enter total functions (@SUM)
5 Copying	Entering data into the spreadsheet	Enter labels Enter values Position labels Format values
6 Comparing	Making visual comparisons of data without the use of software commands	Visually examine budget data and develop layout

*FJA data levels are arranged from the most complex to the least complex
[+]Software commands are arranged within each level from least complex to most complex

Figure 5: Example of FJA Training Applied to Budget Task

will depend upon the complexity of the functional area task and the level of expertise that the user has reached with the software. The user will not always employ different software with the same level of expertise, since tasks using different software applications may differ in complexity. Training should be linked to the complexity of the task the user is expected to accomplish.

Implications for EUC Training

Dodge and Lindholm (1987) note that there are probably 50 ways to train a user. However, most of them are inefficient and/or ineffective (Mackay, 1987; Hughes, 1986; Mykytyn, 1988; Sein et al., 1987). The reason for this is that they focus on the software rather than on the task.

The FJA hierarchy of functions suggests an entirely different approach to EUC training than is commonly practiced. The FJA approach suggests that the focus should be on the task the end user is to perform. Within the task domain, training proceeds from the least to the most complex subunit of the task and the software commands necessary to accomplish each subunit.

If a task only requires the worker to perform lower-level functions such as comparing and copying, the FJA framework suggests that no need exists to train them in computing, analyzing, or other higher level functions. Therefore, the level of required training is dependent upon the accurate identification of all processes necessary to complete the task. This task analysis may require more time using the FJA framework than was previously allocated. However, the time savings will be realized in the training programs and in the end user's effectiveness.

FJA also provides a useful framework for developing data to be used in achievement and performance tests focusing on job content. The task data translate directly to information on the questions of "how to" and "know how" knowledge or skills, especially in performance on machines (Fine, 1986). It is an excellent means for developing performance standards in relation to job content. The paradigm, "To do this task, to these standards, the worker needs this training" establishes the task relevance of the standards and the degree to which they must be achieved for satisfactory performance (Fine, 1986).

FJA produces communicable information about productivity. Since each task ends with a result and the results must add up to required outputs, management can track the efficiency and effectiveness with which jobs are designed to achieve management's goals and objectives. Through the use of the FJA framework, managers may realize that certain tasks should be grouped together, and, therefore, job descriptions could be streamlined to reflect more similar tasks. This would allow users to attain a higher level of expertise in fewer areas rather than dividing their efforts over numerous areas.

The validity and usefulness of the FJA framework for EUC training need to be investigated. Several questions that need to be addressed are identified in the following section.

Defining the Research Agenda

The FJA classification has been extensively tested in a wide range of applications. Its utility as a framework for EUC training has not, however, been examined. Research questions which need attention include:

•Will users trained based upon the FJA framework express different levels of satisfaction with their training than users not trained with the FJA framework?

•Will users trained within the FJA framework learn faster or slower than those not trained with the FJA framework?

•Will the retention of users be higher, lower, or the same in an FJA training framework as those trained in a non-FJA framework?

•Will user productivity levels be affected by the training framework employed?

•Will the command of the software and its capabilities be affected by the type of training employed?

•Will FJA enhance users' building of mental models?

•Will users' information processing strategies be more effective if they are trained within an FJA framework?

•Will the simple-to-complex-functions concept facilitate their problem solving processes?

•Will the process of simple-to-complex-functions training frustrate users?

These questions are illustrative of the research issues that need to be addressed. With the increase in EUC, and the concomitant increase in training budgets, the importance of effective training for the software use has become more imperative.

References

Benson, D.H. (1973). A field study of end-user computing: findings and issues. *MIS Quarterly, 7*(4), 35-46.

Carroll, J.M., & Carrithers, C. (1984). Training wheels in a user interface. *Communications of the ACM, 27*(8), 800-806.

Carroll, J.M., Mack, R.L., Lewis, C.H., Grischkowsky, N.L., & Robertson, S. (1985). Exploring a word processor. *Human-Computer Interaction, 1*(3), 283-307.

Carroll, J.M., Smith-Kerker, P.L., Ford, J.R., & Mazur-Rimetz, S.A. (1988). The minimal manual. *Human-Computer Interaction, 3*(2), 123-153.

Dodge, M., & Lindholm, E. (1987). The spectrum of user training. *Information Center, 41*(9), 47.

Doll W.J., & Torkzadeh, G. (1988). The measurement of end user satisfaction. *MIS Quarterly, 12*(2), 259-273.

Ein-Dor, P., & Segev, E. (1988). Information resources management for end user computing: An exploratory study. *Information Resources Management Journal, 1*(1), 39-46.

Fine, S. A. (1986). Job analysis. In Berk, R. A. (Ed.), *Performance assessment* (pp. 53-81). Baltimore: Johns Hopkins University.

Fine, S.A., & Wiley, W.W. (1971). *An introduction to functional job analysis.* Kalamazoo, MI: The W. E. Upjohn Institute for Employment Research.

Hughes, C.T. (1988). Adequacy of computer training for the non-data processing managers. *Journal of Systems Management, 39*(6), 32-35.

Mackay, J.M. (1987). *Expert/novice problem solving behavior: A comparative study of task and technology.* Unpublished doctoral dissertation, University of Texas, Austin.

Mackay, J. M. & Lamb, Jr., C. W. (1989). *EUC training that makes sense.* Unpublished working paper, Texas Christian University, Fort Worth.

Magal, S.R., Carr, H.H., & Watson, H.J. (1988). Critical success factors for information center managers. *MIS Quarterly, 12*(3), 413-425.

McCormick, E.J. (1976). Job and task analysis. In Dunnette (Ed.), *Handbook of industrial and organizational psychology* (pp. 651-696). Chicago, IL: Rand McNally.

McCormick, E.J. (1979). *Job analysis: methods and applications.* New York, NY: AMACOM.

Milkovich, G.T., & Newman, J.M. (1987). *Compensation*. Plano, TX: Business Publishers, Inc.

Mykytyn, P.P. (1988). End user perceptions of DSS training and DSS usage. *Journal of Systems Management, 39*(6), 32-35.

Nelson, R.R., & Cheney, P.H. (1987). Training end users: an exploratory study. *MIS Quarterly, 11*(4), 547-559.

Rivard, S., & Huff, S.L. (1988). Factors of success for end user computing. *Communications of the ACM, 31*(5), 552-560.

Sein, M.K., Bostrom, R.P., & Olfman, L. (1987). Training end users to compute: cognitive, motivational and social issues. *INFOR, 25*(3), 236-255.

United States Department of Labor, Manpower Administration. (1972). *Handbook for analyzing jobs.* Washington, DC: Government Printing Office.

United States Department of Labor, Manpower Administration. (1977). *Dictionary of occupational titles* (3rd ed.). Washington, DC: Government Printing Office.

Wetherbe, J.C., & Leitheiser, R.L. (1985). Information centers: A survey of services, decisions, problems, and successes. *Journal of Information Systems Management, 2*(3), 3-10.

Part IV
Artificial Intelligence and Microcomputer Technology

As micro systems mature, we have seen the introduction of artificial intelligence technologies to enhance the abilities of the system while decreasing the repetition of some tasks. This had led to the necessity of managing this new approach to end user computing. Part of the challenge lies in implementing strategies to keep pace with the ever-spiraling technological changes. Leopoldo Gomoets (An Architecture to Manage Artificial Intelligence Systems in a Microcomputer Environment) addresses these concerns and structures an architecture to deal with present and future AI systems management. In addition, he discusses future developments that he sees as impacting the effective organizational implementation of AI. D.G. Dologite (Software Selection: A Knowledge-Based System Approach) adds to this perspective by giving us a prototype to assist the large organization in purchasing and evaluating software. It allows an organization to broaden its support and quality of service in the software selection area without adding more staff.

Chapter 8

AN ARCHITECTURE TO MANAGE ARTIFICIAL INTELLIGENCE SYSTEMS IN A MICROCOMPUTER ENVIRONMENT

Leopoldo A. Gemoets
University of Texas at El Paso

This chapter has been motivated by the advent of the microcomputer and the subsequent introduction of networks and Artificial Intelligence (AI) technologies. The management of such innovative resources is the challenge that often means growth or obsolescence to the individual, the department, the division and the entire organization.

Compilation and research of success and failure data and concepts with respect to technology transfer over the past three years have singled out, among other things, management style and management innovation as a principal factor in successful technology absorption by business environments (Gemoets, 1989). One product of this effort has been the investigation and design of management architectures by a process of reviewing and evaluating previous management experience in terms of new technol-

ogy. Because technology enters a business and industry with such speed, there is usually not sufficient
time to test management architectures in the classi-
cal sense of measuring impact of change. This has
been a limiting factor for research on the study of
information resource management styles.

This chapter is composed of two major sections.
The first describes the proposed management structure in general terms of a matrix made up of the
interests of six participating entities with respect to
thirteen management information issues. The matrix
can be used to combine conditions for different information projects. The second section enters the relatively unknown area of three future developments
that may impact business organizations: synthetic
expertise, network mentality and database mining.
The combination of these perspectives with the microcomputer may truly form tools and opportunities to
meet the information challenge of this decade.

The utilization of microcomputer technology
offers challenge and opportunity to traditional resource management methods. The power and flexibility of the microcomputer makes possible a wide range
of group, section, department, and even corporate
level tasks to a larger range of individuals. In this new
environment, old functional protocols serve little or no
organizational purpose and become obsolete. The
management of functional divisions requires a new
structure and a new paradigm of purpose and style if
it is to effectively employ this new resource (Tom,
1987).

Traditionally, communication flows between the
organizational levels follow a well-defined pattern in
which upper management requires middle management to collect and organize the information gathered

by the operational level (Anthony, 1965; Neumann & Hadass, 1990). The microcomputer attached to information networks can transcend these organizational boundaries by offering more direct information coupling between upper management, operations, and the user.

A new element is introduced by this more intimate connection. In the age of yearly, quarterly, and even monthly reports, the period between reports acted as a buffer for errors, inconsistencies, and other data quality issues. The age of the microcomputer, with its faster and more innovative perspectives, imposes data quality and accessibility requirements of a new order. Actions, commitments and decisions that could be delayed until all data had been received and checked must now be made as soon as the microcomputer puts it before management. This "just in time" decision requirement will motivate management to adapt to a new technology. In a microprocessor environment, managers require a new architecture and methodology. The manager must look at the data quality and access as resources to be managed. The definition and identification of quality data is a challenge for present and future information managers.

The microcomputer permits the management of very high density and flux of data. The representation and extraction of goal-oriented information from large and complex data sets is outside of unaided human capacities under these information loads. The reliable and timely utilization of so much data appears to be beyond traditional computer techniques. To meet this new challenge, the technology for developing and maintaining knowledge and relationships as compact information resources is being developed under the name of Artificial Intelligence (AI). This technology is truly revolutionary in the sense that it not only processes data as a set of unrelated facts but establishes relationships utilized by human-like or human-equivalent reasoning. The convergence of the micro-computer and AI technologies at this period in the information age serves to show how technology evolves to meet challenges at a new scale of performing tasks.

AI technology represents an environment that may equalize the human scale to the sheer volume and dynamic nature of information. AI is not only essentially a new programming language that will supplement or replace COBOL, C and even present Fourth Generation Languages, it is also a new paradigm and perspective for the management, not of data nor even information, but of the knowledge and relationships embedded in databases. Since it is a new environment with a new product, its management and development will require new methods and approaches. These methods will be based on goals that assume and require knowledge as a resource, not simply information or data. A critical and practical comparison of traditional and AI information systems management is being developed. The verification, documentation, and supporting resources to bring about effective AI projects is subject to research. Issues of the management of knowledge, expertise, reasoning and relationships include their description, storage, representation, verification, and maintenance. All these concepts fit into general management schemes. Specific management methods are being designed and tested. However, the information managers will have to adapt to these schemes (Reitman, 1990).

The combination of microprocessing and AI technology is poised to break down the traditional managerial structure and channels used to account for resources. Functions and tasks may be performed in almost complete isolation from the rest of the corporation. Microcomputer-based expert systems give sufficient power to a single or small group of individuals to function as effectively as a large organization. There arises the need to give management a new architecture by which a management methodology can be established for the microprocessing and AI systems environment.

In this chapter the reader must be aware that terms such as "data", "information" and "knowledge" have a unique and discreet meaning. In subsequent discussions "data" is a collection of figures annotated as an event in time or place. "Information" is the set of common or exclusive relations among data or events of a single class. "Knowledge" is the set of relations between conditions and events from diverse classes with causality and time sequence accounted for.

The reader may find that simulation and modeling are more closely related to information than knowledge. Correlations and formulae developed either statistically or deterministically are examples of information. Pattern recognition or definition of the inclusive/exclusive relationships are examples of knowledge. Trends is a synonym for pattern recognition. Knowledge is considered to be a process of concentrating information into a compact form of exclusive actions. For example, knowledge is the set of rules which identifies the level of the risk of a $100,000 loan for a new client moving from a competing institution. An Information profile (balance sheet) is but a record of the client's previous transactions and financial condition. And finally, data supports the information profile. These three elements (data, information and knowledge) are significantly different but always intimately meshed. It is the knowledge element which will be discussed in this chapter.

Technology Transfer: Past, Present and Future

A working concept of technology's influence on business methods may motivate a change in management style. This section will include the historical perspective of microcomputer and artificial intelligence potential. Although technology depends on conditions and opportunities to become an applicable and economic tool, it must also contain the essence of a solution in order to initiate experimentation.

The microcomputer found its place in business by allowing the user to implement the supplementary tasks of reporting and utilizing data in unique and often creative ways. These were the very tasks that made up the bulk of the DP backlog. The DP and IS priority has been the support of 'standard' tasks required by upper management. However, the micro came in with unexpected extras: text and word processing, electronic mail, desk top publishing, database query, graphics and COLOR. These capabilities were beyond the DP department and its mainframes.

Decisions are key products provided by all levels of employees. Present management apparently tends to limit these products, thereby limiting access to information that serves to give value to decisions. Over the last twenty years the computer has made information easier to organize, thus improving common decision making; it is now progressing in its capacity to support decisions of deeper perspective and complex composition the limits of which are not yet defined. As decision-making potential diffuses through an organization, problem solving reaches the individual level as shown in Figure 1. This diagram overlays the historical pattern of technology with the advances in problem solving over the last fifty years, orienting the user toward the potential implied by emerging technology while staying in touch with historical causes of progress. The reader is challenged to imagine the next or fourth stage beyond Knowledge Base technology.

Artificial Intelligence Technology

AI is a maturing technology and its position in business is not yet fully defined. Its future will depend on the class of opportunities it faces and on the imagination with which it is applied. As an introduction to this technology, AI will be defined from various perspectives, since at this time no one can tell which is the most effective. From a management perspective one needs to understand these four basic characteristics of AI:

- How different is AI from other information resources?
- What are AI resources made of?
- What are the expected products or services from an AI application?
- What resources and commitments are necessary to implement, support and maintain AI?

Note that we will not attempt to discuss the class of problems that should and should not be approached by AI.

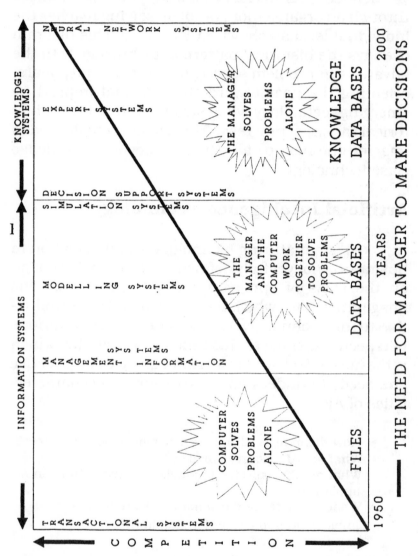

Figure 1. Problem Solving Architecture

Artificial Intelligence endeavors to make machines such as computers capable of displaying intelligent behavior, i.e., behavior that would reasonably be regarded as intelligent if it were observed by humans (Holsapple & Whinston, 1987). Two cornerstones of intelligence are the ability to reason and to communicate. These, in turn, represent two principal areas of research in the AI field. This research has led to the development of practical techniques for building software that enables computers to understand natural language and to solve problems requiring reasoning, not just "dumb" data processing. These systems are now producing results that are more or less comparable, although not equivalent, to what would be expected from a human. Practically, AI is an approach for speeding up simple tasks such as word spelling for word processors, or organizing and searching for data satisfying well-stated conditions for "intelligent" databases.

Expert Systems

In an introductory handbook on Artificial Intelligence (AI), Mishkoff defines expert systems or "knowledge-based systems" as computer programs that contain both declarative knowledge (facts about objects, events, and situations) and procedural knowledge (information about courses of action) to emulate the reasoning processes of human experts in a particular domain or area of expertise. Harmon and King (1985) define expert systems as AI programs designed to represent human expertise in a specific domain. "Expert Systems have the potential to make a competitive difference in industry, academia, and government, yet there is little knowledge on how to manage these complex software tools" (Sviokla, 1989, p. 65).

Typical expert system application areas include diagnosis, planning, instruction and management, monitoring, and design. Internally, an ideal ES can be characterized as including the following (Rolston, 1988):

- Extensive specific knowledge from the domain of interest
- Application for heuristic analysis
- Support for heuristic analysis
- Capacity to infer new knowledge from existing knowledge
- Symbolic processing
- An ability to explain its own reasoning

The variety of available expert systems now has sufficient breadth and depth, as shown in Table 1, to make them a serious information tool (Schutzer, 1990). This list includes most aspects of management and does not include medical systems, manufacturing, weather and environmental advisors, electronics, oil & gas and most of the science and engineering disciplines. Note the innovative nomenclature, such as "financial engineering", that is an indicator of new classes of services that can be formed by linking financial and engineering methodologies through expert systems.

Expert Systems are composed of at least three basic entities: the knowledge base, an inference engine, and a user interface applied to a specific body of knowledge called domain. The knowledge base contains rules expressing an expert's heuristic for the domain. The inference engine is made up of logic rules that are used to control how the rules in the knowledge base are used or processed. The user interface allows

- Intelligent filtering of the news
- Intelligent front end to multiple heterogeneous database
- Smart financial analyzer
- Text and message repair
- Smart spreadsheet
- Interactive knowledge-directed simulation
- Business planning, forecasting, and competitive assessment advice
- Intelligent customer advisor
- Customizing catalogs and sales campaigns
- Sales and marketing prospecting and profiling
- Investment advisor
- Tax advisor
- Audit planning
- Financial engineering ideas generation
- Intelligent market minder and filter

- Analysis of merger and acquisition candidates
- Hedging and risk assessment advice
- Interest rate and stock price forecasting
- Corporate credit analyzer
- Insurance underwriting advice
- Credit card authorization
- Fraud detection
- Monitoring and policing trades
- Automatic order processing
- Intelligent equipment leasing analyzer
- Residential appraisal
- Health claims adjustment
- Office relocation planning
- Graphics selection advice
- Smart message center

Table 1. Expert System Business Applications

communication or interaction between the expert system and an end user.

Knowledge-based systems are another branch of artificial intelligence (Charniack & McDermoot, 1985; Gallagher, 1988; Martin & Oxman, 1988). Typically, knowledge-based systems enable users to consult an expert system as they would an expert adviser in order to diagnose what might be causing a problem, to figure out how to solve a problem, to determine how to perform a task, or to make a decision. They can also answer various levels of questions as may be needed to reach goals. They can make recommendations regarding the problem or decision at the end of the consultation, and, when asked by a user, can explain the reasoning steps used to reach its conclusion. These systems are called knowledge-based because they are largely based on expert knowledge and the expert reasoning process (called heuristic).

Knowledge compilation, organization and representation are as important as databases were in the seventies and eighties. Knowledge acquisition is concurrently referred to as the most important aspect of expert system development and the most problematic (Hayes-Roth et al., 1983; Shaw & Gaines, 1986). It alternately has been tagged "knowledge extraction," "knowledge elicitation," and "knowledge acquisition." It refers to the "transfer and transformation of problem-solving expertise" from a knowledge source (e.g., human expert, documents) to a program. This procedure is considered an emerging technology composed of a mix of disciplines from psychology, cognition, perception, learning and other sciences.

Neural Networks

A neural network is one of three types of neurocomputing. Neural network usually refers to software simulations of neurocomputing, which commonly utilize the back propagation technique popularized by Dr. John Hopfield of the California Institute of Technology. It is characterized as a network because, like other communications networks, it is composed of interconnected processing elements (Caudill, 1987). "Neurocomputers have the potential to revolutionize the design and execution of complex simulation models of managerial and/or economic phenomena involving numerous, highly diffused elements" (Trippi & Turban, 1989, p. 92).

A neural network at a bank has been trained to identify and verify handwritten signatures. The signature is captured using a video camera and then input into a neural network, where it is compared to a number of samples of a customer's signature form which it learns. Then the signature is fed into a second neural network, which makes the decision to verify or reject the signature as genuine. This system is achieving 96 percent to 98 percent accuracy, with a false alarm rate of 2 to 4 percent.

Another neural network that has received considerable attention is Netalk, created by Terrence Sejnowski at Johns Hopkins University in Baltimore, Maryland. He trained Netalk to translate ASCII text into understandable, spoken English speech. When it first spoke, Netalk babbled like an infant. But after 16 hours of learning to match text and phonemes, the neural network was able to speak at the level of a child six years old.

Artificial Intelligence in the form of expert systems, neural networks, natural language processing or other reasoning or cognitive technologies offers a new tool for dealing with the complexities of the information age. To date this tool has gone through enough applications that its general introduction to business resources can be expected, not just predicted. The establishment of the PC or microcomputer is serving as a technology transfer platform for AI. The only remaining milepost is the recognition of this technology as a competitive need by top management. However, without a management architecture to control and oversee the combined power and impact of the microcomputer and AI, these technologies may be relegated to insignificant corners of the business environment. With over 2,000 applications operating worldwide and 10,000 being developed (Thompson & Feinstein, 1990), the need for a management strategy is imminent. The following section will deal with one set of management strategies from the point of the AI-micro-mainframe resource manager.

Management Architecture: Micro/AI

The present status of information resource management represents the results of years of experience, tradition and discipline encompassing many environments and technologies. As in any management task, information management involves a mixture of art, science, intuition, common sense, risk taking and luck. The major challenge has always been to meet the complexity and immediacy of requirements and interests that must be balanced with available resources. It is now certain that the users overwhelmed the information resources at the end of the seventies. The microcomputer came to the rescue by becoming the relief valve for the information manager.

Now that the micro has established itself as a firm and necessary resource, information management must deal with it on its own unique terms. Distributed resources are different from centralized resources but not necessarily better or less costly. In addition, the microcomputer has been largely responsible for the advances made in AI in the eighties. The innovations in AI technology could not have evolved in the limited access and restrictive environment of the mainframe. AI is a microcomputer environment solution to specialized problems and is about to be applied to the wider environment and problems of the entire corporation.

The management of AI applications and their unique environment is a new challenge. Present AI systems have been relegated to specialized tasks which very much isolate the applications from the mainstream. This isolation has been premeditated as management looks for experience to judge the new technology. Maintenance, monitoring and other diagnostic and advisory roles are only the tip of the AI potential. AI applications are reaching into the information mainstream as they mature and management understands and exploits their utility. To prepare for AI as a mainstream information tool, the manager must first recognize that useful AI applications will be multi-dimensional with very large or even global (corporate) scope. These applications will require a management perspective to develop that potential. One special trait of AI applications is that they are goal driven. These systems search for the information and tasks necessary to fulfill a goal, given a set of conditions defining the state of the environment. As the goals expand away from individual or functional maintenance tasks into department, division and corporate scope, the AI applications will absorb data and resources to reach the level of those goals. Thus management needs to be prepared to determine and implement the level of perspective required for AI. For this reason the information manager position has taken on a new importance for the success of corporate AI. "In considering ESs, a manager should be concerned not only with ES itself, but with the process by which the ES is adapted, and the overall process of creating and using ES" (Sviokla, 1989, p. 65).

The management structure of architecture for AI, as outlined in Table 2, correlates the issues of information management with the different perspectives that may arise for an AI application. This structure has been developed according to terms that

Management Issues	Enduser Participation	Management Participation	Mainframe Management	IS Management Participation	Information Center Participation	Outside Consultant Participation
Steering committee	Primary Planning	Planning Approving	Similar	Primary Planning	Advisory	Optional
Budgeting	Primary Planning	Planning Approving	As Needed	Necessary		
Internal Controls	Monitor	Monitoring Controlling Approving	Similar	Optional	Optional	
Documentation	Primary Approving	Approving	As Needed	Primary	Primary	As Needed
Communications	Optional	Approving	Advisory	Primary	Primary	Advisory
Security	Necessary/ Optional	Monitoring Controlling Approving	Primary	Primary	Advisory	Optional
Standards	Necessary	Approving	Advisory	Primary	Primary	Optional
Data Administration	Advisory	Controlling	Advisory	Primary	Primary	Optional
Data Relations	Primary	Controlling	As Needed	Primary	Primary	Optional
Application Interfaces	Advisory	Controlling	As Needed	Primary	Primary	Optional
Staffing		Planning Approving		Primary	As Needed	
Training	Primary	Approving		Advisory	Primary	Optional
Disaster Recovery Plan	Primary	Approving	Advisory	Primary	Optional	Necessary

Table 2. Management Architecture for AI Systems

management is presently applying to the application of other information tools. The relevance of each of these issues to the success of an applications is known to vary. The reader should use judgement to focus on the issues pertinent to a project.

The structure of management is elicited from the common interests represented by the various participants in the information project. There are six categories of participant interests: 1) end user, 2) senior management, 3) mainframe or hardware management, 4) IS management, 5) information center and 6) outside consultants. Any one of these may motivate and initiate an information project. In the AI environment all will be required to define, implement, maintain and utilize the system.

The end user and senior management represent the business reason for a project and should include customer, client, government and all participants in the business environment of the project. The manager has the responsibility to ensure that these two classes of participants are heavily represented to cover the multi-dimensional nature of AI projects. The hardware, software, analysis and development resources are represented by the three classes of information professionals. In addition, IS should represent the database resources and technology already existent in the company. These three groups are mainly concerned with compatibility and interface issues of the project, including the decision to purchase new platforms and software tools.

The consultants serve to fill in the gaps in the domain of the business applications and the technology. The manager needs the consultant to negotiate the conflicts that will arise during the definition of the project. The source of the consultant can be internal to the organization at the discretion of the project leader and the budget.

Steering Committee

During traditional IS development, the primary function of the steering committee has been to identify, approve, prioritize and fund projects identified by the Information Systems groups (Eliason, 1989). Functional executives knowledgeable not only of the business environment but also familiar with the corporate automation culture of the organization make up the committee.

Management needs not only to shape information systems to fit corporate business strategy but to make information systems an integral part of that strategy (Howard & Duvall, 1988). The successful information systems managers will be those who align their information systems' objectives with the overall objectives of the companies they serve. Top management has little interest in the state-of-the-art information technology unless the information provided can be directly linked to an impact on business performance (Zawrotny, 1989).

Peter Drucker (1967) wrote:

An organization is not like an animal, an end in itself, and successful by the mere act of perpetuating the species. An organization is an organ of society and fulfills itself by the contribution it makes to the outside environment.

This certainly applies to the information systems groups which need to manage the AI technology with consideration that the organization is going to use information strategically. Alignment of corporate goals during a period of transition in the development of a distinctive technology such as AI systems can produce a cutting edge advantage. Finally the steering committee must learn to manage knowledge systems as well as information systems while retaining the perspective of the entire organization.

Budgeting

The prime responsibility of middle management to allocate strategic resources for the operation of the organization has been an important function. Budget levels have always been important in the management of computer resources (Frand & McLean, 1986). Allocating resources for an expensive emerging technology is a laborious and difficult management task. However, justifying corporate investment for AI technology is not a difficult task. Provided that the organization thoroughly understands its mission and its environment, justification of AI technology by measuring benefits is feasible. Thompson and Feinstein (1990, p. 95) have expressed that

> Well-selected, well-implemented expert systems applications should have little difficulty in passing investment hurdle rates. In fact, expert systems should be one of the most lucrative capital investment opportunities available. Leveraging personnel resources to achieve increase in productivity is cited as a key benefit by many organizations.

Budgeting of resources consisting of personnel, hardware, software and necessary development costs is tactically necessary for the organization to adopt AI systems and as the potential to exercise the potential of options on future opportunities.

If the organization invests in AI-systems development in an aggressive form, i.e., adequately allocating capital to perform the basic functions of complementing AI technology, they will become more prepared for the next technology wave, including neural networks, parallel processing, other branches of AI and expert data bases. Each forward step the organization takes allows it to capitalize on future developments (Thompson & Feinstein, 1990).

Internal Controls

The feedback system of internal controls consists of end-users, methods and procedures, data storage hardware and software. Controls ensure that data is valid to the business, that files and knowledge bases are protected against unauthorized access, that disaster and recovery procedures are available. The Internal Control Subsystem manages systems performance (Whitten, Bentley & Barlow, 1989).

With the introduction of AI tools, these are additional control requirements:

- Interface Software Management and Control
- Knowledge Management and Control
- Inference Engine Management and Control

The software engineer manages and controls development of AI by ensuring that the methodology for software development includes the Internal Control Subsystem. This Subsystem consists of the establishment of formal reviews to ensure compliance of internal control procedures and walkthroughs during the system development phases. The establishment of AI system competency against known or modeled knowledge standards of consistency and/or completeness require the design and establishment of such standards. These standard-making tasks may be distributed among the steering committee, end-user and management.

Documentation

Procedures in the mainframe environment have been designed so that the mainframe can stand alone from operators and end users. PC systems cannot stand alone and perform; therefore users must be informed of various operations through documentation. User documentation consists of written or visual explanations that, in principle, show "what the application software does, how it works, and how to use it" (Doll, 1987). It has also been suggested that the use of an information system is directly related to the user community's sense of satisfaction (Bailey, 1983). It has been concluded that user satisfaction is strongly influenced by a system's documentation (Gemoets & Mahmood, 1990). During the above investigation, it was noted that users emphasized, as a matter of both primary and secondary interest, documentation completeness. The process, if followed, should enhance the IS manager's control of resources by releasing time spent in explanations and training. AI systems are expected to be very powerful and their utilization correspondingly successful only if there is good user understanding. At the same time, since AI are domain or application constrained, the systems themselves must have embedded documentation. The documentation will probably be inserted into user interfaces. As the systems interact with the user and their data, requests for data and direction may occur; these requests must be framed in the user's perspective. It is expected that the bulky user's handbooks will be reduced in size as interaction (text or voice) replaces them.

AI systems documentation should include the following characteristics:

> Provide formal instructions for its use;
> Explain its capability;
> Be well organized;
> Provide the means to review and judge it;
> Be concise; and
> Be complete.

Communications

Workstations are becoming increasingly powerful and will be the platform of choice in a corporate computing environment. Workstations have given the computing environment a new dimension, called Desktop mainframes. These will provide the end user with the power of a mainframe on a desk. The workstation combines the power of computation and the ability to integrate information across the corporation. This new environment will integrate the AI systems' functionality well. However, different machines will need to exchange information without any changes in command language or without physical intervention. Machines will need to operate other machines having different operating systems. With these interactions of machines and software sharing not only information but knowledge under an open system, a manager can implement this architecture.

The newest resource across corporate America is telecommunications technology. The information integration promised by the Integrated Services Digital Network (ISDN) would support any futuristic development in AI systems. ISDN will provide corporate-wide access for data, text, voice, and video devices which may then be integrated by AI systems with Digital Video Integration (DVI). Effective management of telecommunications is becoming increasingly important to managing information as a critical organizational asset (Szewczak & Snodgrass, 1989).

Security

Monitoring and controlling physical and conceptual resources are functions of middle management since the systems act on information. Protecting AI technology as a corporate resource is a fulltime activity. In the early days of computers, security of the corporate processing function was dedicated to physical security. Computer sites were protected against disasters such as fire, floods, and power outages. The introduction of more complex transactional processing (banking, insurance industry) having more sophisticated software increased the need to protect programs from unauthorized and/or illegal usage. The advent of microprocessing brought the need for protection of communication links and terminal access.

The overall design of security systems for AI technology depends on management assessment of threats to the organization and its resources. Threats according to Tom (1987) are defined as the dangers to which an organization and/or system can be exposed. Studies have confirmed that not only fraud and embezzlement are possible security problems, but also the theft of data for the purpose of selling it to a third party. The destruction of data has also been a threat over the last five years. In the environment of AI systems, not only are data, information, software and hardware involved but also knowledge. The loss of data or data ending in the wrong hands cannot be compared to knowledge ending in the hands of a competitor. A knowledge base can represent the expertise, facts and concepts of individuals which could sum up to hundreds of years of preparatory experience. A challenge certainly exists for the security manager to design security systems to prevent corporate experience from going somewhere else.

Security systems for AI systems can be administered by a security manager implementing three safeguards (Highland, 1984):

> administrative
> physical
> technical

Administrative Security: Set of policies and procedures and standards to execute software

Physical Security: Measures to reduce or prevent disruption of service, loss of assets or unauthorized access to equipment, data and/or information knowledge.

Software Security: Internal control measures which are built into the software as sub-systems. (internal controls is a management issue discussed in another section.)

Standards

The approach to control standards (managing the software development) of micro-based AI software which has been developed by the end-user with or without the assistance of the information systems group is a management issue. End users can be expected to develop AI systems using expert systems shells and neural network software. However, the question of ownership responsibilities, such as support and maintenance of these AI systems, has not clearly been identified. To date, neither a development technique nor a life cycle for AI systems has been identified.

The likely usefulness of Software Engineering in development of Artificial Intelligence systems has been recognized by authorities in Artificial Intelligence (Barstow, 1988; Simon, 1986). Papers on specific expert systems reported that the detailed description of the problem has been prepared before any Artificial Intelligence code has been written (Bobrow, Mittal, & Stefik, 1986). In other words, successful expert systems' developers have been using the standards of structured systems analysts during systems development. Applying structured systems analysis as a standard in the development of AI systems, results in the following benefits (Alpar, 1990):

• Documents are created that can be used for communication among domain experts, knowledge engineers and end users;

- The documents represent a logical basis for system partitioning;

- Changes in user requirements or problem under standing can be easily located and conceptually addressed.

Thus structured specifications strongly enhance the communications between knowledge engineer, application specialists and end user. Standards should be an integral part of internal operating procedures. A set of standards must address policies and procedures in the following areas: Coding documentation, data dictionary, language, shell, library, man-machine interface, internal control, and training (Mahmood & Gemoets, 1990).

Data Administration

The days of the data administration function consisting of developing and maintaining a data dictionary are long gone. Today, data administration is much more complex. With the advent of new technologies like AI systems, data administration consists of identifying data models, business models, and other analytical techniques to structure the information needed to support corporate goals and objectives. The data administration group is responsible for the management of corporate data resources, evaluates user needs, weighs them against long-term data resources development objectives, assigns individual priorities, presents them to the steering committee for approval, and finally devises a data resource development plan based on the approved priorities (Tom, 1987). Along with the tasks above, the administration

group is responsible for issues of information ownership and data standardization. Although the user has
become more actively involved in developing systems,
the information systems staff, with their overall awareness of corporate business process and data resource
requirements, are likely to identify better a set of
system requirements. Certainly the data interface
between the Data Base Management System (DBMS)
and the knowledge base is a technical task that needs
to be defined by the data administration group.

Information Integration

In a centralized, mainframe environment, it is
much easier to monitor and control the organization's
use of data. On the other hand the microprocessor
environment requires the definition of data usage by
various systems. This is difficult to accomplish but
necessary for the integration of the information environment.

The basic information architecture of the 1990s
will be physically a three-tiered structure of workstations on local area networks, departmental computers
and large-scale data processing centers (Nolan, 1988).
Users will expect on-demand access to all data pertaining to their files, databases or knowledge bases.
The user will additionally expect to access any level of
the architecture and the ability to interface both
hardware and software systems. This futuristic technology is based on relational database technology.

For the 1990s and beyond, relational DBMSs
will be the rule rather than the exception in building
information architectures (Dadashzadeh, 1990).
Relational DBMSs is another management consideration for the new direction of database concept being

utilized for the representation of rules. The rules-based data base (Knowledge-base) needs to be integrated with DBMS. When the additional power afforded by the deductive capabilities of knowledge-base systems is integrated into DBMSs, seamless integration of an organization's expert system applications with its database becomes a reality.

Data Relations

The meaning and value of data is determined by the number of relations or conditions associated with the set or individual item. Present corporate data has explicit and implicit relations tied to it. Explicit relations associate a customer (account), time of day, time of year to a transaction. Implicit relations are those activities and transactions NOT performed. For instance, a customer purchases a VCR but not any video tape or batteries. The latter may imply negative factors associated with a company's tapes and batteries. AI systems will be performing the search for positive, negative and null relations in corporate databases. Therefore the manager must be ready to link the AI systems to the corporate data systems, be they historical or active, in a manner consistent with AI relation-seeking techniques.

The manager must develop very explicit and accurate descriptions of data resources. These include:

1) Hardware compatibility between AI platform and database.
2) Structural compatibility between AI data requirements and data. (Eight, sixteen and

thirty-two bit formats.)
3) Intelligent Data dictionaries.

The management goals for data relations should include:

1) Reducing data/AI problems to minimum.
2) Minimizing the impact of data quality and structure on the success of AI.
3) Updating and correcting the data structure inventories through the corporation with potential AI applications in mind.

Centralized and decentralized data is a consideration that arises from the scope and perspective to be assigned by AI tools and applications. Since users generally have limited knowledge of data base technology and its unique characteristics, the database interface and preparation planning rests with DBA groups.

Tennebaum (1990) describes the need to have clear data accessibility and data need limitations. Usually the local information groups should provide the necessary data access design; otherwise consultation with DBA specialists will prove to be cost effective.

Application Interfaces

As AI expands from locally, insulated functions, to global, corporate level perspectives, its major success factor will be the human system interface. "Different classes of users require significantly different sorts of interactions (Wexelbat, 1989).

At no other time in systems development has interface success seemed so critical. The critical assessment of loan application risks, and sales leads cannot be hindered by cryptic user requirements. A new level of utility for interfaces cannot be over emphasized. At the same time, new methods and tools offer new means of meeting the challenge of the interface. The manager must profile the users' modes of utilizing information. These modes must be judged for their effectiveness factors. A user profile must be added to the system analysis tasks. The system interface may become a sub-specialization in the AI industry. Here we can only describe the types of user modes one may expect. There are various profiles that are classified by the intensity of the input, interaction and activity:

1) Input   - Structured (forms, profiles,etc.)
                    - Specific facts (data entry)
                    - Data streams (time series)
                    - Preprocessor (correlation, etc.)

2) Interaction - Avoid surprises (lead to goal)
                    - Prepare user for difficult or adverse response
                    - Be prepared to back up statements
                    - Use true inquiries.

3) Activity   - The product in AI session is a decision in the form of tasks
                    - Present tasks in users' terms

4) Hold and   - Make sure systems can be held while
    Return   other tasks are attended. AI should be more flexible to hold and continue.

5) Recovery   - System failure, user error or bad data AI can be more robust to external failure since it relies little on procedures and more on data.

6) Innovation - The system must be capable of responding to users motivated to innovation and creativity.
                    - Do not give all users the same dialogue

7) Documentation - User must believe the AI is reliable
through meaningful explanation and
discourse.

Various approaches are being developed by the AI industry to meet the interface challenges.

User profiles   - User identities and responses are
evaluated to level of expertise
- Coach/teach dialogue and
strategies may be effective.
- Adapt system interactions to user
expertise

Expert/   - Teaching and training strategies
Instructor   embedded in system.

Staffing

In the 1980's, Universities responded to the increase in staffing demands for new AI groups by training more AI specialists. Industry, financial institutions and the defense organizations have been hiring people with strong mathematical backgrounds and training them in AI systems. The rate of progress of an organization involved in AI technology partly depends on the availability of AI-trained professionals and of non-AI trained specialists in areas such as software engineering management,knowledge engineering, AI training, marketing, market support, technical writing; and upon the availability of experts in specific industries including banking, insurance, engineering, travel, and finance. Although the estimated number of AI-trained experts is said to be fewer than 2,000 people worldwide (Millson, 1985), an organization must rely on hiring its expertise for its success in this emerging technology. The following is a set of options which management has available for the staffing administration task:

1) The first AI-trained expert to be hired should have not only the proper training but also much experience.

2) A team of AI-trained experts are hired to support and collaborate with the first-hired core person.

3) Consultants or a consultant team can be brought into develop the first few projects or to develop in-house expertise.

4) Professional meetings can be utilized for the out reach of AI professionals.

Training

Training is the bridge between technology and its application. In the environment of microcomputers and AI, the information manager faces a unique challenge. Training must include the users, the information professionals, technicians, operators and maintenance personnel. It is ironic that in the era of personal computing, so many persons are needed to maintain the competitive edge.

Some of these services may be provided by external resources which may well be equipped with expert systems and other AI tools. But as the organization advances in its implementation of technology, training becomes a tactical and strategic issue. The training of the users has been found to be the success or failure factor for the microcomputer. Most "spreadsheet experts" remember how poorly they were utilizing this tool until some formal training was obtained. As more functions, settings, options and peripherals combine to make even simple software complex, training awareness becomes a more critical necessity.

The success of any organization to survive in its environment is related to management ability. If problem-solving skills are deficient in any of the critical areas of management decision-making, then the small business owner-manager must improve those skills through the use of appropriate educational programs, consultants, AI or none-AI based computer software, or some combination of these.

Disaster Recovery Plan

Disaster is any unexpected disruption that causes losses in terms of company's competitive advantage in the market and deviation from standard operating procedures (Hiatt & Motz, 1990). The organization can not afford to gamble on the unexpected event happening, because it will happen. The impact of the occurrence needs to be assessed beforehand, and necessary and extensive preparations are required for safeguarding the organization's resources against disaster before it occurs to protect it against loss of time and money.

Knowledge base systems consisting of data bases, ruled bases, inference software as well as the overall interfacing software packages need to be protected. The loss of a knowledge base in an expert system or the proprietary neural network software to examine credit could be compared to the loss of a key person. A key person in an organization could very well represent the life of the corporation. Fortunately most AI systems are based on microprocessors and there is no need for a HOT-SITE (A fully equipped and operational data processing facility that is provided by a commercial service (Johnson, 1989, p. 60).

The organization needs to have the knowledge base, data base files and software stored in an off-site facility which is protected against fire, water, and other damaging factors. In the event of a disaster, hardware can be readily acquired by either buying or leasing it off the shelf. Provisions should be taken to ensure that compatible microcomputer and peripherals are available in the specification of a plan. If there is more than one expert system in operation, prioritizing the systems as well as other applications should be performed by conducting a risk analysis to quantify the impact of a disaster. A plan activation procedure will ensure that all information systems are operational within a predesignated time frame.

Trends and Emerging Technologies

Synthetic Expertise

System management based on advanced technologies is a combination of applied experience with previous technology and adaption to the variations and opportunities offered by the new. Developing and exploiting the opportunities based on new technology is the major task of the manager, an important roll in the technology process. If the manager is not able to find an advantage to technology, it will wither and disappear.

In this section three business opportunities based on AI are described. While the management structure described earlier is still needed, the definitions of the advantage to be gained is introduced here. An interplay of the management style of the reader with these emerging applications hopefully will be motivated.

These applications are synthetic expertise, database mining and network mentality. Their common characteristic is the higher utilization of existing resources and personnel. Their advantages include better quality service through more adequately informed decisions; stronger integration of corporate resources; and equalization of capabilities for the individual worker and the small entrepreneur.

The reader has been introduced to the concept of AI and to a structure for managing the resources developed with AI within micro and mainframe environments. To reiterate, a practical definition of AI is that it is a technology for synthesizing, discovering and utilizing relationships from data in all forms. The manager must consider such relationships as the sources to be managed in the future business environment. These resources are now being called knowledge and the technology is called knowledge engineering. The most compact way to appreciate this innovation is through the term information concentrators. Knowledge and its utilization are several levels removed from data processing both in concept, development and managing. Due to the nature of knowledge, this technology is expected to transcend present management and business environment.

Consider this example of how diverse resources interact at levels beyond our present understanding. Consider the myriad soft and hard rules necessary to run an enterprise. These rules are usually compartmentalized or grouped into disciplines or responsibilities of accounting, engineering, management, law and so on by processes which can best be described as convenient to a human scale of understanding.

One way to find the level of coupling for diverse activities is to hire consultants whose product is simply expertise. The capability to hire the right consultants is dependent on the size of the enterprise's financial resources. AI has the potential to synthesize some expertise and concentrate it down to the size, availability and economics of managing a system through a PC or some very compact tool.

The economic balancing of synthetic and consultant expertise is expected to be a new key element in new business environments. AI in the form of expert systems and neural networks can serve as a knowledge equalizer among businesses of different financial edge. But the synthetic expert adds an additional edge beyond experience. Whereas a consultant is aware of an industry or some segment of a business, synthetic expertise can be made deeply aware of the particular enterprise that invests in it. Thus AI systems can be current in relevance and their expertise expressed in terms of the business at hand.

Synthetic expertise is not expected to give a competitive edge. On the contrary it will remove the edge enjoyed by those with larger resources. It has an equalizing effect. AI will generate a proliferation of competing equals. Small or large firms can compete at equal knowledge footing. With distributed knowledge the formation of distributed corporations can occur. A quasi-corporation can be built of any group of small businesses with joint goals and disjoint capabilities. As long as communication and knowledge is equally available, independent businesses may synthesize the power and utility of the present corporation. Under this structure a business can be part of various independent enterprises. Resource equality permits the simple meshing of distributed expertise. AI is expected to alter the way the corporation applies data and information resources.

Database Mining

Consider the large number of enormous databases taking up space in the vaults of most of the world's institutions. There is no human capacity to mesh these resources into meaningful wholes. Although the human capacity to recognize patterns is still without peer, only AI in the form of neural networks, expert systems or other unknown tools has the required elements to synthesize patterns from such large data storage. The success and failure factors for plans, products, methods, sales campaigns, financial strategies for the last twenty to thirty years is hidden in data which is now almost forgotten. The identification of the knowledge resting inside our data banks recently has been given the name of database mining. "All it takes to get started with database mining is a statistically valid historical database and someone who is interested in developing tools, such as neural network software, to work with it" (Rochester, 1990).

Consider the synthetic capacity to look at very large volumes of data. These systems are goal oriented: 1) expert systems are wired to satisfy the given inquiries by activating the rules (knowledge base) as required by the given conditions, 2) Neural Networks are configured to minimize the number of errors in recognizing the pattern presented to their inputs. Neural systems are now being loaded with the data from video images to recognize objects and to store them in very small codes. One can just as well load these systems with sales, marketing and other data to recognize patterns and trends. The basic problem with this application is that one does not get the correlations and econometric parameters of previous technologies. We have to look for the practical aspect of neural network mining and learn to utilize these new tools.

Network Mentality

The diffusion and distribution of service resources are generating new structures which we can define as networks whose capabilities and control require a new style or approach to management. This statement requires some background to explain.

At present Anthony's model of management structure implies top to bottom, single path communication and localized service or task centers. This model also implies and requires unique and specific decision-making responsibilities detached from the task implementation responsibilities. In this pyramidal structure the decision must travel unique pathways. Loss of these paths through inefficiency or other reason downgrades the decision making process. When the pyramid is too tightly put together, a loss of communication channels or their quality affects the integrity of the corporation.

When one attempts to diagram the management structure which may be applicable in the future, in the manner of Anthony's model, one encounters interesting difficulties. In Figure 2 one finds the management pyramid with its three-level structure which has served us so well. The usual two-dimensional structure can be seen to be gaining three-dimensional characteristics. Technology in the form of advanced information systems appears to have transcended our previous management structure and may be ready to cause a change or "mutation" in such structure. This diagram is inadequate and misleading at present because it directs thinking into old-fashioned corners. The reader needs to rearrange this structure so that it represents more realistically the management environment relevant to microcomputers, artificial intelligence and other existent or emerging information technologies.

The distribution of resources creates a whole set of interconnected paths which allow the sharing of decision- and task-making responsibility in unique and unfamiliar ways. Shared resources thus present a new challenge to management. For instance, the selection and purchase of these resources must now be made with a much broader outlook. The sharing of hardware resources such as printers, disk space, high and low capacity memory, high and low capacity CPU time, fonts, software and even personnel makes their optimal selection a serious matter. And when one considers the sharing of data and information among distributed users, a whole new set of considerations arises. Embedded in this pool of interconnected resources is the potential extension of individual capabilities. The extended individual can be expected to produce extended and even unexpected results whose value-added is heretofore unknown.

The future manager should not expect the same old task to be performed better or faster. The future manager should expect results that transcend the present task's potential. Instead of considering simple increments in productivity, we should expect incre-

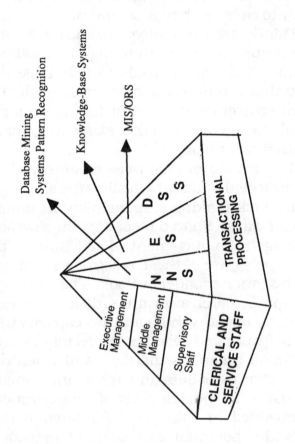

Figure 2. Knowledge Systems

ments in relevant productivity in the future. The adding of the term 'relevant' comes about through the benefit of information which permits the general worker to understand relevant objectives and make informed decisions with higher value.

Let us discuss the potential obsolescence on the making and use of the beloved quarterly report. The reporting capacity of the shared resources networks allows one to expect 'real-time' or 'as-needed' monthly, quarterly and even yearly reports. These reports can be updated by the network in the midnight to dawn interval when load on the resources is low. However, we cannot expect the utility of the weekly or quarterly reports to remain constant when reporting transcends them with 'real-time' capabilities. The response and planning reserved to these periodic information concentrators can be and must be done on an equivalent 'real-time' basis. The planning paradigms are expected to mutate into an 'in-touch' approach responding to personal or people priorities rather than to the reporting environment as is done now. The responsibility and challenge to future management is to utilize shared resources to stop serving the medium and return to serving the customer and people.

The obsolescence of the quarterly and yearly reports also may affect the present planning mentality. Planning may be relegated to enhancing the communication environment with the 'external' environment to enhance information resource. This would be analogous to the linking of the cash register to inventory and manufacturing scheduling systems. Channels of communication with financial, supply, service and other support services then enhance the capability to support the 'in-touch' or 'as needed' requirements. The bottom line will be so tightly bound to the free, reliable and relevant flow of information that strategic plans may have to be developed in terms of information revenue and flow.

Since communication implies a mutual transfer of information, the external world must also be allowed to 'peek' into the operation of the company. This is a higher level than merely letting a customer's transaction activate the inventory, receivables and accounting systems. A customer should be able to estimate or 'see' the state of inventory, sales force, supply and other parameters relevant to his or her operation. This intimate touch between customer and operations and planning is difficult to estimate or describe. The mutual dependence between customer and supplier will require ever increasing communication for day-to-day and hour-to-hour operation.

Conclusions

This chapter has offered a wide view of the impact Artificial Intelligence will have on the information manager. The sections on the micro and mainframe should have motivated the reader to look into experience and define how technology impacts our business environment. Most should have gone through enough technological changes to have definite perspectives of new technology. The collection of these perspectives motivated the preparation of the architecture to manage the potential impact expected from AI. Much of the discipline learned by the information manager will be found to be useful. Structured planning and systems analysis will always be with us. But even these tools have to be refined for the challenge of AI.

Just as the mainframe technology forced a new

management structure on business, creating CIO's, the PC-AI technology is poised to force a new, presently unknown, structure. New, yet undeveloped, paradigms can be expected to make adequate use of these new resources challenging our management styles.

Business leaders will still have the main function of innovating or implementing innovation, as they always have. This time, however, innovation will be their main (if not sole) product.

The challenge introduced by the microcomputer is only the tip of a management challenge which will affect us the rest of the decade. The technologies arising out of Artificial Intelligence are barely infiltrating the organization. The future moment in time when these methods reach the level that they need to know about the entire organization is what this chapter has been describing.

In order for the present information manager to obtain an instinct for the impact of technology, we have reviewed the history and impact of the minicomputer on information. The reader should have been able to read the message that what the micro did for the user in data manipulation and organization, Artificial Intelligence is about to do in knowledge, relationships and decision manipulation. The level of awareness that can be reached by all users, not just top management or a few select observers, with the aide of AI can but change the organizational paradigm of our business.

Three possible products of artificial intelligence have been discussed for their potential for altering organizational structures. Synthetic expertise developed from expert systems and neural networks technology can equalize financial, negotiating and administrative capacity sufficiently to make the Fortune 500 an irrelevant concept. This technology can provide the organizational structures for business to be formed not as divisions of a conglomerate but as coalitions of independent services directed toward common business objectives. The information barriers that prevent such diffuse or distributed administration may be overcome in such a way that Anthony's model of organization becomes obsolete. In a world where anyone can make well-informed and sophisticated decisions, the vice-president, among other management levels, becomes obsolete. The whole information extraction system which makes up the structure of the present corporation may one day sit on a desk in the shape of a super-microcomputer, intelligently reviewing what the rest of the world is doing at 2 A.M., while its owner sleeps.

The seeds for such information concentrators may lie in pioneering concepts such as database mining and network integration. However, in the meantime the present information manager is challenged by the incremental advances toward that ideal. The management paradigms of today should be considered to have short life span. The manager is challenged to adapt styles compatible with the resources arising out of technology.

References

Alpar, P. (1990). Toward Structured Expert Systems Development. *Expert Systems with Applications*, Vol. 1, pp. 63-70.

Anthony, R.N. (1965). Planning and Control Systems: A Framework for Analysis. Harvard University Graduate School of Business Administration, Studies in Management Control. Cambridge, Massachusetts.

Bailey, J.E., & Pearson, S.W. (1983). Development of a Tool for Measuring and Analyzing Computer User Satisfaction. Management Science. 29, 6. pp. 519-529.

Barstow, D. (1988). Artificial Intelligence and Software Engineering. In *Exploring Artificial Intelligence*, H. Schrobe (Ed.). San Mateo, CA: Morgan Kaufmann, pp. 641-670.

Bobrow, D.G., Mittal, S., & Stefik, M., (1986). Expert Systems: Perils and Promise. *Communications of the ACM*. 29, pp. 880-894.

Caudill, M. (1987). Neural Networks Primer. *AI Expert*. San Francisco, CA: Freeman Publications.

Charniack, E., & McDermott, D. (1985). *Artificial Intelligence*. Reading, MA: Addison-Wesley.

Dadashzadeh, M. (1990). Database Management Systems: The Foundation for Information Architecture. In M. Khosrowpour & G.J. Yaverbaum (Eds.), *Information Technology Resources Utilization and Management Issues and Trends*. Harrisburg, PA: Idea Group. pp. 239-273.

Doll, W.J., & Torkzadeh, G. (1987). The Quality of User Documentation. *Information and Management*. 12, 6, pp. 73-78.

Drucker, P. (1967). *The Effective Executive*. New York: Harper & Row.

Durr, M., & Walker, D. (1985). *MICRO TO MAINFRAME: Creating an Integrated Environment*. Reading, Massachusetts: Addison-Wesley Publishing Company.

Eliason, A.L. (1989). *Systems Development Analysis, Design, and Implementation*, Second Edition. Little Brown Glenview, II: Scott, Foresman. p. 58.

Frand, J.L., & McLean, E.R. (1986). *Third Annual UCLA Survey of Business School Computer Usage*. Graduate School of Management, UCLA.

Gallagher, J.P. (1988). *Knowledge-Based Systems for Business*. Englewood Cliffs, NJ: Prentice-Hall.

Gemoets, L.A. (1989). An Information Systems Technology Profile of the Maquiladora Industry. *Southwest Journal of Business & Economics*, Volume VI, No. 4, Fall, 1989. pp. 7-13.

Gemoets, L.A., & Mahmood, M.A. (1990). Effect of the Quality of User Documentation on User Satisfaction with Information Systems. *Information and Management*, *18*. pp. 47-54.

Gianturco, D.J. (1988). *Microcomputers. Corporate Planning, and Decision Support Systems*. Westport, CT: Greenwood Press.

Hayes-Roth, F., Waterman, D., & Lenat, D. (Eds.) (1983). *Building expert systems*. Reading, MA: Addison-Wesley.

Harmon, P., & King, D. (1985). *Expert Systems*. New York, NY: Wiley.

Hiatt, C., & Motz, A.A. (1990). Disaster Recovery Planning. In M. Khosrowpour

& G.J. Yaverbaum (Eds.), *Information Technology Resources Utilization and Management Issues and Trends.* Harrisburg, PA: Idea Group., pp. 449-471.

Highland, H.J. (1984). *Protecting your Microcomputer System.* New York, NY: John Wiley & Sons.

Holsapple, C.W., & Whinston, A.B. (1987). *Business Expert System.* Homewood, IL: Richard D. Irwin Inc. p. 4.

Howard, P.D. &, Duvall, T.J (1988). When Systems Don't Support Strategy. *Information Strategy: The Executive's Journal*, 4(2), pp. 16-21.

Johnson, B. (1989). Captive, Cold, Hind, Hot, Warm: Which Kind of Site is Best?. *Disaster Recovery Journal*, January, 2(1), 60.

Mahmood, M.A., & Gemoets, L.A. (1990). Building Effective Expert Systems: An In Depth Analysis of Managerial Issues. In M. Khosrowpour & G.J. Yaverbaum (Eds.), *Information Technology Resources Utilization and Management Issues and Trends.* Harrisburg, PA: Idea Group.

Martin, J., & Oxman, S. (1988). *Building Expert Systems.* Englewood Cliffs, NJ: Prentice-Hall.

Millson, D. (1985). Wanted Software Professionals. *Computer Language*, (October), pp. 51-55.

Mishkoff, H. (1985). *Understanding Artificial Intelligence.* Dallas, TX: Texas Instruments Publishing.

Neumann, S., & Hadass, M. (1990). On Decision Support Systems. *I/S ANALIZER for Information Systems Management*, (February), 28(2), Review 22 (Spring/1980). pp. 77-84.

Nolan, R.L. (1988). MIS in the Next Decade. *Information Week.* January 4, 1988. pp. 26-28.

Perry, W.E. (1985). *THE MICRO-MAINFRAME LINK.* The Corporate Guide to the Productive Use of the Microcomputer. New York, NY: John Wiley & Sons.

Reitman, W. (1990). Managing the Development of Generic Expert Systems Products. In De Salvo & Liebowitz (Eds.), *Managing Artificial Intelligence & Expert Systems.* Englewood Cliff, NJ: Yourdon.

Rolston, D. (1988). *Principles of Artificial Intelligence and Expert Systems Development.* Sunnyvale, CA: McGraw-Hill Book Company.

Schutzer, D. (1990). Business Expert Systems: The Competitive Edge. *Expert Systems with Applications*, 1(1), 17-21.

Shaw, M.L.G., & Gaines, B.R. (1986). Interactive elicitation of knowledge from experts. *Future Computing Systems*, 1(2), 151-190.

Simon, H. (1986). Whether Software Engineering Needs to be Artificially

Intelligent. *IEEE Transactions on Software Engineering.* SE-12, pp. 726-732.

Sviokla, J.J. (1989). Expert Systems and Their Impact on Firm: The Effects of Plan Power Use on the Information Processing Capacity of the Financial Collaborative. *Journal of Management Information Systems. Vol. 6*, No. 3, Winter 1989-90. pp. 65-84.

Szewczak, E.J., & Snodgrass, C.R. (1989). ISDN as an Information Resource for Strategic Management of Multinational Firms. *Information Resources Management Journal. Vol. 2*, No. 3. pp. 15-25.

Tannenbaum, (1990). Installing AI Tools into Corporate Environments. *AI Expert.* May, 1990.

Thomson, D.M., & Feinstein, J.L. (1990). Cost Justifying Expert Systems. In DeSalvo, D.A. & Liebowitz, J. (Eds.), *Managing Artificial Intelligence & Expert Systems.* Englewood Cliff, NJ: Yourdon. pp. 93-121.

Tom, P.L. (1987). *Managing Information as a Corporate Resource.* Glenview, IL: Scott, Foresman and Company.

Trippi, R., & Turban, E. (1989). The Impact of Parallel and Neural Computing on Managerial Decision Making. *Journal of Management Information System. Vol. 6*, No. 3, Winter 1989-90. pp. 85-98.

Wexelbat, R.L. (1989). On Interface Requirements for Expert Systems. *AI Magazine.* Fall 1989. pp. 66-78.

Whitten, J.L., Bentley, L.D., & Barlow, V.M. (1989). *Systems Analysis and Design Methods.* Second Edition. Homewood, Ill: Irwin.

Zawrotny, S.B. (1989). Key to IS Success: Alignment with Corporate Goals. *Information Resource Management Vol. 2*, No. 4, p. 32.

Chapter 9

SOFTWARE SELECTION: A KNOWLEDGE-BASED SYSTEM APPROACH

D.G. Dologite
Baruch College - City University of New York

Human expertise is being lost in the microcomputer support area of many organizations. This seems inevitable because contact between qualified individuals and the end-user, as well as vendor, communities present opportunities that encourage many job shifts (Heltne, 1988; Nunamaker et al., 1988). Among the many problems this drain creates, one can be singled out for a relatively risk-free pilot application of knowledge-based, or expert system technology: the screening of software packages before purchase by an organization.

Several factors make the software selection problem appropriate for knowledge-based system (KBS) development. The primary one is that the expertise needed to do this task is becoming scarce within the organization. Another is that screening software for

Previously published in the Journal of Microcomputer Systems Management, Vol. 2, No. 1
© Idea Group Publishing

acquisition is a well understood task (Hayes-Roth et al., 1983; Rauch-Hardin, 1986;Waterman, 1986).

The Software Selection Assistant (SSA), described in this paper, demonstrates a KBS approach to preserve valuable expertise used to support the software screening task. In addition, SSA will be shown to help support a related software selection task. It concerns servicing the increased end-user demand for assistance in selecting software appropriate for their particular application.

Organizations find that a poor overall fit of packaged software with end-user requirements causes not only package disuse, but also a more important loss in potential end-user effectiveness (Dickson et. al., 1985; Hartog & Klepper, 1988). This makes the matching of software with end-user tasks a high-priority issue in many organizations (Gerrity & Rockart, 1986; Rockart & Flannery, 1983).

The key factors that make this related problem appropriate for KBS development are: expertise is needed in many locations, and the solution has a high payoff (Harmon, Maus, & Morrisey, 1988; Waterman, 1986).

In general, SSA will be shown to be a useful tool which enables an organization to broaden its support and quality of service in the software selection area without adding more staff.

The KBS approach described in this paper can be generalized and applied in other organizations that have similar software selection tasks to support. In the following sections, SSA's phase one screening module for software acquisition is detailed with a focus on background models in the literature, operation, and construction. A discussion of SSA's phase two evolutionary direction into the end-user and package matching function follows. Conclusions are then drawn as to the SSA experience and, finally, areas are pointed out that are of interest to practitioners and researchers experimenting with KBS systems to solve software selection problems.

Screening Module Background

Previous work related to the software screening purpose of SSA is found in non-knowledge-based system studies. Work by Hasty, Herbst, and Mahmood (1989), Dologite and Levine (1985), Needleman (1988), Archer (1988), and Ryan (1987, 1988) demonstrate systematic approaches to finding a few software pack-

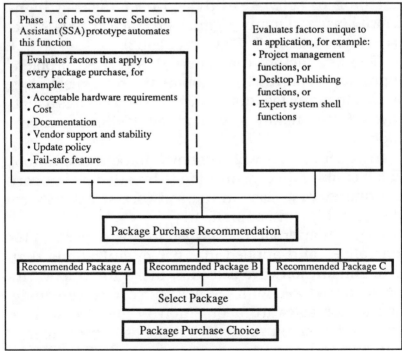

Figure 1: Functional Breakdown of the Software Package Selection Task

ages worth further intense evaluation prior to the selection and acquisition of a single best one.

SSA's approach is anchored in the software evaluation and selection model proposed in Dologite (1981, 1982, 1985), Dologite and Mockler (1988) and diagrammed in Figure 1. It consists of a two-part procedure. One part includes the evaluating factors that are relevant to any package selection effort, whether the package belongs to the project management, expert system shell, desktop publishing, or any other application category. These factors include evaluating, for example, a package's costs, vendor support, market acceptance, and update history.

The second part of the software selection model that serves as SSA's conceptual frame concerns evaluating a package's application-specific factors. As an example, for a project management package, it considers factors related to project scheduling, calendaring, and resource allocation. Although this part requires expert judgment, it deals with a new set of specialized selection criteria for each new software package selection effort. This part, therefore, is retained in SSA's plan as a manual procedure. The data collected during this procedure, however, serves as the input stream to SSA's second phase which is described later.

It is important to establish that there is no right or wrong order for performing the first two procedures shown in Figure 1. In some cases, only if a package meets generic guidelines related to cost, vendor support, or other conditions, is it examined further. In other cases, the presence of application-specific factors may determine whether or not it is screened for "generic" features. In all cases, organizational requirements will guide the procedure.

In many ways, SSA's screening module traces its

genealogy to Coopers and Lybrand's legendary Exper-TAX KBS (Shpilberg, Grahm, & Schatz, 1986). Exper-TAX actively guides staff accountants through the client information gathering process, then analyzes and synthesizes the information to identify the basic tax accrual and planning issues. Similar to Exper-TAX, SSA's procedures were previously performed using manual questionnaires and checklists. Now both SSA and ExperTAX function as "intelligent" questionnaires to actively guide staff professionals through the data gathering phase. Both systems improve the quality of the information gathered and, among other benefits, facilitate the training of new staff.

Operation of SSA's Screening Module

As diagrammed in Figure 2, a software selector carries out a consultation with SSA's screening module through the user interface. The selector, who evalu-ates one candidate package at a time, is asked a series of questions about the package's characteristics and the organization requirements. SSA then makes a recommendation about whether or not to consider purchasing the package.

The factors covered in SSA to help a software selector arrive at an informed decision are: costs, documentation, market acceptance and update his-tory, vendor support and stability, operating system support and requirements, hardware support and requirements, third-party support, fail-safe consid-erations, and ease of use. Such factors are widely sup-ported by the literature for screening packages (see, e.g., Hasty et. al., 1989; Dologite, 1982, 1988, 1985, 1981; Dooley, 1987; Downing-Faircloth, 1985). These sources should be consulted for a full explanation of these factors which is outside the scope of this paper.

During the questioning segment, a selector is given a range of answers, as the following examples from the documentation section illustrate:

• How do you rate the User Guide for understandability by nontechnical personnel?

> 1 = good
> 2 = satisfactory
> 3 = poor

• Is the User Guide indexed so users can easily find answers to questions?

> 1 = yes

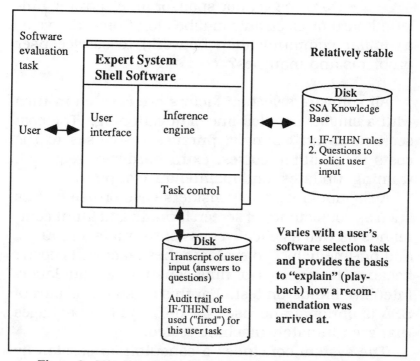

Figure 2: User Interface with the Software Selection Assistant

2 = no

The questioning that ensues parallels that of filling out a paper questionnaire. But, as Basden (1984) and Shpilberg et. al. (1986) observe, the KBS advantage is in "intelligently" selecting and ordering questions. For example, to the question "Does the vendor offer after-sale support?," a "no" response ignores any further questions about vendor after-sale support while a "yes" response triggers related questions such as:

• Is vendor support available through a toll-free 800 telephone number?

• Does the vendor sponsor an electronic bulletin board or electronic mailbox (on CompuServe or a similar communication network) to service user problems and inquiries?

All software selection factors are covered in turn with a similar detailed line of questioning. The cost section, as an example, pursues responses to the costs for multiple copies, extra hardware required, training, updates, and maintenance support.

An optional section considers ease-of-use factors such as consistency of screen formats and input commands as well as effectiveness of tutorials, manuals, and on-line help. To evaluate these factors is costly because it requires a time-consuming and labor-intensive hands-on test. For this reason, this part of SSA is optional and used for only the few packages that are ultimately machine-tested.

The system concludes a consultation session by rating the package based on the selector's responses to questions. The SSA prototype is limited to making a final recommendation of favorable (a candidate package should be highly considered), satisfactory (a package should be further evaluated for suitability), and unfavorable (a package should not be considered further).

At any point during a consultation, a selector may want to ask why a particular question is asked or a recommendation is made. By typing "why," SSA displays the knowledge-base entries and selector responses that influence the specific question or recommendation. SSA builds an audit trail of a session's events, as diagrammed in Figure 2, which enable it to respond to a "why" request.

SSA Construction

SSA was developed on a microcomputer using the M.1 expert system shell by Teknowledge, Inc. This shell was identified as promising for a first-cut prototype and works on IBM-compatible computers, the planned system delivery environment.

As with all expert system shells, only the knowledge base had to be developed from scratch. The knowledge base contains the recorded expertise gathered from interviews with resident software selection experts, supplemented with additional data about software selection from observations and researched sources (e.g., Brownstein & Learner, 1982; Buckland, 1985; Dologite, 1985, 1988; Flores, 1986; Frankel & Gras, 1983; Hasty et al., 1989). The data gathering procedures used reflect normal knowledge elicitation practices (see, e.g., Harmon et al., 1988; Hayes-Roth et al., 1983; Schneiderman, 1986; Winston, 1984). The collected expertise was then represented in the knowledge base as an interrelated set of IF-THEN rules.

Rules are one common form of knowledge representation in knowledge-based systems (Barr & Feigenbaum, 1981; Brachman & Smith, 1980; Woods, 1983). For example, the following rules were formed to record how a software selection expert evaluates a package's documentation:

Rule-47:
if user-guide = good and
other-manuals = good and
on-line-help = good and
installation-guide = yes and
third-party-aids = yes
then documentation = good.

Rule-93:
if documentation = good and
costs = low and
background = favorable
then package-gen = favorable.

In this case, Rule 47 determines that if the user guide, other manuals, and on-line help are rated as good, and the package supplies an installation guide with third-party books or other aids providing additional support, then the document category receives a good rating. This result cascades down to other rules, such as Rule 93, which refine the evaluation criteria even further to end at a single recommendation.

Rules are supplemented with a set of related questions which are used to solicit input during a user session or consultation. This input style, where the system poses questions and the user is expected to provide answers, allows the system to be in control.

In effect, the system functions as an intelligent tutor and uses a dialogue style which studies show is effective in such situations (see, e.g., Sleeman & Brown, 1982).

Together the questions and rules constitute the system's knowledge base. A program built into an expert system shell called an "inference engine" controls the logic search through the knowledge base, fires the appropriate rules, tracks the inference process and communicates with the user through the user interface. As evident from Figure 2, the inference engine is the central component in an expert system shell.

To organize the rules and related user questions in the knowledge base required first developing a paper model of the decision-making process for the software selection task. The method described in Mockler & Dologite (1988) was used which involved creating a dependency diagram, as shown in Figure 3. It details the interrelationship of the selection criteria, the legal values for each factor, and the information to be input by the user. The diagram is supplemented with a decision chart, such as the example given in Figure 4, which functions as a key to identify which combinations of "IF" premises result in which "THEN" conclusions. Decision charts and dependency diagrams are prepared for each decision group or rule set.

Creating a paper model of the SSA prototype represented 80 percent of the work to construct the system. The final step required converting the paper model into the formal rules and questions that are keyed into the microcomputer data file which becomes the system knowledge base. The conversion step is relatively straightforward.

After debugging the knowledge base of syntax and

logic errors, the system was tested. The approach to validation was to let less experienced personnel involved with software selection, but not involved in the development of SSA, conduct independent tests of the system's performance. The validators processed several cases that had recently been completed and compared the system's response with the actual outcomes. They also ran tests of new cases in parallel with the old manual process. Results of these exercises indicated that SSA supported software selectors in the task of collecting information and analyzing it to arrive at a recommendation better than the former paper method.   The issues raised about question wording and sequence were used to fine-tune the system.

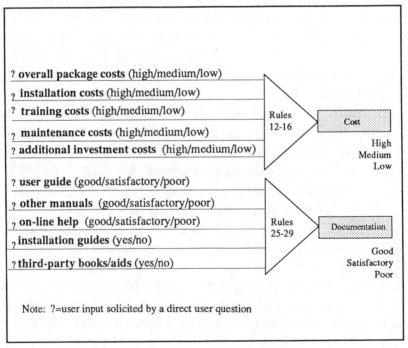

Figure 3: Partial Dependency Diagram

IF										
Package in General (Rules 41-58)	FFS	FFF	SSU	F	S	any	SUU	U	U	any
After-Sale Support (Rules 59-76)	FFF	FUU	FUF	S	any	S	SFS	U	any	U
Other-Features (Rules 77-94)	FSF	UFS	UFF	any	S	F	USS	any	U	U
THEN										
Favorable	XXX	XXX		X	X	X				
Satisfactory			XXX				XXX			
Unfavorable								X	X	X

Figure 4: SSA Decision Chart-Partial Rule Set

Evolving the Prototype

The prototype created in phase one of SSA's development is designed to be reused for every software package acquisition effort. Its success depends on a separate evaluation of a software package's application-specific features. Because the features examined to select a project management package are useless when evaluating an expert system shell package, this application-specific evaluation is not appropriate for KBS implementation and so is performed off-line. The information gathered during this task, however, became the input for phase two of SSA's development effort. It focuses on creating reusable application-specific KBS support modules for the related problem of matching end-users with pre-selected software packages. The case of matching end-users with expert system shell software was the focus of the first phase two module.

The task performed by SSA's phase two modules has precedents described in the literature by Nunamaker et. al. (1988), Heltne et. al. (1988), Masud & Kolarik (1987), Chang (1987), and Laporte (1987). One main motivation behind such efforts is a concern to ensure that the software recommended to perform an end-user's task is appropriate.

In SSA's approach, as well as in most other systems that inform the design of a phase two module, end-users themselves are expected to use the KBS. End-users were, therefore, heavily depended on for feedback throughout the development of the phase two prototype module. Their input especially helped to determine the sequence and nature of questions asked to identify end-user computer ability and hardware environment issues. In general, the steps used to develop, construct, and validate the phase two prototype module followed the pattern already described for SSA's screening module.

Any end-user consulting the prototype module, the Software Selection Assistant/Expert System (SSA/ES), answers questions about computer literacy and task requirements such as:

• Do you consider yourself a beginner, average, or experienced microcomputer user?

• Do you have a preference for the method used to represent knowledge in the knowledge base (e.g., rules, objects, semantic nets, etc.)

• Will any input come from signals sent by automated machinery (signal processing)?

Some of these questions may never be asked, depending on an end- user's response to previous questions.

The phase two design calls for recommending software based on a list of organizationally-supported packages. As an example, expert system software is available in:

• Easy-to-learn packages, like 1st Class or VP Expert, for end-users who indicate little or no experience and limited application needs

• High-end PC-based packages, like Level 5, GoldWorks, and GURU, for end-users with requirements to interface with other applications and a need to do custom programming.

SSA's design of narrowing an end-user's requirements and ability to a category with specific recommended packages attached to it is much like that described by Nunamaker (1988), Heltne et. al. (1988), and Chang (1987). It allows flexibility to add, change, or delete packages as desired without requiring substantial changes to the rules.

This design contrasts with the KBS described in Masud & Kolarik (1987) which matches an end-user with any one of three computer-aided-design (CAD) packages. Should one package be deleted or added to the CAD system, theoretically, considerable changes to the rules would be required. An early SSA version attempted this approach and found it too rigid for cases where the software category is not mature enough to have stabilized on a few dominant package choices.

SSA's follow-on phases include matching modules for project management and desktop publishing software packages, among others. In the long run, these SSA application-specific modules are expected to be linked together through a master module. Mainframe-based designs that would be appropriate models for this phase are described in Chang (1987), Heltne et. al. (1988), and Nunamaker et. al. (1988). Variations for a microcomputer implementation remain to be worked out.

Discussion and Conclusions

SSA is an experimental knowledge-based system project that is still evolving. The system is expected to always be in an "evolving" state. It is well accepted that any development of a knowledge-based system is an incremental process of building prototypes that become more "expert" during the on-going development process (Buchanan et al., 1983; McDermott,

1984).

In the organization where the SSA prototype modules are being concept tested, preliminary results are positive. The screening module serves a purpose similar to ExperTAX (Shpilberg, 1986), which functions as a repository of corporate knowledge. In the SSA case, the focus is on software package selection. Both KBS render the using organizations less vulnerable to a knowledge and experience drain in the wake of employee turnover.

In use, SSA functions as a guide for less-experienced personnel who perform software acquisition tasks and as a personal tutor to accelerate the software selector training process. Similar advantages of other KBS performing such tutorial roles are widely documented in the literature (see e.g., Basden, 1984; Madni, 1988; Rauch-Hardin, 1986). In SSA's case, as in others, trainees benefit from the explicit knowledge of the company's definitive experts stored in the KBS, instead of being trained by co-workers or less-knowledgeable instructors. Also, because it is no longer necessary for a human expert to be devoted to the training process, overall training costs are reduced.

In general, SSA's screening module, as well as the matching modules, serve to standardize procedures and raise the level of task performance wherever they are used throughout the organization. This finding is similar to one of the major results Coopers and Lybrand experience with ExperTAX. In both cases, the KBS incorporates expertise from some who are expert in the data gathering process and others who are expert in summarizing results and constructing viable alternative strategies. Through integrating all the experts' collective specialized knowledge, the resulting KBS provides a consistent quality of response in a more efficient manner than would result from any one expert acting alone.

In the case of SSA's matching modules, end-users receive the best consulting advice the organization can offer on selecting software for a specific application, wherever they are located. Harmon et al. (1988) and others point out the potential of KBSs being particularly helpful in places where a few key individuals are in short supply. Also, as Hammond (1982) observes, a KBS can offer users access to data on their own terms so that they can solve their own business problems.

As a result, end-user dependence on microcomputer support personnel is reduced. Because the matching modules free the microcomputer support staff from handling many routine requests, they are able to concentrate on other more pressing issues.

SSA's approach to the two software selection tasks discussed in this paper, screening packages and matching end-users with packages, can be generalized and applied in other organizations with similar functions to support. Because the screening task is an administrative function that is well understood, with literature sources to backup any expertise that may be scarce, it is a relatively risk-free way to explore the benefits of using KBS in the microcomputer support area. Considerably higher payoffs are to be realized, however, by using KBS technology to match end-users with appropriate software. Putting the right software tool in the end-user's hands is vital if, as has been predicted, they will comprise 75 percent of the total computing capacity of the typical American corporation in the 1990's (Dickson, et al., 1985).

Areas for Further Study

Much work remains to be done on SSA which may suggest some issues and areas that could be conducive to future study by practitioners and researchers. One such area is to explore the development of an expert-level and a novice-level version of the screening module for software selectors. As has been found by Madni (1988), after a user becomes trained in a task supported by a knowledge-based system, the system is abandoned by that user. So an expert, or "coarser-grain," version is being considered to function as a quick reference guide to cover only the critical points for software selectors who become more experienced.

Another area to explore is the development of a two-part approach to SSA's matching modules. One module could ask for end-user profile information, such as computer experience and hardware environment. This information could be saved for automatic reuse with any application-specific inquiry the end-user makes. Although such a "User Profile" has been implemented on a mainframe system, where control and update are centralized (Nunamaker et al., 1988), the logistics of implementing this on a distributed microcomputer-based system must be worked out.

SSA modules are easily maintained by adding, deleting, or changing rules. Updated knowledge bases require, however, labor intensive distribution to ship floppy disks or telecommunicate KBS files to various locations. It is possible that a more efficient solution to roll knowledge bases out to users might involve a centralized bulletin board or other system.

In general, SSA could be improved with a more feature-rich expert system shell which provides links to other applications. This development would enable software selectors a convenient spreadsheet format to explore various package weighting and rating alternatives, such as those found in Shoval and Lugasi (1987), Downing-Faircloth (1985), Rastani and Rijo (1985), Schoemacker and Waid (1982), Sharpe (1969), and Tell (1976). The system could also provide end-users with a way to sample the recommended software immediately.

A more powerful shell should also allow more control over the user-interface design which could provide users with some relief from the present rigid question-and-answer dialogue. Ideally, experienced users should be given control of the process (Carrol & McKendree, 1987;Mackie, 1980) and be allowed to insert free-flow text whenever it is considered necessary to make a note.

Although SSA is still developing, and presents implementation challenges for further study and work, preliminary results are encouraging. The system proves to be a useful tool which enables an organization to broaden its support and quality of service in the software selection area without adding more staff. It effectively demonstrates the potential of using KBS "software to select software."

References
Archer, N. P. (1988). End user software selection. *Journal of Systems Management, 39*(7), 32-39.

Barr, A., & Feigenbaum, E. A.(Eds.) (1981). *The Handbook of Artificial Intelligence* (Vol. 1). Los Altos, CA: William Kaufman.

Basden, A. (1984). On the application of expert systems. In *Developments in Expert Systems*. New York: Academic Press.

Brachman, R. J., & Smith, B. C. (Eds.) (1980).*SIGART Newsletter: Special Issue on Knowledge Representations*, 70.

Brownstein, I., & Learner, N. B. (1982). *Guidelines for Evaluating and Selecting Software Packages*. New York: Elsevier.

Buchanan, B.G., et al. (1983). Constructing an expert system. In F. Hayes-Roth, D.A.Waterman, & D.B. Lenat (Eds). *Building Expert Systems*. Reading, MA:

Addison-Wesley, 127-167.

Buckland, J. A. (1985). *Critical Technology Report: Selecting Software Packages for End Users.* New York: Chantico Publishing Co.

Carrol, J.M., & McKendree, J. (1987). Interface design issues for advice-giving expert systems. *Communications of the ACM, 30*(1), 14-31.

Chang, E.C.-P. (1987, December). Using expert systems to select software for traffic analysis. *1987 Winter Simulation Conference Proceedings,* 828-37.

Dickson, G. W., Leitheiser, R. L., Wetherbe, J. C., & Nechis, M. (1985). Key information systems issues for the 1980s. *MIS Quarterly, 8*(3), 135-148.

Dologite, D.G. (1981). Small business computer acquisition. *Journal of Systems Management, 32*(3), 34-40.

Dologite, D.G. (1982). Evaluating packaged software - avoiding the landmines. *Data Management, 20*(1), 20ff.

Dologite, D.G. (1985). *Using Small Business Computers.* Englewood Cliffs, NJ: Prentice-Hall.

Dologite, D.G., & Levine, D. M. (1985). Comparative analysis of word processing packages. *Journal of Systems Management, 36*(9), 8-17.

Dologite, D.G., & Mockler, R.J. (1988). *Using Microcomputers.* Englewood Cliffs, NJ: Prentice-Hall.

Dooley, B. J. (1987). Caution: Evaluating software. *Datapro Directory of Microcomputer Software, 7*(7), MS99-701-071 - 072.

Downing-Faircloth, M. (1985 September). General software testing procedures. In *Datapro Reports on Microcomputers,* (Vol. 2). Delray, NJ: Datapro Research Corporation.

Flores, I. (1986). *The Professional Microcomputer Handbook.* New York: Van Nostrand Reinhold.

Frankel, P. & Gras, A. (1983). *The Software Sifter: An Intelligent Shopper's Guide to Buying Computer Software.* New York: Macmillan.

Gerrity, T. P., & Rockart, J. F. (Summer 1986). End-user computing: Are you a leader or a laggard? *Sloan Management Review,* 25-34.

Hammond, L.W. (1982). Management considerations for an information center. *IBM Systems Journal,* 21(2), 131-161.

Harmon, P., Maus, R., & Morrisey, W. (1988). *Expert Systems Tools and Applications.* New York: John Wiley.

Hartog, C. & Klepper, R. (1988, August 27). Business squeeze pushes software sales up 184%. *Computerworld,* 55-58.

Hasty, R. W., Herbst, A. F., & Mahmood, M. A. (1989). Microcomputer software evaluation and selection strategies. *Journal of Microcomputer Systems Management, 1*(1), 8-19.

Hayes-Roth, F., Waterman, D. A., & Lenat, D. B. (1983). *Building Expert Systems.* Reading, MA: Addison-Wesley.

Heltne, M. M., Vinze, A. S., Konsynski, B. R., & Nunamaker, J. F., Jr. (1988). ICE: Information center expert, A consultation system for resource allocation. *Data-*

base, 19(2), 1-15.

Laporte, P. (1987, December). On the design of an expert system as an aid to the use of scientific software. *Eighth International Conference on Computing Methods in Applied Sciences and Engineering*, 519-530.

Mackie, R.R. (1980). Design criteria for decision aids: The user's perspective. In *Proceedings of the Human Factors Society 24th Annual Meeting*, Santa Monica, CA. 80-84.

Madni, A. M. (1988). The role of human factors in expert system design and acceptance. *Human Factors, 30*(4), 395-414.

Masud, A.S.M., & Kolarik, B. P. (1987,March). Microcomputer- based knowledge system for CAD software selection. *9th Annual Conference on Computers and Industrial Engineering*, 26-28.

McDermott, J. (1984). R1 revisited: Four years in the trenches. *AI Magazine, 5*(3), 21-32.

Mockler, R.J., & Dologite, D. G. (1988). Developing knowledge-based systems for strategic corporate planning, *Long Range Planning, 21*(1), 97-102.

Needleman, T. (1988, April/May). How to select an accounting package for your clients. *Computers in Accounting*, 52-??.

Nunamaker Jr., J. F., Konsynski, B. R., Chen, M., Vinze, A. S., Chen, Y. I. L., & Heltne, M. M. (1988, January). Knowledge- based support for information centers. *Proceedings of the Twenty-First Annual Hawaii International Conference on Systems Sciences*, 96-105.

Rastani, J., & Rijo, C. (1985, March). Software selection made easy. *Infosystems*, 92-93.

Rauch-Hardin, W. (1986). *Artificial Intelligence in Business, Science, and Industry*. Englewood Cliffs, NJ: Prentice-Hall.

Rockart, J. F., & Flannery, L. S. (1983). The management of end user computing. *Communications of the ACM*, 776-784.

Ryan, H. W. (1987). What envelope? *Journal of Information Systems Management, 4*(4), 52-56.

Ryan, H. W. (1988). Experimenting with the envelope. *Journal of Information Systems Management, 5*(2), 72-79.

Schneiderman, B. (1986). *Designing the User Interface: Strategies for Effective Human-Computer Interaction*. Reading, MA: Addison-Wesley.

Schoemacker, P., & Waid, C. (1982). An experimental comparison of different approaches to determining weights in the additive utility model. *Management Science, 28*(2), 102-196.

Sharpe, W. F. (1969). *The Economics of Computers*. New York: Columbia.

Shoval, P., & Lugasi, Y. (1987). Models for computer system evaluation and selection. *Information and Management, 12*(3), 117-129.

Shpilberg, D., Graham, L. E., & Schatz, H. (1986). ExperTAX: An expert system for corporate planning. *Expert Systems, 3*(3), 136-151.

Sleeman, D., & Brown, J.S., eds. (1982). *Intelligent Tutoring Systems*. New York: Academic Press.

Tell, B. (1976). A comparative study of four multiple- criteria methods. In H. Thirie, and S. Zionts, S., (Eds). *Multiple Criteria Decision Making*. New York, NY: Springer-Verlag.

Waterman, D. A. (1986). *A Guide to Expert Systems*. Reading, MA: Addison-Wesley.

Winston, P. H. (1984). *Artificial Intelligence*, 2nd ed. Reading, MA: Addison-Wesley.

Woods, W. A. (1983). What's important about knowledge representation? *IEEE Computer, 16*(10), 22-27.

Part V
Microcomputer
Security and
Protection

Increases in organizational resources are generally matched by an enhancement of the protection of that resource. However, the one area where this has not occurred is with computer-based information systems (CBIS). Numerous surveys show that most organizations do not have adequate security plans in place. Kai Koong and Roland Weistroffer (Managing Microcomputer Security) present options in developing security and disaster recovery plans to protect organizational information and applications. Hindupur Ramakrishna and Bindiganavale Vijayaraman agree that businesses are underprepared for dealing with disasters involving their CBIS and they present several examples of disasters, organizational issues in preparing to meet possible disasters, and solutions to prevent them. Cherie Werbel and Phillip Werbel (The Changing Environment of Software Copyright: The Case of Apple Computer v. Microsoft Corp.) presents an acknowledgement of a different kind of security problem, i.e. software copyright infringement. They discuss the recent Apple computer vs. Microsoft and Hewlett-Packard and how lawsuits are being used to protect software development techniques.

Chapter 10

MANAGING MICROCOMPUTER SECURITY

Kai S. Koong and H. Roland Weistroffer
Virginia Commonwealth University

Computers and information technology have added a new dimension to the management of businesses. To many efficiently operated firms, information output from computer based systems is equally, if not more, important than the other two scarce resources, namely skilled labor and capital. This is because information technology has changed the way corporations compete (McFarland, 1984). To those business managers and executives who know how to utilize it effectively, information is a strategic weapon in the battle against competitors and unreliable suppliers. As a matter of fact, the ability to access and use information will more and more dominate any power struggle, be it an economic, political or social one (Naisbitt, 1984).

Unfortunately, information technology has its downside as well. User-friendly hardware and software have made information technology widely available, and anyone with a microcomputer, a modem, and the required technical skills can gain access to networked computer systems. Thus the computer has become a potential tool for illicit intrusion into information banks. Furthermore, the computer itself has become a target of possible abuse or sabotage. Natural disasters pose an additional threat to information systems, their effects often compounded by poor management.

Numerous accounts of security failures and crises have been published in the literature. Table 1 shows a few of these cases. The listed incidents are not isolated misfortunes. A number of research studies have reported on the magnitude of computer security failures. The statistics are mind boggling and should induce business managers and executives to allot more attention and resources to this growing problem in computerized information systems. A few of these reports are summarized in Table 2.

The problems with computer security can be expected to continue to increase in the 1990s and beyond. An estimated ninety percent of all minicomputers and mainframes that are sold or leased in the United States have some form of communication capability (Bidgoli and Azarmsa, 1988), and the reliance on computer networks is increasing steadily. The communication capability makes computer systems more vulnerable to deliberate as well as accidental damages. Just what is the magnitude of this problem? A request placed in a metropolitan area electronic bulletin board for virus attacks resulted in more than one hundred such attacks in just a few hours (Johnston, 1988)! This shows the potential danger computer systems are faced with currently. In

1. An employee hated his job and quit. Before he left, he added instructions to a computer program that would result in other software being erased two years after his departure from the company (Capron and Williams, 1982).

2. The chairman of a life insurance company used a computer to steal 200 million dollars over a period of four years (Keough, 1989).

3. Several employees at a major computer company manipulated inventory records by diverting an estimated 20 million dollars worth of equipment to dummy accounts (Ball, 1988).

4. A graduate student infected computer systems of the US Department of Defense and of various universities with a computer virus. Damages are estimated to be over 100 million dollars (Phelps, 1989).

5. A fire at a major utility company caused some three million dollars worth of damages. Key documents and papers in the computer system were destroyed (Tucker, 1987).

Table 1: Cases of Security Failures

1. Among American businesses, computer crime accounts for an estimated five billion dollars in losses annually (Esters, 1989), but only ten percent of all detected computer crimes are reported to authorities (Bakst, 1987).

2. According to 1986 statistics on the banking industry, the amount of revenue lost to computer fraud was ten times greater than the amount lost to robbery (Ginn, 1989).

3. I n 1989, about 350 thousand computers were infected by viruses (Cullen, 1989), and according to John McAfee, the cost of the "Internet Worm" incident that affected some six thousand computer systems is estimated at 97 million dollars (NCCCD, 1989).

4. A company that is hit by a computer security failure can lose as much as fifty percent of its functionality in less than five days (Menkus, 1988). The day-by-day decline in business activities due to a company data center being struck by disaster is shown in Figure 1.

5. The average company will lose two to three percent of its gross sales within eight days of a sustained computer outage. If the crisis exceeds ten days, it is unlikely to recover. In fact, fifty percent of companies suffering this magnitude of a loss will go out of business (Toigo, 1989).

Table 2: Computer Crime Statistics

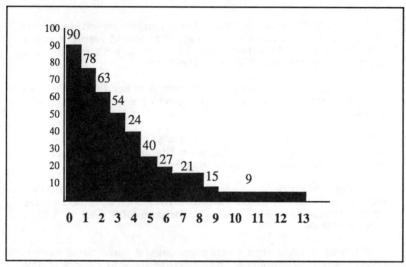

**Figure 1: Approximate Decline in Operational Business Activities
After a Complete Data Center Failure**

view of developing technology and the further increase in computer literacy and accessibility in society, one can only guess at the extent of the danger to information systems in the future. Managers and executives act wisely by developing effective defense mechanisms now. Though it may sound like a cliche, the adage "an ounce of prevention is better than a pound of cure" applies more than ever.

The State of Microcomputer Security

From small family businesses to multinational corporations, the microcomputer, or personal computer, has become a crucial tool for supporting a wide range of business activities. Linked to larger computers via networks, its use ranges from office applications such as word processing, through database queries, to strategic decision support modelling. As with larger computer systems, microcomputers are frequently targets of abuse. In addition to that, they

1. In July 1988, there were 44 personal computer based disaster recovery software packages in the market with prices ranging from $450 to $35,000. Most of these packages had become available only in the preceding 24 months. By January 1989, five more packages had been introduced.

2. According to the National Center for Computer Crime Data, the average facility has 1,224 microcomputers, 96 minicomputers and 10 mainframes. The average annual damages due to abuse and crime in this microcomputer dominated environment are 109 thousand dollars in monetary losses, 365 hours of lost employee time, and 26 hours in lost computer time (NCCCD, 1989).

3. It takes 19 days to re-create one IBM AT 20 megabyte hard disk containing sales and marketing information, at a cost of 17 thousand dollars. If the disk contained accounting information, specialists at the 3M Corporation estimated that the operation will take 21 days at a cost of about 19 thousand dollars (Aaland, 1988).

4. Using personal computers, a group of teenagers, called the Milwaukee 414 Club, cracked the access controls of over sixty industry and government computer systems (Cronin, 1986).

Table 3: Some Facts and Developments in Microcomputer Security

are often the medium through which illicit access to other computer systems is gained, via computer networks. Unfortunately, in many organizations, big or small, microcomputer security and disaster recovery planning are regarded as unimportant and a waste of time and money (Usdin, 1987). Cronin (1986) calls this indifference to the problem a managerial blind spot. Table 3 shows some facts and developments that may serve to rouse attention to the seriousness of the microcomputer security problem in the work place. These facts should not be totally surprising to knowledgable managers and executives who use microcomputers in their firms. After all, personal computers are designed for maximum accessibility and convenience. They are cheap, yet powerful machines, and with their small size and easily interchangable hardware parts, they challenge the very issue of security and control by their own design.

An obvious first step needed to confront the problem of microcomputer security is educating the users and managers on the subject. Traditionally, American businesses have relied on universities and colleges to provide for such needs. Unfortunately though, the universities in the United States are doing an abominably poor job in regard to computer security education. According to a study cited by the National Center for Computer Crime Data, only seven percent of business schools offer courses in computer security. Although most schools provide at least some coverage on this crucial topic in other information systems courses, ten percent provide no coverage at all (NCCCD, 1989).

Even though formal education about the subject may not always be readily available, there exists an abundant amount of literature covering the various aspects of security. Some of the questions a neophyte may raise are:

1. What exactly is microcomputer security?
2. What is the profile of a computer system intruder?
3. How can an intruder be detected?
4. When is the development of a microcomputer security plan cost effective?
5. What are the elements of a strategic microcomputer system security plan?

Knowledge of the answers to the above questions will assist managers in developing effective measures to counter potential computer crime and the effects of natural disaster. Some answers to these questions are provided and discussed in the following sections of this paper. An in-depth study of these topics is especially recommended for managers and executives responsible for sensitive or classified information, or those working in establishments with a prior poor record with regard to microcomputer-based system security.

Microcomputer Security Defined

It is difficult to provide a precise delimitation of the field of microcomputer security. Essentially, microcomputer security includes all aspects of protecting assets in a computer environment where micocomputers dominate. These assets may be information, hardware, software, peripheral supplies, people, communication media, processing capabilities and money (Cooper, 1989). Microcomputer security thus may be defined as a system of safeguards for protecting a microcomputer based information system from the effects of deliberate or accidental damage. This system consists of a collection of methods, mechanisms, and procedures that are applied to reduce or remove the threats to the assets in a microcomputer system.

Threats, by definition, include (1) people who are adversaries, and (2) happenstance due to people or nature. Adversaries may be spies, terrorists, criminals, disgruntled customers or former employees, or just individuals seeking a challenge at the border line of what is legal or proper. The offenses carried out by these adversaries all have in common that a microcomputer is either the tool or the target. According to the Computer Crime, Criminal Justice Resource Manual published by the U.S. Department of Justice, these transgressions are labelled as computer abuse, computer crime and computer related crime (CCCJRM, 1979). They generally fall into the categories called sabotage, theft of services, and property crimes (Wolk and Luddy, 1986), and account for about 45 percent of all computer related afflictions (Schreider, 1988). The other 55 percent are caused by happenstance, which includes accidents, mistakes made by people, hardware failure, software errors, communication loss, and problems with the computer environment, such as power failures. Natural disasters, such as lightning, earthquake, wind, tornado, flood, and electrostatic discharge also fall under this category (Cooper, 1989).

No microcomputer security system will ever be foolproof. The presence of such a system should not be viewed as a panacea against deliberate or accidental loss: A persistent adversary is likely to find some way of thwarting the system. But an effective microcomputer security system will make it much more difficult for the antagonist to succeed, and it will minimize the loss incurred if disaster does strike.

Microcomputer security should be viewed as a defense system. A single security measure is unlikely to provide satisfactory protection. Multiple layers of controls and recovery planning are needed to minimize the risk of loss. This means that managers should view the security of microcomputer systems from the perspective of risk management.

Management Concerns in Microcomputer Security

Profile of Perpetrators

Most microcomputer crimes are considered white collar crimes. Potential transgressors can be distinguished by their skills, knowledge, and access

1. The ages of perpetrators range from 18 to 46 years, with a median age of 25.

2. Many perpetrators attended a college or university where attacking campus computer systems was not only condoned, but often encouraged as an educational activity.

3. The perpetrators are often highly skilled technicians, over-qualified for their job, highly motivated, and possibly frustrated by the daily routine.

4. Crimes are often performed in the transgressor's own job specific area. That way the perpetrator is not as easily identified, as the crime is committed in a position of trust. In a study conducted by the American Bar Association, 77 percent of the 160 cases investigated fell in this category (Reel, 1989).

5. Most computer crimes are committed by more than one person. This is probably because a single person may not have the skill, knowledge, and access required to complete the crime. In the microcomputer environment, this holds especially for networked systems.

6. Groups of people working together may encourage and stimulate one another to engage in unauthorized acts, resulting in a kind of competition to perform pranks.

7. To most perpetrators, harming individuals is immoral, but causing damage to the computer system is not. This Robin Hood syndrome is based on the belief that they are harming only the computer or its contents, not the organization or its owners and employees.

8. The computer is a challenge to the intellectual capability of the transgressors. They consider the crime or abuse a game, and don't feel that they are causing any real harm. It is important to point out here that these perpetrators are rarely caught. According to the United States Federal Bureau of Investigation, computer related crimes are often the most elusive types of cases to investigate (Sessions, 1989). There are no geographical limitations, and the entire illicit act can be carried out in nanoseconds.

Table 4: Profile of Computer Criminals

with respect to the computer system. Unfortunately for most businesses, the group of people with access to the assets, and with the operational, programming, and other skills needed to commit computer crimes, is fairly large. However, some common traits of perpetrators and their crimes have been identified in the literature, and the profile given in Table 4 may assist managers and executives in developing effective strategies to combat computer crime (Wolk and Luddy, 1986).

Managers' Response to Computer Crime

An issue of concern to management should be the fact that, historically, the courts have given relatively light sentences to convicted computer criminals. Also, companies may find it not cost effective to prosecute a perpetrator. Companies often will not prosecute in case of computer crime or abuse, because managers fear that it may result in bad publicity. In fact, they may even promote offenders to buy their silence (Parker, 1983). Worse though, steps to ward off future crimes are seldom taken, for fear of adding complexity to the computer system and driving up cost figures: It may easily take thirty to fifty staff members to examine and rectify a security problem (Scisco, 1988).

A study by Straub (1990) revealed that of 268 disclosed computer abuse incidents, only 50% were detected through system controls; a further 16% were uncovered through purposeful investigation, and 41% were discovered by sheer accident. The study also reports that of these 268 incidents, only 24 (or 9%) were turned over to police or other external authorities; in 19% of all cases no disciplinary action at all was taken. In half of the 24 cases reported to police the perpetrators were known. Of these, 7 (or less than 3% of the 268 abuse incidents!) resulted in conviction.

These facts on computer abuse and the profile of perpetrators hopefully will convince business managers and executives of the importance of having a microcomputer security plan in place. Potential computer abusers must be convinced that computer crime is likely to be detected and will result in prosecution. The profile shows that the typical computer abuser is highly competent and lacks satisfaction and challenge in his or her job. Management must therefore try to fulfill this need for challenge by matching employee qualifications and task complexity. Moreover, management must promote corporate loyalty among their employees, by creating a climate of mutual trust: Employees should feel that the company is committed to the long term well-being of its employees. Such lifetime employment management practices explain why few computer crimes are committed by employees of Japanese businesses (Uzawa, 1989). This is one area where American managers and executives can learn from their Japanese counterparts.

Structured Approach to Microcomputer Security Management

Effective microcomputer security systems and policies should be developed using the same systematic approaches that have been proven successful for the protection of larger computer systems. The advantages of using a structured systems approach are well documented in the literature, especially with respect to accountability, clarity, and maintainability. Consistency in approaches also permits firms to lower operating costs. In such a top-down approach, the microcomputer security management process is divided into modules, and the employees become active partners in the program, helping the successful implementation of the security system. The steps in the development process are:

1. Problem Recognition/Opportunity Identification
2. Identification of Alternatives
3. Feasibility Analysis and Selection of Best Alternative
4. Implementation of the Best Alternative
5. Follow-up

In the following, the five steps of this process are discussed in more detail.

Problem Recognition/Opportunity Identification

The key to identifying security improvement opportunities is the presence of corporate goals in

---

1. Protect the system from unauthorized access
2. Protect specific data and programs from unauthorized use or manipulation
3. Ensure access and service to legitimate users
4. Preserve the integrity of the system

Table 5: Goals in Support of Microcomputer Security

---

1. A defined and documented microcomputer security policy
2. Operating standards and procedures
3. An outline of responsibility for microcomputer security
4. A personnel security program
5. A complete asset-threat inventory

Table 6: Strategies for Microcomputer Security

support of a safer microcomputer work facility. Four major goals are indicated in Table 5. Protecting the system from unauthorized access prevents the "bad guys" from sabotaging or abusing the microcomputer system. Even legitimate users may not have unlimited access to all programs and data that are stored on a file server of a network. Some data must be protected from unnecessary viewing in order to preserve the privacy of individuals, or to prevent the competition from gaining access to information of strategic value. Further, the integrity of the data must be preserved, i.e. data and programs must be protected from illegitimate alterations. To ensure proper access and service to legitimate users, components of the system must be protected from unnecessary tie-ups by other users. Lastly, the integrity of the system as a whole must be preserved, in the sense that the proper operation of the system should be ensured at all times; in case disaster does strike, however, it must be possible to restore the system in reasonable time and at reasonable cost.

To ensure the successful implementation of security measures, senior management should provide the strategic endeavors (Fine, 1983) listed in Table 6. Managers must be careful not to implement overly rigid security measures, so that the legitimate usage of the microcomputer information system is not unnecessarily obstructed. Whenever improvements to the microcomputer security system are proposed, managers need to investigate all costs and benefits of these new measures. This is further discussed in step 2, the identification of alternatives.

Most problems with microcomputer security systems are relatively easily detected and corrected. With microcomputer systems that are not connected to a communications network, most security problems are related to hardware and software failures, theft, and calamities caused by forces of nature. Periodic inventory audits will enable the detection of most thefts. Knowledge of previous disasters at the site and annual inspections of the microcomputer facility by professional inspectors will reduce the risks of accidents and natural disasters.

Damages to hardware and software can be detected using various disk operating systems commands. For example, the CHKDSK command enables a user to check for existing problems on a computer disk. A number of utility packages, such as PC TOOLS and NORTON UTILITIES do an excellent job checking the problems on the server of a network. Many of these utilities can also be used to correct minor problems, once identified. As an example, program and data tamperings may be detected by simply using the DIR command to list the complete directory of a disk and observing for changes in file sizes, access dates, and increases or decreases in the number of files.

Identification of Alternatives

Various measures can be implemented to support the four major goals in microcomputer security stated in Table 5. These may be grouped under the following headings:

A. Protection from unauthorized access
B. Preventing data and software compromise
C. Safeguarding the facility against natural disasters

Protection from Unauthorized Access. Access to a system includes physical access as well as logical access. Physical access refers to the ability to enter the building or room that houses the components of the system, such as micromputers, peripherals, and data disks. Preventing unauthorized physical access also precludes logical access, as long as all computers are stand-alone. If the microcomputers are connected to communication networks, then logical access must be addressed separately. Controlling physical access in this case only protects the assets from physical abuse or sabotage. Deliberate or unintentional damage to data and programs, and even the crashing of the network, is still possible via communication lines.

Physical access to microcomputer equipment may be controlled at four different levels (Bowers, 1988): (i) perimeter; (ii) portal; (iii) space; and (iv) object. Perimeter protection involves controlling the area surrounding the building or place housing the equipment. Portal protection refers to controlling the entrance to the facility where the equipment is kept. Space protection involves monitoring the inside of the facility, and object protection deals with security measures for individual items of microcomputing equipment. Examples of security equipment that can be used for controlling physical access are alarm systems, television cameras, identification cards, keypad access control systems, and card key systems.

Logical access deals with authorization and authentication, namely, deciding on who should have access, and monitoring and enforcing the access rights (Gasser, 1988). Authorization may be granted at different levels or for different parts of the micro-computer based information system. In communications networks, access control may be achieved through call-back devices, passwords, and encryption algorithms. One or all of these methods can be selected as effective security measures.

Preventing Data Compromise. Data and programs in microcomputer environments are especially vulnerable to unauthorized use and manipulation. This includes the invasion of privacy of information, and the alteration of data and programs for criminal purposes, such as making changes to inventories or accounts, or infecting the system with a computer virus.

Managing this aspect of microcomputer security involves two separate areas: Protection from users and protection from viruses and worms. Specification of the type of use and limitation of specific users to certain data files are possible controls that may be used to protect the data integrity from users. Transaction logs allow the monitoring of these control measures, by keeping a record of who accessed which file at what time. A general precaution to reduce the threat of virus infections is to limit the exchange of programs and data and to not permit booting from unknown floppy disks. The main problem in recovering from a virus is not loss of data, but the near certainty of reinfection if the proper recovery procedures are not followed (McAfee, 1989).

Passwords may provide some protection from virus or worm infestations, however, some sophisticated viruses and worms incorporate password guessing algorithms. The increase in processing speed achieved by newer hardware aids the invaders in this endeavor. Some worms also use their own version of the encryption algorithm, which may be faster than the one used by the system. The worm thus can repeatedly guess at the password, encrypt it, and compare it to the encrypted version of the correct password kept by the system. Keeping the encrypted

1. Shut down the system
2. Reboot from a clean operating system floppy disk
3. Backup all data files onto newly formatted floppy disks; do not use backup utilities from the infected hard disk
4. Backup only those batch files that are familiar
5. Perform a low level format of the infected hard disk and restore the operating system to it
6. Replace all executable programs from original distribution packages
7. Restore the backup data files
8. Reformat all suspect floppy disks

Table 7: Procedure For Recovery From Virus Infections

passwords in hidden or *shadow* files rather than in public files, makes it more difficult for a worm or virus to crack it (Seeley, 1989).

Several special anti-virus software products are available. These fall into three main categories: (i) infection prevention products; (ii) infection detection products; and (iii) infection identification products. Infection prevention products are programs that will stop certain generic viral replication processes or prevent some initial virus infections. Infection detection products are meant to detect infections soon after they occur, generally identifying the specific area of the system that has been infected. Infection identification products identify specific known viral strains on already infected systems, and may be able to remove the virus, thus returning the system to its pre-infected state.

If a virus infection has been detected, the procedure for recovery given in Table 7 will generally prevent reinfection.

Protecting the Facility from Natural Disasters. Natural disasters such as fires, floods, and earthquakes can cause serious damage to a microcomputer system. Information on previous occurrences of such disasters in the area, and how they affected microcomputer based information systems, will help managers evaluate the risk associated, and the need for security measures. Hiring an experienced building inspector to conduct periodic checks of the facility for signs of structural damage can help detect potential problems before any serious loss occurs.

Feasibility Analysis and Selection of Best Alternative

Four types of feasibility analyses are needed for evaluating microcomputer security systems: (1) economic feasibility, (2) technical feasibility, (3) schedule feasibility, and (4) organizational feasibility. Economic feasibility refers to the ability to pay for the implementation of specific security measures. Technical feasibility deals with the existence of the technology and the availability of technical experts for implementing security alternatives. Schedule feasibility is concerned with being able to meet the timeframe required for implementing security measures without having adverse effects on operations and productivity. Finally, organizational feasibility relates to whether a security alternative can be implemented within the organizational structure of a corporation. However, many microcomputer based information systems are used by smaller firms, in which organizational feasibility may be less of an issue.

Cost-benefit analysis is a useful tool for the evaluation of security alternatives. A possible approach to determining the expected losses is to develop a cost-precision matrix, using the annual loss expectation formula or ALE (Perry, 1985). With the help of such a table, a manager or executive can identify and decide on the optimum mix of controls to minimize the cost of security.

Implementation of the Selected Alternative

The implementation of a microcomputer security system must be planned very carefully. For the system to be effective, appropriate training must be conducted for the different groups of people involved. The users of the microcomputer facility should be convinced to fully support all the control measures, and they should know their own roles in maintaining security or in recovering the system in the event of disaster. Documentation on the security system should be retained in an easily accessible location for the use of all employees.

To make sure that the new security measures are effective in the real day-to-day operation of the facility, an acceptance test is highly recommended. This is done by comparing the post-implementation performance to the pre-implementation expectations. Quality assurance statistics, disaster testing, and security audits are some of the approaches that can be used for this (Perry, 1985). When no concrete data is available, employee opinion polls on the effectiveness of the implemented measures may be used. Specifically, the users should be asked whether they believe that the established critical success factors for the system have been met.

Follow-Up

Follow-up refers to the continuing process of keeping a microcomputer security system functioning. Follow-up includes upgrading and extending the security system as needed. It must be kept in mind that threats to microcomputer based information systems are not stagnant. As technology changes, new threats will appear, whilst earlier ones may lose their relevance. New technology may also allow newer and more effective security measures, requiring changes to or replacement of the security system.

Disaster Recovery Planning

The ten practical guidelines in Table 8 are provided to assist managers in the development and maintenance of a more secure microcomputer based information systems environment. This list is not exhaustive, but it may serve as a first step toward the building of a safer microcomputer environment. Equally important to the implementation of security control measures, however, is the development of a comprehensive disaster recovery plan. The primary goal of a disaster recovery plan is to keep the business running. A disaster recovery plan should contain the following four major components (Burch, 1989):

    (a) prevention plan,
    (b) contention plan,
    (c) recovery plan, and
    (d) contingency plan.

The prevention plan deals with avoiding disaster from happening in the first place, and most of this paper is devoted to such issues. The contention plan covers the disaster situation and should include guidelines for emergency shutdowns, instructions on protecting documents or equipment in case of an

1. Develop a corporate microcomputer security policy

2. Identify consistent microcomputer security objectives throughout the organization

3. Establish critical success factors to evaluate the microcomputer security system

4. Assess the feasibility and cost of security measures

5. Involve employees and managers as much as possible in the development of the security system, and make sure that top management fully understands and supports the project

6. Create a security quality assurance function

7. Establish a microcomputer security task force

8. For large microcomputer facilities, appoint a chief security officer

9. Recognize that management is responsible for a security problem, if one exists

10. Do not wait for a problem; rather, look for potential areas where security can be a problem and develop means to counter it

Table 8: Guidelines for Maintaining Security

evacuation, location of contingency processing facilities, and information on people or services to contact in case of emergency. The recovery plan handles the restoration of the system and must include instructions on backup procedures, a categorization of subsystems into critical, secondary, and tertiary, and procedures for restoring the system. Finally, the contingency plan deals with keeping the business running through the emergency. It must identify the critical functions of the system and provide alternative procedures for carrying out these functions. Exhibit F depicts the disaster recovery plan as a hierarchical model.

The implementation of the disaster recovery plan can be done in three stages (Miller, 1986): evaluation, procedurization, and validation. In the evaluation stage, subsystems are evaluated according to their importance in supporting critical functions, objectives are set for recovery, and resources needed to satisfy these objectives are identified. In the procedurization stage, user procedures for manually processing the critical and secondary subsystems during an interruption period are developed, as well as procedures for maintaining backups and documentation. The validation stage involves exercising the disaster recovery plan, as well as the on going administration of the plan.

All these measures will incur additional operating costs, and some managers and executives may not feel well disposed toward developing a comprehensive security system for their microcomputer- based information systems. In fact, the average business can expect to pay a low six figure amount per year to attain effective risk reduction (Cox, 1989). However, it is important to bear in mind that in the absence of a well-managed microcomputer security system, minor problems can cause major damages. Conversely, with an effective microcomputer security defense system and a good disaster recovery plan, even a major calamity may cause only manageable losses.

References

Aaland, M. (1988). Preventing computer disaster. *Working Women*, November, 88.

Ball, M. (1988). To catch a thief. *Security Management*, March, 72.

Baskt, S. (1987). Computer security: A management issue that must be reckoned with. *The Office*, August, 10A.

Bidgoli, H., & Azarmsa, R. (1988). Computer security: New managerial concerns for the 1990's and beyond. *Journal of Property Management,* October.

Bowers, D.M. (1988). *Access control and personal identification systems.* Boston: Butterworths.

Burch, J.G. (1989). Disaster recovery plan: A moral and professional responsibility. *Internal Auditor,* June, 43-47.

Capron, H.L., & Williams, B.K. (1982). *Computers and data processing.* Menlo Park: Benjamin Cummings.

CCCJRM (1979). *Computer crime, criminal justice resource manual.* Washington: U.S. Department of Justice.

Cooper, J.A. (1989). *Computer & communications security: Strategies for the 1990s.* New York: McGRaw-Hill.

Cox, R. (1989). Continuing education. *American Banker,* May 23, 17.

Cronin, D.J. (1986). *Microcomputer data security: Issues and strategies.* New York: Prentice Hall.

Cullen, S.W. (1989). The computer virus: Is there a real panacea?. *The Office,* 109.

Esters, S. (1989). Avoid it like the plague: Protecting yourself from computer virus attacks. *Black Enterprise,* 19.

Fine, L.H. (1983). *Computer security - A guide for management.* London: Heinemann.

Gasser, M. (1988). *Building a secure computer system.* New York: Van Nostrand Reinhold Publishers.

Ginn, R.D. (1989). The case for continuity. *Security Management,* 33, 87.

Johnston, P. (1989). It pays to test all assumptions, *ComputerWorld,* 23.

Keough, H.R. (1989). An inside job. *Security Management,* March, 13A.

McAfee, J. (1989). The virus cure. *Datamation,* February 15, 29-40.

McFarland, W.F. (1984). Information technology changes the way you compete. *Harvard Business Review,* May-June, 98-103.

Menkus, B. (1988). No vaccine to ward off effects of virus attacks. *ComputerWorld,* 27, 58.

Miller, H.M. (1986). Disaster recovery planning. *Journal of Systems Management,* March, 25-30.

Naisbitt, J. (1984). *Megatrend.* New York: Warner Books.

NCCCD (1989). *Commitment to security.* Santa Cruz: National Center for Computer Crime Data.

Parker, D.B. (1983). *Fighting computer crime.* New York: Scribner's.

Perry, W.E. (1985). *Management strategies for computer security.* Boston: Butterworth.

Phelps, F.E. (1989). Bug bytes. *Security Management*, September, 85.

Reel, N. (1989). Data security: Can your computer keep a secret?. *Computing for Business*, April, 32.

Schreider, T. (1988). PC packages will assist but not carry. *ComputerWorld*, July 11, S9.

Scisco, P. (1989). No such thing as a small mishap. *ComputerWorld, 21*, S1-S7.

Seeley, D. (1989). Password cracking: A game of wits. *Communications of the ACM, 32*(6), 700-703.

Sessions, W.S. (1989). An FBI perspective on computer crime and viruses. *Computer Security: Issues & Trends*, 1.

Straub, D.W., & Nance, W.D. (1990). Discovering and disciplining computer abuse in organizations: A field study. *MIS Quarterly, 14*(1), 45-60.

Toigo, J.W. (1989). *Disaster recovery planning: Managing risk and catastrophe.* Englewood Cliffs: Prentice-Hall.

Tucker, E. (1987). After fire: Picking up the pieces. *Washington Post*, December, B1.

Usdin, S. (1987). Like it or not plan for a disaster recovery. *The Office, 105*, 90 & 92.

Uzawa, M. (1989). Computer security in Japan: Increasing concern during the 1980s. *Computer Security: Issues & Trends*, 15.

Wolk, S.R., & Luddy, W.J. (1986). *Legal aspects of computer use.* Englewood Cliffs: Prentice-Hall.

Chapter 11

THE CHANGING ENVIRONMENT OF SOFTWARE COPYRIGHT: THE CASE OF APPLE COMPUTER V. MICROSOFT CORP.

Cherie Sherman Werbel
Ramapo College of New Jersey

Phillip A. Werbel
Attorney-at-Law

"Apple wins first round in software-copyright case" was the highlight of the Law Section of The Wall Street Journal on March 20, 1989 (Schmitt, 1989). Richard Sherlund, vice president of investment research at Goldman Sachs & Co. stated, "I think the whole industry is stunned by this announcement." In Big Board trading, Hewlett-Packard slipped $2, Apple fell slightly, and Microsoft fell $4.75.

What was the nature of Judge William Schwarzer's decision and why was it so unexpected that it upset an entire industry? How did the legal and social environment that fostered the decision develop? What is the long-term impact of this decision on corporations, software developers, and consumers? These are the questions we can hope to answer by analyzing

Previously published in the Journal of Microcomputer Systems Management, Vol. 1, No. 2
© Idea Group Publishing

*the history and progression of software copyright deci-
sions, and the latest chapter in this saga, the case of
Apple v. Microsoft.*

Introduction

How does the law provide for the protection of
intellectual property, such as software, and why are
computer programs often copyrightable but not patentable? There are three principal categories of intellectual property protection: patent, copyright, and
trade secret (Lieberman & Seidel, 1988, pp. 716, 719,
728).

A *patent* provides a 17- year monopoly over the
use of a work; an invention is the property of its owner
and cannot be produced and sold by anyone else. To
qualify, an invention must be novel, nonobvious, and
useful. Patentable items include processes, manufac-
tures, machines, and improvements. Unpatentable
items, which are specifically excluded, encompass
printed matter other than designs, naturally occurring substances, methods of doing business, ideas,
scientific principles, and mental processes. The social
consequences of patenting these sorts of items, thus
preventing their free and widespread use, would certainly be negative. Even when a patent is granted and
use of an invention restrained, the patent-holder is required to fully disclose the particularities of his invention in the interests of the long-term benefit to society.

Copyright offers a more limited protection for a
period equal to the author's life plus 50 years, or in the
case of work done for hire, for 75 years. Copyright,
unlike patent, does not protect an idea, merely an
expression of an idea. This allows two items of
software to have a far greater similarity than, say, two

patentable devices. The software items could be used in nearly an identical fashion to accomplish the very same purpose. The attempt to discriminate idea from expression, and thus the copyrightable from the un-copyrightable, has been the basis for much legal hairsplitting and will be discussed in greater detail with regard to specific cases. For a work to be copyrightable, it must be original and tangible. Copyright grants the owner the exclusive right to reproduce and distribute the work, and to prepare derivative forms of the work, rather than a right to exclusive use ("Copyright," 1983, p. 1733).

The third form of intellectual property protection, trade secret, has less applicability to the software arena. A *trade secret* is "information, including a formula, pattern, compilation, program, device, method, technique, or process that: (1) derives independent economic value, actual or potential, from not being generally known to, and not being readily ascertainable by proper means by, other persons who can obtain economic value from its disclosure or use, and (2) is the subject of efforts that are reasonable under the circumstances to maintain its secrecy" (Current, 1988, p. 91). So by definition, a trade secret is only valuable as long as it is kept secret, and it is virtually impossible to keep software "secret" (Lieberman & Seidel, 1988, p. 719).

Early Computer Litigation

The roots of copyright dispute and the struggle to determine what is copyrightable date back to 1907 and the case of *White-Smith Music Publishing Co. v. Apollo Co.* The issue in this case was whether copyright protection extended to a player piano roll. In this instance, the Supreme Court held that a piano roll was not a copy of a musical composition because it was in a form that could not readily be perceived (Lieberman & Seidel, 1988, p. 728). Since that time, copyright protectability has been extended and expanded to include works in any tangible forms of expression from which they can be communicated either directly or with the aid of a machine. The Copyright Act of 1976 specified that the following types of works were eligible for copyright protection: literary works; musical works; dramatic works; pantomimes and choreographic works; pictorial, graphic, and sculptural works; motion picture and other audiovisual works; and sound recordings ("Current, " 1988, p. 23). Computer programs belong in the category of literary works (Clapes, Lynch, & Steinberg, 1987, p. 1524). In 1980, Congress defined a computer program as "a set of statements or instructions to be used directly or indirectly in a computer in order to bring about a result" ("Copyright", 1983, p. 1726). It has been argued that a computer program, because of its abstract nature, can be categorized as an idea and is not patentable.

During the 1970s, the Patent Office did not grant software patents. Software was considered equivalent to mathematical equations, which are clearly ideas, and therefore unpatentable. However, in 1980, the Supreme Court deviated from this standard and ruled that the inclusion of software in a patentable process did not make the process unpatentable. The case in point focused on a program that determined when rubber was cured inside a mold. This set the precedent that as long as a computer program was part of a process, it was, indeed, patentable. Today, any program is patentable as long as it is described as a process of some kind (Bulkeley, 1989, p. B1).

Patents have traditionally carried a lot of weight in the courts, due to an extensive review procedure that generally takes 32 months, and infringement has often carried large penalties. However, lack of software expertise in the Patent Office has led to patenting of routine software techniques, according to Jeffrey Tarter, editor of *SoftLetter*, a Cambridge, Massachusetts newsletter. Because software techniques and the software marketplace move so rapidly, small companies have less ability to patent their work than to copyright it, which is a simple, and quick process. The disparity between large and small developers, in conjunction with the intellectual property, system has the potential to create an environment that stifles rather than promotes creativity. It has been speculated that Visicalc, the first spreadsheet program, would be patentable today (Pollak, 1988, pp. 1, 8). Had this occurred, Lotus 1-2-3, Excel, and a whole host of spreadsheet software might never have been developed. The purpose of intellectual property law and, in particular, copyright law is to encourage disclosure of intellectual and aesthetic ideas to the public but, at the same time, to secure a fair return for an author's creative labor in order to motivate such labor ("Copyright," 1983, p. 1723). There is an inevitable tension between these two goals.

Prior to the recent surge of computer litigation, another early case, *Baker v. Selden*, helped to set the stage. In this instance, a system of bookkeeping had been duplicated and the original author sued. The Supreme Court held that the blank account-books, or forms, which constituted the system were not copyrightable. This argument has been used by software companies to justify copying of computer screens, which they attempt to classify   in the same category as blank account-books.

Literal Copying

In computer law, there have been three recent phases of litigation. Phase one, which began in the 1970s, concerned exact duplication of software. The legal issue to be decided was whether computer programs were copyrightable at all.

The case of Apple v. Franklin (1983) typified this era. Franklin Computer developed and marketed a computer clone which was 100% compatible with Apple computers. The issue was whether the Apple-soft operating system, a portion of which was embodied in hardware or read-only memory (ROM), and was copied by Franklin, was subject to copyright protection. The court held that embodiment in ROM, although a novel format at the time, did not deprive a program of legal protection. Further, both source code and object code were determined to be protected by copyright. Finally, operating system programs, like application programs, are protected, despite the fact that their instructions implement methods, processes, ideas, and systems, which themselves are not ordinarily copyrightable. Franklin's desire to manufacture compatible equipment was found to be no defense against copyright infringement and did not justify it.

Non-Literal Copying

Phase two involved non-literal copying. The major issues were whether duplication of the outline, structure, and flow of a program constituted copyright infringement and whether mere translation of software to a different operating environment constituted infringment.

The case of *Whelan Associates, Inc. v. Jaslow Dental Laboratory Inc.* (1987), was the highlight of this phase. A program written for dental laboratory management on the IBM PC, in the BASIC programming language, was held to infringe upon the copyright of a dental laboratory management program written for the IBM Series I computer, in Event Driven Language. The court found that structure, sequence, and organization (SSO) of a computer program can be protected and that such protection extends beyond protection for literal code. There was judged to be a substantial similarity between the two programs, established through expert testimony and lay observation. The so-called ordinary observer test was used to determine substantial similarity. That is, if the ordinary person in the position of the intended audience for the works in question would recognize them as substantially similar, the protected expression has been infringed. This can be characterized to some degree as an "I know it when I see it test" (Jacobellis V. Ohio, 1964). Technical similarities included file structures, screens, and subroutines. The Supreme Court's definition of infringement was clearly in keeping with the traditional principle of "comprehensive non-literal similarity," used to determine infringement of literary works (Current, 1988, p. 29).

The Court also clarified the difference between idea and expression in a computer program. It stated that the purpose or function of a utilitarian work is its idea, while its expression is everything not necessary to the performance of the function. The idea of the dental software was efficient management of a dental laboratory. This idea could be accomplished in a number of different ways, with different file structures, data flows, and so on. These constitute the program's expression.

Recognition of copyright of non-literal expression was taken one step further in *SAS Institute, Inc., v. S&H Computer Systems, Inc.*, 1985. Here, S&H created a virtual copy of SAS 79.5 ported to the VAX environment. The court examined the code and was able to identify changes made for no functional reason other than to disguise a similarity to SAS code. It also noted the absence of any independent design documentation and the duplication of nonfunctional code, identical with SAS code, in the S&H product. Forty-four examples of copying, even in the context of 186,000 lines of code, was found to constitute substantial similarity ("Current," 1988, p. 44).

Look-and-Feel Lawsuits

The most current phase of software litigation consists of the so called look-and-feel lawsuits. In *Digital Communications Associates, Inc. v. Softklone Distribution Corp.* (1987), the arrangement and design of the Main Menu of DCA's CROSSTALK XVI program was held to be infringed by the status screen of Softklone's program MIRROR. Softklone was judged to have copied the "total concept and feel" of the Crosstalk screen. The screen was deemed not to be a merger of expression and idea, which would have made it uncopyrightable, but rather, a product inclusive of both concepts. The use of a screen to reflect a program's status was determined to be an idea, as was the use of a command-driven program or the typing of two symbols to activate a specific command. However, the implementation, which consisted of the headings, the arrangement of the parameter/command terms, highlighting and capitalizing, were judged to be expressions. These expressions were irrelevant to the function of the program and only one of a wide variety of patterns possible.

The court also held that copyright of a computer program does not protect a particular screen since different programs can generate the same screen. DCA had separately registered its status screen and won the case on this basis. A screen was differentiated from a "blank form" because of the large amount of information conveyed (Current, 1988, p. 69).

In *Lotus Development Corp. v. Mosaic Software, Inc. and Lotus v. Paperback Software International,* Mosaic's TWIN program and Paperback's VP-Planner program are alleged to copy the structure, sequence, and organization of LOTUS 1-2-3 (Lewis, 1989). These are ongoing disputes as of this date.

Apple Computer v. Microsoft and Hewlett-Packard

Within this category of look-and-feel lawsuits, *Apple Computer, Inc. v. Microsoft Corp. and Hewlett-Packard Co.* is a precedent-setting case. The roots of this dispute date back to 1982 when Microsoft and Apple entered into an agreement for Microsoft to develop three application programs to be distributed with Apple's planned future computer, the Macintosh (Mac). At that time, the two companies were so entwined that Microsoft had more employees writing software for the Mac than Apple itself.

Apple provided Microsoft with early pre-commercial release prototypes and related confidential documents. These included Mac's visual displays and graphic images. Some of these displays were not original to Apple but had been developed by other companies, such as Xerox, or were in the public domain (Pleadings, 1989). Apple also made personnel from the Apple development team available for technical consultation. There was no attempt to conceal proprietary information.

Through 1985, Microsoft's software was the only Mac software to really sell besides the Apple software that came packaged with the machine. In 1985, the Mac itself was still not selling and Apple went through a major reorganization, replacing Steven Jobs, the company founder and leader, with John Sculley. We can conjecture that this change in command was the beginning of a philiosophical change in business direction that would alter the relationship between Microsoft and Apple.

Because of this ongoing relationship, Microsoft sent a prerelease version of their Windows 1.0 software, a new graphics interface package, to Apple in 1985. Microsoft began to release software development kits so that application programmers could use the Windows system of software to create applications programs that would run in the Windows environment.

In October 1985, two months after receiving Windows, Apple threatened to sue Microsoft for copyright infringement (Pleadings, 1989). In an effort to stem the tide, Apple drafted a memo proposing to restrict the look and feel of Microsoft's future programs to that of the disputed Windows 1.0. The purpose of the restriction was to prevent Microsoft from marketing a competing product that would resemble Mac graphics any more than Windows 1.0 already did. Apple was aware that the programs they had licensed to Microsoft could be used to create Mac-like software. Routines or "parts" of the Windows software could be restructured and reutilized in an entirely different manner, creating a substantially different product.

Apple's restrictive language was rejected by Microsoft and Microsoft countered with its own draft of an agreement (Pleadings, 1989). Under this 1985 agreement, Microsoft Windows 1.0, Multiplan, Chart, Word, File, and Excel, written to run on the Mac, were identified as derivative works generated by Apple's Lisa and Mac graphic user interface programs. Microsoft was granted a license to use these derivative works in present and future software programs. Apple was given a five-year grant to any new visual displays created by Microsoft as part of Microsoft Windows (Pleadings, 1989). Microsoft agreed to hold back a release of Excel, for the IBM PC, to provide Apple with a longer period in which to market the software exclusively.

At this time, Apple undertook other defensive measures to protect its software copyrights. In 1985, Apple also entered into an agreement with Digital Research (DRI). The companies agreed upon and established a procedure to review future DRI products for 'substantial similarity' to the Mac (Pleadings, 1989).

In 1986, Microsoft notified Apple that it was going to issue a press release claiming unlimited rights under the 1985 agreement. Apple objected but

Microsoft went ahead with the announcement (Pleadings, 1989).

During the period 1985-1988, three versions of Windows were released. These were 1.01, in November 1985; 1.03, in August 1986; and 1.04, in April 1987. Version 2.03, the subject of the lawsuit, was released in April of 1987 (Pleadings, 1989).

Concurrently, the Hewlett-Packard Co. (H-P) sought a license from Apple for Mac audiovisual works. They planned to use these works to develop software that would generate a "visual desktop." Apple declined to grant them a license. H-P then obtained license rights to Windows, from Microsoft, and developed a program called New Wave. The product manager for New Wave has described the package as "similar to the Mac" (Pleadings, 1989). By utilizing the routines available in Windows 2.03, H-P virtually reproduced the Mac interface.

In March 1988, Apple filed a complaint against Microsoft and Hewlett-Packard alleging that visual displays and images generated by Windows 2.03 were illegal and infringing copies of Mac audiovisual works and were unauthorized derivative works. The complaint alleged that Microsoft's use of Mac visual display techniques in Windows 2.03 exceeded limited license rights granted by Apple to Microsoft (Pleadings, 1989).

There are two phases to the lawsuit. Phase one is a trial on the 1985 Settlement Agreement limited to issues regarding the scope of the licensing grant and where Windows 2.03 is covered under the license. Phase two will address larger issues of infringement and copying.

Litigation to date in the case of *Apple Computer,*

Inc. v. Microsoft Corp. and Hewlett-Packard Co. consists of no less than eleven motions, cross-motions, claims, counterclaims, and memos. The judge's decision serves to summarize this course of events.

Apple began by alleging copyright infringement. Microsoft moved for summary judgment that Windows 2.03 was licensed while Apple cross-moved for partial summary judgment that Windows 2.03 was unauthorized. The immediate question before the court was the interpretation of the 1985 agreement, which was a question of law. The judge determined that the parties used language showing an intent to limit the license and accompanying release of claims to the visual displays in Windows 1.0 and the named applications programs. The preamble of the agreement defines the subject matter of the dispute as "certain visual displays generated by several Microsoft software products" specified as Microsoft Windows Version 1.0 and certain named applications programs. Microsoft then acknowledges that "the visual displays in the above-listed Microsoft programs are derivative works of the visual displays generated by Apple's Lisa and Macintosh graphic user interface programs." The license is to use these derivative works, only, in present and future software programs. Apple's release covers only Microsoft Windows version 1.0.

A key term is "derivative works." Microsoft is only able to use these specifically licensed visual displays in future versions of Windows or other programs. The judge compared this language with that used in Microsoft's license to Apple. Here the license extends "to use any new visual displays" created by Microsoft.

The judge felt that Microsoft's attempt to differentiate "screen display" from "visual display" was not persuasive. To state that each window is a visual display but the combination of windows is a screen display, and not a derivative work subject to copyright, was in his opinion, quibbling. Because Microsoft drafted the language of the agreement and had the opportunity to be more specific, Apple's interpretation of the agreement was held to control.

Also, Judge Schwartzer stated that whether the screen displays were generated by systems or applications software was irrelevant. The end product, or visual interface, was the subject of the agreement. He held that what Microsoft received was a license to use the visual displays in the named software products as they appeared to the user in November, 1985. Considering the great value to Apple of the graphic interface embodied in its Mac operating system, he deemed it "contrary to reason and common sense to interpret the 1985 Agreement as creating a blanket license the limits of which are defined only by the limits of the ingenuity and skills of programmers." (The precedent for this conclusion is *Howe v. American Baptist Homes of the West* which held that reasonable construction consistent with language of contract must prevail over unreasonable construction.) (Pleadings, 1989.)

The Windows 1.0 operating environment, as shipped by Microsoft, was a tiled window system, which is quite different from the Mac operating system. That is, windows were placed side by side and did not overlap. Windows 2.03, on the other hand, was designed to generate overlapping windows, which is a major feature of the Mac operating system. Clearly Windows 2.03, as well as New Wave, bear a much greater similarity to Mac software than Windows 1.0. The judge held that "it is not reasonable to conclude that Apple gave up this valuable distinguishing feature in the absence of specific language."

The court held that the 1985 Agreement was not a complete defense to the infringement claims for Microsoft for Windows 2.03. Delayed for the next phase of litigation is whether there is a relevant and valid copyright and whether it has been infringed. Microsoft is licensed to use Windows 1.0 and the named applications programs.

The latest wrinkle in the lawsuit, as of this writing, is Judge Schwartzer's preliminary ruling defining the scope of the 1985 license. He indicates that 90% of the items that Apple claimed were wrongfully used by Microsoft and Hewlett-Packard were, in fact, fair game (Schmitt, 1989b). Defense attorneys for Hewlett-Packard suggest that this ruling, if upheld, disposes of most of the controversy; and they are confident that the rest of material in question can be shown to be uncopyrightable. Apple's attorneys contend that the judge is misreading the license, as its intent was to prevent the development of Mac look-alike products and that, on appeal, they will be able to convince a jury. Neither party, despite urging from the court, is ready to settle. The final ruling is expected within the week.

Implications of the Decision

It is speculated that Apple will not appeal this ruling (Schmitt, 1989a). The judge has indicated that he would like to distill from the remaining disputes a few legal questions that he can resolve himself without a lengthy jury trial. This would mean that the decision could be reached in months, rather than years. In the next phase of litigation, Microsoft and Hewlett-Packard will try to weaken Apple's copyright claims by demonstrating that Apple software lacks originality and therefore should not be protected by copyright.

In any event, Microsoft and Hewlett-Packard will try to limit their liablity. Apple had demanded that the sale of New Wave and Windows 2.03 be stopped, that profits from their sale be turned over, and that $50,000 be awarded for each instance of copyright infringement. Windows 2.03 is a big seller for Microsoft but, more importantly, the foundation for the Presentation Manager, which is scheduled to supplant the IBM PC's MS-DOS operating system. Presentation Manager will in all likelihood be far and away the most widely used operating system for personal computers. Much is at stake, not just for Microsoft and H-P, but also for IBM and the user public.

Large amounts of money are involved here, and perhaps the destiny of Apple, Microsoft, and IBM. Were Apple to lose, its plans to increase market share in the business sector would surely be stymied, as it would be giving up its one competitive advantage, an easy-to-use graphic interface. IBM and Microsoft will have to shift gears and alter their strategy for maintaining market share, if their plans to move to a new graphic interface must be aborted. In a larger sense, software development companies and programmers will be put on notice as to just how far they can go in copying ideas and/or expression of ideas in their software.

If the judge decides for Apple, the so-called software/hardware gap could widen. Companies may not be able to build upon earlier versions of software they have licensed and, therefore, the ability to create software which exploits rapidly changing, ever-more-powerful hardware in a timely fashion, will become even more difficult. Consumers may no longer feel secure that a given piece of software will be updated and keep pace with technical developments in the marketplace. Because new software releases are available to licensed owners at a nominal fee, but a new package may run several hundred dollars, software purchases would be scrutinized more carefully and some institutions could be forced to use out-of-date software. Software costs could skyrocket as developers pass along the costs of licensing each new version to consumers.

On the other hand, companies may pour more money into software research and development if software copyright gains strength and they are confident that they can bar other companies from marketing a similar product. The small body of independent software developers may also grow if the return on software development is assured.

At this point, all we can be sure of is that the decision in this case will have far-reaching effects, both negative and positive, and that we can look for further cases of this sort in the near future.

References

Apple Computer, Inc. v. Franklin Computer Corp., 714 F.2d 1240 (3d Cir. 1983).

Baker v. Selden, 101 U.S. 99, 25 L.Ed. 841 (1880).

Bulkeley, W. (1989). Will software patents cramp creativity? *The Wall Street Journal*, (March 14), B1.

Clapes, A., Lynch, P., & Steinberg, M. (1987). Silicon epics and binary bards: Determining the proper scope of copyright protection for computer programs, *UCLA Law Review*, 34, 1493.

Copyright protection of computer program object code. (1983). *Harvard Law Review*, *96*, 1723-1744.

Current judicial developments in copyright protection for computer software. (1988). *Computer software 1988: protection and marketing*. New York: Practicing Law Institute, 23-198.

Digital Communications Associates, Inc. v. Softklone Distributing Corp., 659 F.Supp. 449 (N.D. Ga. 1987).

Jacobellis v. Ohio, 378 U.S. 184, 197 (1964).

Lewis, P. (1989). All's not quiet on the legal front, *The New York Times*, (March 26), 8F.

Lieberman, J. & Seidel, G. (1988). *Business law and the legal environment*. (2nd ed.). New York: Harcourt Brace Jovanovich.

Pleadings in *Apple Computer v. Microsoft Corp. and Hewlett-Packard Co.*, No. C-88-20149-WWS (N.D. Cal. 1989).

.   Complaint for copyright infringment and unfair competition; jury trial demanded
.   Defendant Microsoft's answer, affirmative defenses and counterclaims
. Apple's reply to counterclaims
. Apple's memorandum in support of motion for partial summary judgment
. Defendant Microsoft's memorandum in opposition to Apple's motion for partial summary judgment
. Hewlett-Packard's memorandum in opposition to Apple's motion for partial summary judgment and in support of Microsoft's motion for summary judgment
. Apple's reply to Microsoft's and Hewlett-Packard's memoranda in opposition to Apple's motion for partial summary judgment
. Defendant Microsoft's reply to Apple's memorandum in opposition to motion for summary judgment
. Defendant Microsoft's motion and memorandum in support of motion for summary judgment
. Apple's response to Microsoft's motion for summary judgment
. Memorandum of decision and order

Pollak, A. (1988). The new high-tech battleground. *The New York Times*, (July 3), Section 3, 1,8.

SAS Institute, Inc. v. S&H Computer Systems, Inc., 605 F. Supp. 816 (M.D. Tenn. 1985).

Schmitt, R. (1989a) Apple wins first round in software-copyright case, *The Wall Street Journal*, (March 20), B1.

Schmitt, R. (1989b) Microsoft, Hewlett gain in court battle. *The Wall Street Journal*, (July 24).

Whelan Associates, Inc. v. Jaslow Dental Laboratory, Inc., 797 F.2d 1222 (1987).

Chapter 12

DISASTER PREPAREDNESS FOR MICROCOMPUTER-BASED CBIS

Hindupur V. Ramakrishna
Old Dominion University

Bindiganavale S. Vijayaraman
University of Akron

This chapter is devoted to the very important topic of the disaster preparedness of businesses as it pertains to their computer based information systems (CBIS) and, in particular, microcomputer based systems. Over the past few decades, as computer based systems have become less and less expensive and more and more friendly to use, businesses have come to depend on them for streamlining (and thus increasing the efficiency of) their operations. The recent trend has been to use these systems to gain competitive advantage over the competition. Most organizations recognize (implicitly) the importance of CBIS as an organizational resource that is as important as other resources such as money, materials, machines, and people. However, they do very little to protect themselves from the loss of availability of this resource from disasters.

No one wants to think about disasters, and most believe that disasters happen only to other people's systems. However, as organizations, both small and large, have become more and more dependent on their CBISs, any interruption in the availability of CBIS could lead anywhere from minor inconvenience to a permanent loss of business depending on the duration of the interruption. The seriousness of this fact is not fully understood by most organizations (Colby. 1985; Dugan, 1986; Jelcich, 1987; Rhodes, 1981). Unfortunately, the seriousness of the impact of disaster to a CBIS becomes clear to organizations (as well as individuals) only after the first disaster strikes. For most organizations this lesson may be too costly and for some too late.

However, businesses need not accept disasters to their CBIS as fait-accompli. They can take many preventive measures to reduce the possibility of certain types of disasters, or they can explore and develop contingency measures that could reduce the impact of some inevitable disasters. These measures will in no way guarantee that a disaster will not occur but will reduce the detrimental effect of these disasters on the business.

What exactly is a disaster? According to *Webster's New World Dictionary*, a disaster is defined as "a great or sudden misfortune that results in loss of life, property, etc. or that is ruinous to an undertaking." A CBIS disaster is an interruption in the availability of CBIS when there is a need for it (for business purposes). The interruption could result from unavailability of any element of the computerized system—viz., hardware, software, data, personnel, documentation, supplies, electrical power, or procedures.

For example, just think of what would happen to a business if it lost all of its Accounts Receivables data (both on the computer and hard copy). What would happen to a business if its microcomputer broke down for several days? What would happen if the only employee who is conversant with a particular computer application suddenly falls ill and is not available for a few weeks?

This chapter is devoted to exploring the concept of CBIS Disaster Preparedness. In our discussion, we will mostly concentrate on CBIS that are microcomputer based. Main objectives of this chapter are:

(1) To explore different CBIS disasters and classify them into proper categories.

(2) To explore different organizational issues as they pertain to disaster preparedness.

(3) To present possible solutions to prevent (or reduce the effect of) disasters that are predictable and to present contingency measures for disasters that are not predictable.

(4) To identify and discuss some emerging technologies in the field that could help businesses in preparing themselves for disasters.

In this chapter, we will first give some background to the reader by reviewing relevant concepts and literature pertaining to disaster preparedness. In this section, we will also discuss different categories of disasters and some normal costs associated with them. Then we will provide some justification for serious consideration of this topic by discussing some relevant issues for organizations. Next, we present some possible solutions/remedies to the disasters we discussed in the background section. We have classified the solutions into three categories—preventive measures, contingency measures, and general strategies. Finally, after presenting a brief discussion on future trends and emerging technology we present conclusions about the topic area.

Background

CBIS have become back-bones of a majority of businesses, both small and large. Though the criticality of CBIS differs from business to business depending on the nature of their information-intensive operations, very few businesses can survive without a CBIS. Businesses have become so accustomed to the use of their CBIS in their day-to-day business activities that manual procedures (to fall back on) for some transaction processing are non-existent in many businesses.

What is a CBIS?

CBIS discipline is fairly new and thus there is very little agreement on a single definition. For our purposes, we define CBIS as a collection of elements that are put together to form a synergistic system that supports the information needs of an organization. The needs could be efficiency oriented such as Transaction Processing Systems (TPS), or some needs could be effectiveness oriented such as Decision Support Systems (DSS). For efficiently running/using the CBIS the following elements are necessary:

1. **Hardware**   computer, printer, scanner, etc.

2. **Software**   operating system, application packages, utilities, etc.

3. **Data**   collected and processed to generate relevant information.

4. **Personnel**   needed to operate and maintain the CBIS.

5. **Documentation**   about data, software, etc.

6. **Supplies**   for use with hardware.

7. **Electrical Power** to run hardware.

8. **Procedures**   for smooth operations.

What is a CBIS Disaster?

Unavailability of any one (or more) of the elements listed above, when there is a need for it for business purposes, results in a CBIS disaster. For example, a laser printer that is not available for use due to the unavailability of a toner cartridge constitutes a CBIS disaster just as does an interruption caused by a power outage. Disasters come in many varieties and can cause different types and extents of loss to a business. After briefly reviewing some relevant literature on disaster planning, we will present our comprehensive summary of categories of CBIS disasters.

Review of Literature

In the CBIS literature there are many articles/ reports on disaster planning. Most reports about CBIS disasters are prescriptive in nature. They detail steps to avoid or prevent disasters and steps to develop contingency plans for disasters (Bidgoli, Hossein and Azarmasa, 1989; Boudette, 1988, Clark, 1986; Coffee, 1989; Dugan, 1986; Freeman, 1989; Grindlay, 1985; Hall, 1989; Hill, 1987; Janulaitis, 1985; Jelcich, 1987; Johnston, 1989; Kahane, 1988; Kleim, 1983; Kleim, 1984; Korzeniowski, 1990; Leaf, 1986; Ludlum, 1989; Miller, 1986; Murray, 1980; Moretti, 1986; Passori, 1986; Paul, 1981; Pedigo, 1986; Pepper, 1987; Robbins, 1986; Sensenich, 1985; Thiel, 1984; Whitehead, 1988; Yaremko, 1988). Some others are reports of actual disasters in businesses describing the nature of the disaster, what preventive measures were in place, damage suffered by the business, and lessons learned from the disaster (Baker, 1989; Chandler, 1988; Dissmeyer, 1983; Gardner, 1985; Raimondi, 1986; Robbins, 1988; Ruby, 1986; Weixel, 1989; Weixel, 1989). These articles can be a good source for developing a comprehensive list of past disasters and also for identifying some preventive measures against these disasters.

Another category of articles are product reviews or summaries that describe many different types of technologies to improve disaster preparedness (Smith, 1988). These articles are a good source for identifying disaster preparedness technologies.

Surveys identifying the actual practices in businesses with regards to CBIS disaster prepared-ness are almost non-existent. Some surveys that are reported either have a narrow focus (Christensen and Schkade, 1989) or are mainly aimed at major CBIS in-stallations (Merten and Severance, 1981). This is true for both large organizations (and consequently main-frame systems) and for small businesses (that pre-dominantly use microcomputer systems). However, a recent paper (Ramakrishna and Vijayaraman, 1990) based on a survey of disaster preparedness practices of 67 small businesses with microcomputer based CBIS reports the following:

- More than 50% were not aware of any disaster statistics.

- More than 80% had never assessed the risk to their CBIS.

- About 45% had no plans to protect them from CBIS disasters.

- More than 70% had no special hardware or software to either prevent disasters or to protect them from disasters.

- A majority of these businesses had very little protection from unauthorized access to their systems.

- More than 70% had no insurance against interruption to their CBIS or against loss of business due to CBIS disruption. However, 76% had insurance against hardware and software loss.

- More than 70% perceived their CBIS to be immune from any disaster.

The results of this survey are very revealing. It is shocking, and surprising, to note that a very small percentage of small businesses using microcomputer systems are somewhat protected from disasters, human-made or natural.

Based on the earlier reports/articles, we have developed a comprehensive list of CBIS disasters and also solutions for these disasters. These disasters, categorized appropriately, are presented next.

Categories of CBIS Disasters

There are many types of CBIS disasters. We can classify them into different categories based on which element of the CBIS is affected (or unavailable for use)—i.e., WHAT is affected?—and/or in the cause of the disaster—i.e., HOW did it happen? Based on the CBIS element affected, we can classify disasters into hardware, software, data, personnel, supplies, documentation, electrical power, and procedures. If any one of these, or more than one, is not available for use, a business could have a CBIS disaster. Based on the cause, we can classify disasters as human or non-human, accidental or intentional, or as caused by insiders or outsiders to the business. In Table 1, we have presented an elaborate list of potential disasters to CBIS in businesses classified into the different categories discussed.

For each element, such as hardware, software, etc., the unavailability could result from human-accidental, human-deliberate, or non-human causes. As we can see from the table, it is possible to have the same general category of cause, such as fire, be in all three categories of causes—for example, humans can accidentally or deliberately cause fire damage, or fire can result from a non-human cause such as lightning. Further, it is also possible to have many elements of a CBIS be damaged by the same general cause—for example, fire can cause damage to hardware, software, data, etc. Further, it is also possible for one cause, such as fire, to create other causes, such as smoke and water flooding (as sprinkler systems come into operation), thus creating a chain reaction. Though

	Human		Non-Human
Element	**Accidental**	**Deliberate**	
Hardware	Fire damage Water damage Smoke damage Food/drink damage	Fire damage Water damage Smoke damage Food/drink damage Theft Computer Virus Sabotage	Fire damage Water damage Power fluctuations Computer breakdown
Software	Fire damage Water damage Smoke damage Food/drink damage Misplaced programs Bad modification Erasing by users Computer Virus Reformatting of hard disk Destruction of diskette Erasing by machine failure	Fire damage Water damage Smoke damage Food/drink damage Misplaced programs Bad modification Erasing by users Computer Virus Reformatting of hard disk Destruction of diskette Theft Sabotage	Fire damage Water damage Power fluctuations Computer breakdown Software glitches
Data	Misplaced data Erased data by users Computer virus Power disruption Erased data by machine failure (Hard disk crash, bad disk drive)	Misplaced data Erased data by users Computer virus Power disruption Theft Data tampering	Fire damage Water damage Power fluctuations Power disruption Computer breakdown Software glitches
Personnel	Illness of critical employee	Employee leaving company White collar crime Absenteeism	Death of critical employee
Supplies	Misplace supplies Out of stock supplies	Misplaced supplies Theft Sabotage	Fire damage Water damage
Documen-tation	Misplaced documentation Bad modifications	Misplaced documentation Bad modifications Theft Sabotage	Fire damage Water damage
Elec. Power	Power disruption	Power disruption	Power disruption Power fluctuations
Procedures	Not following procedures Lack of procedures	Not following procedures	

Table 1: Categories of Disasters

the table is quite elaborate and is easy to follow, we will present brief discussions of each of the categories of disasters next.

Hardware

In a CBIS, hardware itself is a system consisting of several components. The severity of disaster caused by hardware failure will depend on the particular component that has failed. Loss or unavailability of hardware could result from many varied causes.

Fire, whether caused by humans or not, results in the most extensive damage to hardware. In most cases the damage is worsened by smoke, heat, and water damage (due to automatic sprinkler systems) that is associated with a fire.

Water damage to hardware can be almost as extensive as that of fire damage. This will depend on the type of disaster. In case of minor flooding due to a broken water pipe or flooding limited to only a portion of an installation, many pieces of hardware may not suffer any direct damage—however, some components could suffer damage due to humidity.

Smoke damage is usually not as extensive as fire or water damage. Depending on the intensity of smoke, hard-disk drives, printers, and few other devices could suffer some minor damage.

Damage due to food/drink is usually limited to highly exposed components of a hardware system—such components as keyboards, printers, etc. The damage is usually caused by spilling food or drink on a component.

Theft could result in extensive loss as any component of a hardware system can be stolen. However, it is usually limited to hardware items that are not heavy and also to items that are readily marketable. Modems, keyboards, lap-top or portable computers, mouse, digitizer tablets, cables, expansion boards, line stabilizers, etc. are the more commonly affected units.

Computer viruses usually do not cause any permanent damage to hardware. However, they can slow the system down considerably and use up a lot of available memory, thus affecting the availability of the system for business use.

Sabotage, a deliberate human activity, can be executed in many different ways— concealing powerful magnets near hardware units, re-wiring hardware, blowing up hardware, etc. Fire, water, and other damage we have discussed earlier are also some methods that can be used for sabotaging hardware.

Power fluctuations can also cause some damage to a few components of a hardware system. Depending on the extent of the fluctuation in electrical power, such components as power units of computers, monitors, etc. could be damaged.

As is true with any machine, computers are also likely to breakdown. Likelihood of breakdown of any component of a hardware system depends on many factors — quality of manufacturing and design, the environment, number of moving parts, etc. Printers, disk drives, keyboards, motherboards, etc. are some examples.

Software

In a CBIS, software is at least as important as hardware. The loss of software could result from many varied causes. Some of these causes are the same as the ones for hardware loss. Here, we will discuss only those causes that we have not discussed under hardware.

Programs can be misplaced by users, either intentionally or accidentally. Users also can modify programs (software) incorrectly, and thus the programs may be useless for some time. Additionally, users can also erase the software, again either intentionally or accidentally.

Computer viruses can also be introduced, accidentally or intentionally by users, into the system, and they may erase or change software, thus rendering the software useless.

Users, either intentionally or by accident, can reformat hard-disks, thus destroying software. Users can also destroy diskettes, by accident or intentionally, thus destroying software.

When hardware fails, it can sometimes erase software. This can also happen when a machine is shutdown due to power failure or due to computer breakdown. Depending on the quality of software, software glitches can cause disruption in the availability of CBIS.

Data

Computer systems will become almost useless without data. As we can see from Table 1, data are also affected by many of the causes that are common to software and hardware. Here we will discuss only those causes that we have not touched upon earlier.

Data tampering can occur when users intentionally try to change some data in order to hurt the business in some way. Also, data that is being worked on at any moment can be lost if there is a power fluctuation.

Personnel

Unavailability of a crucial employee to operate

certain software/hardware can result in a CBIS disaster. Illness of an employee for a period of time that is beyond what a business can live with can be a cause. An employee leaving a business or the death of an employee can also cause disaster. White collar crime committed by an employee could cause a lot of damage to a business.

Supplies

Most computer systems need some supplies on a regular basis. These supplies could be toners for printers, printer ribbons, paper for printers, floppy disks, etc. If these are not available when they are needed, a CBIS disaster results. Most of the causes, such as fire, water, etc., that we have discussed before could result in this type of disaster. If proper procedures for keeping track of supplies are not in place, a business could run out of supplies.

Documentation

Whenever a change is made to any software, it is important to document the change properly for the contingency of losing the modified software. If this documentation is not available when needed, it could result in a CBIS disaster. It is conceivable that some user, intentionally, could modify some documentation incorrectly so as to cause a potential disaster. Some other causes of unavailability of documentation are similar to those of software, data, etc. and have been discussed earlier.

Electrical power

Computer systems can not operate without some form of electrical power. Power disruptions can be caused either intentionally by users or they can be an act of God. This is also true of power fluctuations, i.e., changes in the amount of power available, voltage, current, or cycles fluctuations. These will interrupt the functioning of a computer system and will lead to many types of disasters.

Procedures

Following proper procedures in computer system operations is very important. If such procedures are not followed properly, either by ignorance or intentionally, many different types of CBIS disruptions can occur.

Cost of Disasters

When a CBIS fails, the cost of this failure to a business will be much more than the cost of failed hardware or software. Unfortunately, most businesses insure the system but do not protect themselves from business loss.

Many of the costs associated with a disaster are either intangible or difficult to estimate. Hence, many organizations do not fully understand the costs of CBIS disasters and, consequently, do not bother either to take preventive measures or do contingency planning against disasters.

Costs are difficult to generalize for different kinds of businesses; however, there are some general estimates reported in the literature that businesses can use as a rough guide. The estimates are given below:

• The average company will lose 2-3 percent of its gross sales within 8 days of a sustained computer outage.

• The average company that experiences a computer outage lasting longer than 10 days will never fully recover. Fifty percent will be out of business within 5 years.

• The chances of surviving a disaster affecting the corporate data processing center are less than 7 in 100. The chances of experiencing such a disaster are 1 in 100 [Toigo, 1989 p. xvi].

• Twenty megabytes of lost sales and marketing information take 19 days to re-create at a cost of $17,000. For an equivalent amount of accounting information, the time needed to restore the data rises to 21 days and the cost to $19,000 [Aaland, p. 88].

• More than half the corporations that lose their records due to fire will not survive the next business year [Sampson, 1989, p. 19].

• A company's ability to function after a major disaster slips dramatically, and as much as 50% of its functionality can be lost in less than five days [Daly, 1990, p. 25].

Differences in Micro and Mini/Mainframe Environments

The following are some differences between the micro and mainframe/mini computer environments that are relevant to our discussion of disaster preparedness of small businesses:

• Most mainframe/mini computer environments

are managed by formal DP/MIS departments within organizations. This may not be the case with most small businesses with microcomputer based CBIS.

• Due to the availability of formal training through formal DP/MIS departments, the direct users in mainframe/mini computer environments are more likely to be sophisticated users of CBIS.

• Due to a better understanding of legal requirements for protecting CBIS installations, the mainframe/mini computer environments are more likely to explore the disaster preparedness issue in a formal way.

• Even though small businesses (with microcomputer based CBIS) are less likely to be as prepared as bigger businesses, unfortunately, the likelihood of disasters and also the nature of impact of these disasters are not likely to be any less.

• Small businesses have not had sufficient experience with computer systems to fully realize damages caused by disasters.

Relevant Issues

Disaster preparedness is necessary for businesses to protect themselves from damages resulting from CBIS disasters. These damages can be manyfold: (1) damages to the actual system, (2) damages due to business loss, and (3) damages due to lawsuits against the business. Most businesses protect themselves from damages of the first kind by taking out appropriate insurance coverage. However, the cost of this type of damage is probably the least for any business. Businesses find it difficult to estimate losses due to damages of the second kind, and they do not fully understand (or do not want to understand) damages of the third kind and also the associated costs. The relevant issue for disaster preparedness is not purely a technical one but is more managerial. It is extremely important for businesses to understand the legal and resource management issues.

As we have noted earlier, cost of lost business operations due to disasters is in orders of magnitude greater than the cost of hardware and software damaged. Availability of uninterrupted use of CBIS is an organizational resource. This resource is at least as important as other organizational resources, such as materials, machines, money, or personnel. For example, if some money were lost in a business, the cost of this loss to that business is not only the lost money but also the cost of opportunities lost due to lack of funds. This is also true of computer systems loss. Businesses should understand this and manage it accordingly.

After a disaster occurs, can a business be sued for not being appropriately prepared for disasters? The answer is a definite *YES* in many cases. Most businesses do not understand this liability. The lawsuits can take many forms. Following are some examples:

- Stockholders of the business can claim mismanagement and file a lawsuit. Appropriate legislation exists that makes this possible.

- Computer crime could be in the form of a disaster, and legal actions from many individuals and/or organizations may result. For example, an employee may misuse the CBIS and disclose confidential information about others, or an employee may use the CBIS to commit a crime against some other business.

Many other forms of liabilities exist for businesses, and it is very important for businesses to fully explore these liability issues and take appropriate preventive actions.

In summary, businesses must take a closer look at many issues that are important as they pertain to disaster preparedness and not take a very narrow view.

Solutions/Remedies

Even though all disasters cannot be prevented, the probability of one occurring can be lessened and the likelihood of long-term disruption of business operations can be reduced. The effectiveness of disaster prevention and recovery depends on the type of disaster that may strike the CBIS. In Table 2, we have presented a list of disasters and possible solutions to those disasters. The disasters are grouped into eight categories: (A) hardware, (B) software, (C) data, (D) personnel, (E) supplies, (F) documentation, (G) electric power, and (H) procedures. Solutions under each of the above categories have been numbered. For example, disaster type B) refers to "destruction of diskette." The solutions are grouped into three categories: preventive measures, contingency

DISASTERS RESULTING IN UNAVAILABILITY OF	POSSIBLE SOLUTIONS
A. HARDWARE	***PREVENTIVE MEASURES***
1 Fire damage (1,13-14,16-17,19,26-27)	1 Fireproof Vaults/Safes (A1,B1,C1,E1,F1,A3, & B15-B16)
2 Water damage (14,16-17,19,21,26-27)	
3 Smoke damage (1,13-14,16-17,19,22,26-27)	2 Back-up -- off-site and on-site (B1-B16,C1-C12, & F1-F6)
4 Food/drink damage (14,16-19,22,26-27)	
5 Theft (8-10,14,16-17,19,26-27)	
6 Computer Virus (8-9,11-12,14,16-19,25-27)	3 Uninterruptible Power Supply (UPS) (A8,B12,C6,C12,G1, & G2)
7 Sabotage (8-10,14,16-19,26-27)	
8 Power fluctuations (3,14,19,26-27)	
9 Computer breakdown (7,14-17,19,26-27)	4 Diesel Generators for power (C6, & G1)
	5 Recovery Utilities (B7-B9,B11-B13,C4-C7, & C10-C12)
B. SOFTWARE	
1 Fire damage (1-2,13-14,19,26-27)	6 Password Protection and Data Encryption (B7,B9,C4,C8-C9, & D3)
2 Water damage (2,14,19,21,26-27)	
3 Smoke damage (2,13-14,19,22,26-27)	
4 Food/drink damage (2,14,18-19,22,26-27)	7 Preventive Maintenance of Hardware (A9,B11,B13,C7, & C10)
5 Misplaced programs (2,14,18-19,26,27)	
6 Bad modification (2,10,14,18,26,27)	8 Security (A5-A7,B7-B8,B10,B15-B16,C4-C5,C8-C9,D3,
7 Erasing by users (2,5-6,8-10,14,18-19,25-27)	E5-E6, & F5-F6)
8 Computer virus (2,5,8-12,14,18-19,26-27)	
9 Reformatting of hard disk (2,5-6,10,14, 18-19,26-27)	
10 Destruction of diskette (2,8-10,14,18-19,25-27)	9 Background-check of employees (A5-A7,B6-B10,B15-B16,C4,C8-C9,D3,E5-E6, & F4-F6)
11 Erasing by machine failure(2,5,7,14-15,19,26-27)	
12 Power fluctuations (2-3,5,14-15,19,26-27)	
13 Computer breakdown (2,5,7,14-15,19,26-27)	
14 Software Glitches (2,14-15,26-27)	10 Disabling access to fired employees (A5,A7,B6-B10,B15-B16,C4-C5,C8-C9,D3,E5-E6, & F4-F6)
15 Theft (1-2,8-10,14-15,18-19,26-27)	
16 Sabotage (1-2,8-10,14-15,18-19,26-27)	
	11 Invest in software for Virus detection (A6,B8, & C5)
C. DATA	
1 Fire damage (1-2,13-14,27)	12 Invest in hardware for Virus detection (A6,B8, & C5)
2 Water damage (2,14,21,27)	
3 Misplaced data (2,14,18,27)	13 Install Smoke Alarms (A1, A3, B1, B3, C1)
4 Erased data by users (2,5-6,8-10,14,18,25,27	
5 Computer virus (2,5,8,10-12,14,18,25,27)	
6 Power disruption (2-5,14,20,25,27)	
7 Erased data by machine failure (2,5,7,14,18 (Hard disk crash, bad disk drive)20,22,27)	***CONTINGENCY MEASURES***
8 Theft (2,6,8-10,14,18,27)	
9 Data tampering (2,6,8-10,14,18,27)	14 Insurance Protection (A1-A9,B1-B16,C1-C12,D1-D4,E1-E2,E5-E6,
10 Computer breakdown (2,5,7,14,20,27)	F1-F2, & G1)
11 Software Glitches (2,14,20,27)	
12 Power fluctuations (2-3,5,14,20,27)	15 Service Contracts (A9, & B11-B16)
	16 Hot-Site and/or Cold-site agreements (A1-A7,A9, & G1)
D. PERSONNEL	
1 Illness of critical employee (14,23-24,27)	17 Reciprocal Agreement (A1-A7,A9, & G1)
2 Employee leaving the company (14,23-24,27)	
3 White collar crime (6,8-10,14,18,23,27)	
4 Death of critical employee (14,23-24,27)	

Table 2: Disasters and Solutions

DISASTERS RESULTING IN UNAVAILABILITY OF	POSSIBLE SOLUTIONS
E. SUPPLIES	***GENERAL STRATEGIES***
1 Fire damage (1,14,19,27) 2 Water damage (14,19,21,27) 3 Misplaced supplies (18,19,27) 4 Out of stock supplies (19,27) 5 Theft (8-10,14,18,19,27) 6 Sabotage (8-10,14,18,19,27)	18 Establish Audit-trails (A4,A6,A7,B4-B10,B15-B16,C3-C5,C7-C9,D3,E3, E5,E6,F3-F6) 19 Buy off-the-shelf hardware, software, and supplies. (A1-A9,B1-B5,B7-B13,B15-B16,E1-E6,F1-F6)
	20 Develop Procedures to 'save' in-process working data, on a periodic basis, to a diskette/hard-disk. (C6-C7,C10-C12)
F. DOCUMENTATION	21 Locate Equipment away from water pipes, above ground, and cover equipment as much as possible (A2,B2,C2,E2,F2)
1 Fire damage (1-2,14,19,26-27) 2 Water damage (2,14,19,21,26-27) 3 Misplaced documentation (2,18-19,26-27) 4 Bad modifications (2,9,18-19,26-27) 5 Theft (2,8-10,18-19,26-27) 6 Sabotage (2,8-10,18-19,26-27)	22 Develop policies against eating, drinking, and smoking in computer areas (A3,A4,B3,B4,C7) 23 Train more than one employee in each critical application (D1-D4)
G. ELECTRICAL POWER	24 Develop good operations document for critical applications (D1-D2,D4)
1 Power disruption (3-4,14,16-17,27) 2 Power fluctuations (3,27)	25 Train all users in the proper way to use CBIS (A6,B7,B10,C4-C6,H1)
H. PROCEDURES	26 Identify Leasing Companies in the area (A1-A9,B1-B16,F1-F16)
1 Not following procedures (25,27) 2 Lack of procedures (27)	27 Develop (and test on a periodic basis) a contingency plan against disasters that clearly identifies roles and activities (A1-A9,B1-B16,C1-C12,D1-D4,E1-E6,F1-F6, G1-G2,H1-H2)

Table 2: Disasters and Solutions (Contd.)

measures, and general strategies. We have numbered solutions 1-27.

In the table, for each disaster, we have identified potential solutions and noted them by listing the corresponding numbers (inside the parentheses) associated with these solutions. Similarly, each solution is followed by references, in parentheses, that correspond to the disasters it addresses. A brief description of the solutions and the disasters they address is given below.

Preventive Measures

Loss of hardware, software, data, supplies, and documentation due to fire and smoke and theft and sabotage of software can be prevented by using fire-proof vaults and safes. Hardware can be protected from fire and smoke damage by storing hardware inside fireproof furniture. Disasters due to loss of software, data, supplies, and documentation from fire and smoke can be minimized by keeping backup copies of software and data, copies of documentation, and important supplies in fireproof vaults or safes on the premises.

Loss of software and data due to misplacing, erasing, theft, sabotage, virus, power disruption, fire, and storm can be minimized by making backup copies of the software and data and keeping them in a safe place. It is important to keep the original, and maybe a copy, of software in a safe and secure place on-site and a second copy off-site. If program alterations are made very frequently, it is important to make back-up copies once a month or maybe once a week. Data should be backed up as frequently as the application in question needs it. It is not enough to backup only once a week if hundreds of transactions take place throughout the week, in which case daily backup is necessary. Backup copies can be made either on floppy disks or cassette tapes or both. When backing up data, several approaches may be used. One way is to simply use the DOS copy command. There are various other utility programs that are available for making faster backup copies on diskettes. Another option that is particularly suitable for large applications is to use tape backup units. Whichever method is selected, the practice of creating rolling backups is the safest.

Loss of data due to loss of power supply and power surges can be prevented by using Uninterruptible Power Supply (UPS) units. A standby UPS system provides power without spikes or drops and is generally equipped with battery backup to allow the user enough time to save all the work currently being done before the computer goes down. An on-line UPS has its battery continually charged by utility power and does not have the possible danger of lag between the actual loss of utility power and the beginning of the power from the batteries, which may be long enough to cause damage in some systems.

Disasters could happen when there is a complete disruption of power supply due to storm and other reasons. This disaster could be avoided by using alternative sources of power supply. One such source is diesel generator. Diesel generators can be used to run the CBIS even when there is a disruption of normal power to the computer system.

Accidental erasure of programs and data, loss of data due to accidental reformatting of hard disk and diskettes, and erasing of programs and data due to machine failure can be recovered by using software utilities that specialize in recovering lost information.

Software packages such as PC Tools and Norton Utilities can be used to recover lost data and programs.

Protection against unauthorized use of the system, unauthorized program alteration, data tampering, theft of data, and other white collar crimes can be achieved by having password protection and data encryption methods. Access to files must be limited by specifying passwords. A second password may also be used before certain options can be carried out. The use of passwords will not solve all the problems. Data are particularly vulnerable whenever they are sent between computers over communication lines. To prevent computer eavesdroppers from stealing or maliciously changing data, data encryption methods could be used in which data are encoded so that they cannot be recognized without knowledge of the coding scheme.

Disasters due to computer breakdown and erasing of software and data due to machine failure can be minimized by proper preventive maintenance of hardware. Preventive maintenance means that after a particular interval of time, regular maintenance will be performed on the computer to help safeguard against serious breakdown due to maintenance neglect. This service is very essential if a good performance from the computer is desired. It is important to establish a plan for preventive maintenance at the time of computer purchase to help safeguard against serious breakdown due to maintenance neglect. For a microcomputer, preventive maintenance once a quarter is essential. Regular dusting, cleaning the exterior of the hardware, and cleaning the drives are also important for proper functioning of the computer system.

Security is a very important issue and should be examined thoroughly by the business. In a small business, deliberate damage or theft of the computer system by the employees is less likely to happen. However, taking some security measures like bolting the computer to the desk, locking the computer room, and using an alarm system could prevent even the smallest chances of such disasters. Access to the system should be limited to only those who must use the system. Data and software security can be achieved by locking on-site backup copies of data and programs in a safe place and storing copies off-site. Limiting access to the computer system through the use of passwords and using data encryption methods for communication of data over communication networks are musts.

A background check of employees is very important in preventing disasters due to theft, sabotage, computer virus, destruction of software and data, and other white collar crimes. This would reveal the reasons for leaving previous employment and the character of the employee.

Access to computer system to employees fired from the job should be denied. Passwords to access systems to such employees should be changed, and keys to the computer room should be recovered. This will prevent disasters due to theft and sabotage of hardware, software, data, supplies, and documentation.

Accidental and intentional introduction of a computer virus into the system is difficult to prevent because nobody will know it has happened until the damage is done. A simple guideline to reduce this kind of disaster is not to share disks with other computer systems that are at a higher risk of being infected by a virus and to use only those software obtained from a reliable source. Other hardware and software for detecting a virus can be used to make sure the diskettes are virus free before using them on the system.

Installation of smoke alarms could prevent destruction of hardware, software, data, supplies, and documentation due to fire and smoke damage.

Contingency Measures

Loss of computer hardware, software, data, supplies, and documentation due to fire, water damage, smoke, theft, sabotage, computer virus, and power surges could be covered by insurance. Apart from the above loss, businesses could also suffer loss due to business interruption from CBIS failure. One way to safeguard the business from the financial loss due to any of the above disasters is by covering hardware loss, software loss, CBIS interruption, and business interruption due to CBIS failure by insurance.

Service contracts should be established with the computer vendor or other businesses for supply of a backup computer system in case your system should be lost for an extended period of time.

A hot site is a facility with computers and basic peripherals all hooked up and ready to go that sits there most of the time in reserve and unused. You pay a monthly fee to be a member of the club, in exchange for which you are allowed to use the computer system in case of loss of hardware due to fire, water, smoke damage, theft, sabotage, computer virus, power disruption, and computer breakdown. Some companies also provide mobile hot site (a full facility on wheels) facilities in case you can not get to their facilities. An alternative to a hot site is a cold site (or shell). A cold site is a facility set up with certain basic equipment that can include power, telephone lines, and certain generic peripherals but without the computer itself. This option is attractive to businesses that have lost access to their facility but whose computers are fine, to people who purchase a replacement machine immediately but need a place to set it up temporarily, or to those who have access to a replacement machine. Cold sites are substantially less expensive than hot sites and are more attractive for businesses that can afford to be down for several days while the necessary system is gathered.

Another option to explore is reciprocal agreements with other businesses that use a similar kind of computer system. Such an agreement would give access to the system of the other business (during its slack period of use) until the computer system is again back in working order. The same applies to other businesses in case of loss of their computer systems.

General Strategies

Audit trails could be used to protect the data, reconstruct the data from backup copies in case of loss of a data file, and also help document the evolution of the program through its modification. Audit trail is a method of maintaining detailed records of the changes made to the program or data file. This information is saved in a separate file that can be used in case of loss of data due to disaster to help reconstruct the lost data and program files. Audit trails can also be established for use of hardware, software, supplies, and documentation.

Off-the-shelf systems are put together with hardware, software, supplies, etc. that are readily available from many sources. Using off-the-shelf systems for CBIS should make it easier and faster to recover from disasters such as theft, sabotage, fire, water, and smoke damage. In case of disaster, the business should be able to buy or lease the necessary hardware, software, and supplies and get their CBIS back and running without much delay. For example, a system put together with standard IBM compatible microcomputers and software such as LOTUS 1-2-3, WordPerfect, etc. is much easier to put together (and takes much less time) when disaster strikes. A business using custom-made hardware, software, and supplies, may have to wait a long period of time to get back to normal. It may not be possible to use off-the-shelf systems all the time, but they must be used wherever it is possible.

When power to the computer is cutoff during the updating of data or documents or while developing any application (say, using LOTUS), the information that is stored in the memory will be completely lost. This could lead to a waste of time in re-entering the data entered after the last backup. Procedures to save in-process working data at a regular interval (say, 5 to 10 minutes depending on the amount of data updated) to a diskette or hard disk should be developed. It should be noted that some packages such as WordPerfect provide the option of saving files automatically at a regular interval, whereas packages such as LOTUS 1-2-3 do not.

Disasters due to water damage caused by breakage of water pipes, sprinkler systems, or flood can be avoided by taking some simple precautionary measures such as keeping computer equipment away from water pipes, well above the ground, and covering equipment as much as possible when not in use.

A most common hardware disaster is hard drive crash. This can occur because of the normal wear of mechanical devices. Also smoke from cigarette smoking can greatly reduce the life of the hard disk and could be a factor in the reduction of hard disk reliability. Spilling coffee or any liquid on the keyboard could ruin the keyboard. Similarly, diskettes can also be damaged. It is important to have a policy of no smoking, eating, or drinking near the computer or the computer room.

One type of disaster that is not very often considered until it happens to a firm is the loss or absence of a critical employee. This type of disaster can cause productivity loss to the organization and also time and money to train a new employee. One step is to train other employees in the operation of the CBIS, which could prevent the risk of being disrupted by the loss of an employee who knows the critical aspects of the CBIS operation.

Developing a good operations document for each critical application will be especially useful when the employee responsible for the operation of a particular critical application is either ill or leaves the business. Detailed descriptions of the operations of the critical application should be developed so that other employees can run the application using the document without disrupting the business.

Training and educating all users of CBIS on the proper usage of computers can help prevent disasters such as accidental reformatting of the hard disk, accidental shutting off power, or deleting program or data files. Proper handling of floppy diskettes is important in maintaining the program and data files on floppy diskettes.

Identifying leasing companies in your area of

business will be helpful in case you want to lease computer equipment in the event of loss of computers due to disaster.

Finally, a complete and a thoroughly tested contingency plan against disasters should be prepared and updated periodically. This plan should clearly lay out the activities in case of disaster and should identify the individuals who play the important roles in the event of disaster and the sequence of activities that should be undertaken when disaster strikes the CBIS. This will reduce (or eliminate) the potential disruptions due to CBIS disasters.

Future Trends and Emerging Technology

As we have pointed out in our earlier discussion, businesses can reduce the possibility of disaster to their CBIS through investments in hardware and software. However, this should be complemented by appropriate policies and procedures for CBIS use and also by appropriate contingency planning. Here, we will examine some trends in this regard.

One technology that can make it easier for businesses to back-up their data and software is emerging. This is the technology/concept of Electronic Vaulting. With this concept, using ordinary telephone lines and some telecommunication software, businesses can back-up data/software on a regular basis and store this safely in a remote site. This will reduce the hassles of regular back-up, thus increasing the frequency of back-up.

With the Scanner technology getting better and better, businesses in the future may not lose much data, even if they do not have back-up data in computer-readable storage, as long as they have hard copies of data. This option will become very viable as a fall-back option for many businesses.

With the trend in designing Fault Tolerant Systems, microcomputers with extra hard-disk drives are becoming available now. These disk-drives are designed to continually store data that is being worked on in the volatile memory (i.e., RAM) of computers. In the event of a power failure, recovery of data will be an easy task with these types of computers.

Though some technological solutions are emerging in the arena of disaster preparedness, it is important for businesses to recognize that better preparedness comes from not only technological solutions but also from appropriate policies and procedures for CBIS use.

Conclusions

Our intent for this chapter is to emphasize the importance of disaster preparedness for businesses, to expose readers to many different types of CBIS disasters and to some possible technological and managerial solutions for the disasters, and to look at some relevant issues and emerging technologies. We have intentionally limited the scope of our discussion to businesses that have microcomputer based CBIS.

Businesses in today's competitive world have come to depend on their computer based information systems more than those in the past. They depend on their CBIS not only to streamline their operations (transaction processing operations) but also in many cases to gain a competitive edge. However, it is unfortunate that most businesses do not have a good understanding of the concept of disaster preparedness.

Literature on disaster planning is fairly extensive but is limited in certain aspects. Conceptual
articles that prescribe what businesses should do to
better prepare themselves for CBIS disasters are
many. Actual reports of disasters in businesses that
detail the nature of the disaster, how businesses
coped with the disaster, and what they learned are
also available in plenty. Many articles in the literature
deal with reviews of technological options in preparing
for disasters. However, reports of actual business
practices (and technologies used) regarding disaster
preparedness of small businesses are lacking in the
literature. Some surveys of this type that do exist
report findings that are very disheartening.

CBIS disaster results in the unavailability of
one or more elements of the system when there is a
need for its use for business purposes. The disaster
could result from unavailability of hardware, software, data, personnel, supplies, documentation, electrical power, or procedures.

CBIS disasters can be classified based on (1)
what is affected or (2) how it happened. The first
classification deals with which element of the system
is not available, such as hardware, software, etc. The
second classification deals with whether the cause
was human or non-human, whether it was intentional
or accidental, and whether it was caused by insiders
or outsiders. We have developed and presented an
extensive table that looks at these issues. For each
one of the possible disasters, we have also identified
many solutions that could be used to reduce the
possibility of disasters.

We have also identified many issues that businesses should consider when they try to understand
the concept of disaster preparedness. The issues are

not just technical in nature but are more managerial. It is also important to realize that businesses may have a legal obligation to manage computer resources as carefully as they manage other resources.

We have also highlighted many differences between the computing environments of micro and mini/mainframe computers. It is important for small businesses to understand that they are as likely to encounter disasters as are bigger businesses, but they are less likely to be prepared.

In our discussion, we have also presented some brief details about emerging technologies in the field of disaster preparedness. These technologies may make it a little easier for businesses to be prepared for certain types of disasters. However, it is important to note that most types of disasters can be prevented (or the possibility and extent of damage can be reduced) only through following appropriate policies and procedures and through the development of good contingency plans.

Computers are very reliable tools for the most part. However, as they age their reliability drops. To be able to use the technology, businesses must develop appropriate environments for CBIS so that a continued (and uninterrupted) use can be derived from those systems. This is crucial for most businesses, and, if not properly prepared, businesses may cease to be in business due to extensive losses incurred because of interruption in their operations. This calls for CBIS disaster preparedness, the topic of this chapter.

References

Aaland, Mikkel. (1988, November). Preventing Computer Disasters. *Working Woman*, pp. 88-92.

Baker, Sharon. (1989, March 13) Guard the Line of Retreat. *Computerworld*, pp. 84.

Bidgoli, Hossein, and Reza Azarmsa. (1989) Computer Security: New Managerial Concern for the 1980s and Beyond. *Journal of Systems Management*, 40(10), pp. 21-27.

Boudette, Neal E. (1988, November 7). A Piece of the Rock for Computers. *Industry Week*, pp. 85.

Chandler, Doug. (1988, August 29). Disasters Underscore Importance of Having Backup of Vital Data. *PC Week*, pp. 83-84.

Christensen, Steven R, and Lawrence L. Schkade. (1989, March 13). Surveying the Aftermath. *Computerworld*, pp. 81-82.

Clark, Orvin R. (1986, October 22). Computer Disaster Recovery Planning. Paper presented at the *Annual International Meeting of the American Society of Business officers*, San Francisco, CA.

Coffee, Peter. (1989, October 2). Virus Fears Cloud Other, More Likely Hazards. *PC Week*, pp. 46.

Colby, Wendelin. (1985, October). Disaster Recovery Plan? Nah... It'll Never Happen to Us!. *Infosystems*, pp. 32-36.

Cummings, Steve. (1987, January 27). No Matter What, PC Downtime is Money Lost. *PC Week*, pp. 105-106.

Daly, James. (1989, February 20). No Excuse for Unpreparedness. *Computerworld*, pp. 25-28.

Dissmeyer, Virgil M. (1983, May-June). Are You Ready to Meet a Disaster? *Harvard Business Review*, pp. 6-12.

Dugan, Ed. (1986, January 27). Disaster Recovery Planning: Crisis Doesn't Equal Catastrophe. *Computerworld*, pp. 67-72.

Freedman, David H. (1980, October). Are You Ready for a Disaster. *Infosystems*, pp. 106-112.

Gardner, Jeffrey E. (1985, November 25). How to Assemble a Comprehensive Disaster Recovery Plan. *Computerworld*, pp. 70-71.

Grindlay, Andrew. (1985, Spring). Can Your Business Survive a Computer Disaster? *Business Quarterly*, pp. 10-14.

Hall, Dan. (1989, August). Turning up the Heat on Disaster Plans. *ABA Banking Journal*, pp. 35-39.

Hill, Thomas. (1987, June 23). Power Protection: Users Say They're Worth the Bucks. *PC Week*, pp. 67-68.

Janulaitis, Victor M. (1985, February). Creating a Disaster Recovery Plan.

Infosystems, pp. 42-43.

Jelcich, Susan. (1987, September 15). Power Protection Awareness May be Increasing, but Education is Still Needed. *PC Week*, pp. 145-146.

Johnston, Robert E. (1989, March 13). It Pays to Test All Assumptions. Computerworld, pp. 88.

Kahane, Yehuda, Neumann Seev, and Charles S. Tapiero. (1988). Computer Backup Pools, Disaster Recovery, and Default Risk. *Communications of the ACM*, 31(1), 78-83.

Kleim, Ralph L. (1983). Disaster Prevention. *Journal of Systems Management, 34*, 10-11.

Kleim, Ralph L. (1984). Disaster Prevention and Recovery for Microcomputers. *Journal of Systems Management, 35*, 28-29.

Korzeniowski, Paul. (1990, February). How to Avoid Disaster With a Recovery Plan. *Software Magazine*, pp. 46-55.

Leaf, Jesse J. (1986, July 15). Staying in Power. *Datamation*, pp. 67-72.

Ludlum, David. (1989, June 12). One Step Ahead of Disaster. *Computerworld*, pp. 105.

Merten, Alan G, and Dennis G. Severance. (1981). Data Processing Control: A State-of-the-Art Survey of Attitudes and Concerns of DP Executives. *MIS Quarterly, 5*(2), 11-32.

Miller, Howard W. (1986). Disaster Recovery Planning. *Journal of Systems Management, 37*(3), 25-30.

Murray, John P, and Auerbach Editorial Staff. (1980). How to Develop a Contingency Plan. *Information and Records Management, 14*(6), 38-42.

Moretti, Mike, and James Cavuoto. (1986, July 8). Variety of Power Snags Can Plague the PC User. *PC Week*, pp. 166-168.

Passori, Al. (1986, January 27). Contingency Planning Options Protect Corporate Data Assets. *Computerworld*, pp. 73-74.

Paul, Roger L. (1981). Recovery from Disaster. *Journal of Systems Management, 32*(2), 18-21.

Pedigo, Joe. (1986, March 12). Disaster Recovery: Making Plans that Could Save Your Company. *Computerworld*, pp. 49-88.

Pepper, Jon. (1987, July 14). Ease of Use, Education Help Deter Corporate Backup Disasters. *PC Week*, pp. 115-119.

Raimondi, Donna. (1986, November 17). Hot Sites: Disaster Plan Douses Flames. *Computerworld*, pp. 1-6.

Ramakrishna, H.V., and B.S. Vijayaraman. (1990). CBIS Disaster Preparedness of Small Businesses with Micro-computer Based Systems: Survey Findings. *Proceedings of the 21st Annual Meeting of Decision Sciences Institute,* San Diego.

Rhodes, Wayne L. (1981, July). What Good is Data Without a Computer.

Infosystems, pp. 58-62.

Robbins, Renee M. (1986, July). Taking the Disaster Out of Recovery. *Infosystems*, pp. 38-44.

Robbins, Renee M. (1988, January). Trial by Flood. *Infosystems*, pp. 40-46.

Ruby, Daniel. (1986, July 15). Corporations Are Learning to Protect PC Data. *PC Week*, pp. 37-44.

Sampson, Karen L. (1989, June). Records Management Can Reduce Business Risks. *The Office*, pp. 14-19.

Sensenich, John F. (1985, November 25). Choosing a Backup Facility: Check Staff, Hardware, Extras. *Computerworld*, pp. 71-72.

Smith, Kenneth F. (1988, February). Power Controls: the Trend Toward Internal Systems. *The Office*, pp. 83-86.

Stair, Ralph M. (1983). Computer Disaster Planning for the Small Business. *Journal of Small Business, 21*(3), 13-18.

Thiel, Carol Tomme. (1984, November). Disaster. *Infosystems*, pp. 26-32.

Toigo, Jon William. (1989). *Disaster Recovery Planning: Managing Risk and Catastrophe in Information Systems*, Englewood Cliffs, NJ: Yourdon Press.

Weixel, Suzanne. (1989, March 13). Survivors Know the Value of Preparedness. *Computerworld*, pp. 75-78.

Weixel, Suzanne. (1989, March 13). Most Accidents Happen When Companies Neglect the Basics. *Computerworld*, pp. 82.

.Whitehead, Janet C., and Diann Conyers. (1988, January). Survival in a Computer Environment—The Synergistic Approach. *Records Management Quarterly*, pp. 8-14.

Yaremko, James F. (1988, March). Make a Plan for PC Disaster Recovery. *The Office*, pp. 54-96.

Part VI
Microcomputer
Education and
Training

Early microcomputer education consisted of teaching programming technique. Then, with the advent of user-friendly software and hardware, the focus of training switched to teaching particular software application packages. Now, with the role of the micrcocomputer taking on a more managerial perspective, it is time to once again shift the focus of the training of the end users. Both chapters in this section discuss the absence of this shift. Henry Collier and Carl McGowan (Computers in Education and Training) look at the possible applications of microcomputers in business education and training. They outline the advantages and dangers of using the computer in classroom situations. John Lanasa (Microcomputer Education: Are Institutions of Higher Learning Providing Effective Microcomputer Training to Future Business Leaders?) investigates the need for today's business student to be educated about the current and future potential of microcomputer technology. He argues that students need more than just the familiarity with the few limited business applications that most school offer as a part of a specific discipline.

Chapter 13

COMPUTERS IN EDUCATION AND TRAINING

Henry W. Collier
University of Wollonngong

Carl B. McGowan
University of Missouri-Columbia

This chapter presents an in-depth examination of the use of computers in higher education and training programs. The examination is not limited to classroom use in colleges and universities, but will present many different computer applications to diverse learning tasks.

As we know, computers are a relatively new tool that can be used by educators and trainers. Many of us can remember the first university and business computers and how they fit, or didn't fit, into university curricula. Many 1960's business and science students learned computer programming rather than computer literacy in their undergraduate programs. Punched cards were fed into the card readers by student assistant "technicians" and paper tapes were fed into the teletype machines in a slightly more interactive mode. Nevertheless, computers of the 1960's were big machines; they were mainframe computers with all the attendants and staff, air conditioning, and the mysticism surrounding these electronic devices.

Businesses began to discover the value and benefits of computers almost as soon as they were introduced. Highly repetitive tasks were automated or computerized. Payroll accounting was one of the first business tasks delegated to the computer, and business managers found that the computer was very cost effective in preparing payroll checks for employees. Many arithmetic errors were eliminated because the computer simply did not make computational errors.

However, the computer performed the tasks programmers told it to do, rather than the tasks managers wanted it to do. In order to get the computer to do what they wanted it to do, managers found that they had to use some of the resources they had saved in eliminating staff that performed the repetitive tasks, to hire computer programmers. In some sense, costs were shifted from one administrative expense to another, and more highly paid, staff. Mainframe computer installations still require relatively large support staffs. Even though mainframe computers are expensive to own and operate, we believe that there will always be a use for the large mainframe and super computers. In some businesses, large computers are more cost-effective than smaller mini or microcomputers. However, the decreasing cost per unit of computing makes microcomputers very cost-effective. Networking makes the use of the microcomputers much easier and even more cost-effective.

We must always remember that we've come a long way in computing in the last 30 years. Many of our university students have hand-held calculators that have more computing power than the so-called mainframe computers of 1960. The Hewlett-Packard Model 41 is a very powerful hand-held machine indeed!   The TI Business Edge performs many calculations that were difficult on the mainframe computers of the early 1960s.   Now we, in 1990, seem to be entering the "portable computer" stage of development. We have 32 -bit machines capable of shared processing available right now.

Our rate of change in computing technology appears to be growing at an increasing rate. How does all this fit into the process of education and employee training? As more and more people have access to computers and computing, we can delegate the more repetitive learning tasks, particularly those tasks of knowledge and comprehension, to computers. The computer can be used for measuring whether the student has achieved the educational or learning objectives.   One of the most efficient uses of the computer is for testing. Software programs exist, and have existed for many years, where the student or trainee can sit down with a computer and select an objective test that measures whether the candidate has achieved the objectives of an academic course.

Several computer application specific journals exist. While most computer users know about publications like *BYTE, PC Computing,* and *PC Week,* many less well-known journal exist. Some of these lesser-known journals are listed in Table 1

Background

Applications

The history of computer use in education and training shows applications from art to zoology.

1. The Computer Assisted Composition Journal
   Johnson State College
   Johnson, VT 05656

2. Collegiate Microcomputer
   Rose-Hulman Institute of Technology
   Terre Haute, IN 47803

3. Computers and the Humanities: Journal of the
   Association for Computers and the
   Humanities
   Kinwer Academic Publishers Group
   P.O. Box 358 Accord Station
   Hingham, MA 02018-0358

4. Academic Computing: Covering Computer Use in
   Higher Education
   Academic Computing Publications, Inc.
   200 West Virginia
   McKinney, TX 75069-4425

5. Florida Educational Computing Quarterly
   Panhandle Center of Excellence in Mathematics,
   Science, Computers and Technology
   Florida A&M University, College of Education
   Tallahassee, FL 32307

6. Social Science Computer Review
   NCSU Box 8101
   North Carolina State University
   Raleigh, NC 27695

7. CALICO Journal
   Computer Assisted Language Learning and
   Instruction Consortium
   CALICO 3078 JKHB
   Brigham Young University
   Provo, UT 84602

Table 1: Additional Computer Application Specific Journals

While this chapter concentrates on applications of computers in business education and training, it is worthwhile to examine some of the uses in other disciplines. Since there is so much literature in the field of computer education and training, we have restricted our discussion to books, papers, and articles written between 1980 and the present. While some of the work before 1980 is relevant, we believe that more current works are of more use to decision makers. The thrust of this chapter is to discuss the uses of microcomputers in education and training; and, quite simply, microcomputer use before 1980 is limited. It has only been in the last 10 years that educators and business managers have had real access to computers. Far more software exists now than in 1980, and the software is far more powerful and comprehensive. We must remember that the first microcomputers had 64K working memories and 160/180K single sided disk storage. Many early microcomputers used cassette tape storage. As we enter the 80486 chip age, we are working with 640K main memory, expanded and extended memories ranging to 16M and affordable personal hard disk drives approaching 300M. Even the floppy disk drive capacity has been increased to 1.44M and 1.2M for the 3 1/2" and 5 1/4" drives respectively. Many of the "desktop" 80386/80387 microcomputers of 1990 have far more computing power than the mainframe computers of 1960 that occupied a whole floor of a multi story "computer center."

Role of the Computer in the Arts

In arts education, Andris (1989) discusses and describes the use of recent developments in microcomputer technology in the production of artworks. This article explains how digitizers and paint programs may be used in art education. Hapgood (1989) describes computer animation and how it may affect people's lives. This chapter discusses examples of computer animation use in education and the more traditional research sciences. Television coverage of the space shuttle flights and the Voyager missions often contain computer simulations of the missions. Walter (1989) reports on the controversy of using computers in the art classroom. Using the computer conflicts with traditional pedagogical methods in art(s) education. Walter also comments on the lack of useful software for art education.

Other computer applications in arts education are explored by Warren (1989) who discusses the role of computers in color theory, graphic arts and decorative design.

Solomon (1989a) discusses the role of the computer in an art program in a magnet high school. This chapter shows us what one teacher can do if there is support from the administrators of the school. Solomon (1989b) explains how the teacher in a school for the arts uses computers to help students learn about music theory. The paper also explains how, with MIDI (Musical Instrument Digital Interface), students can create, hear, and see the results of their applications of the theory.

Role and Scope

What is the role and scope of computers in education? Is there a single answer to this question? When we examine the different types and levels of education, we think the answer is no. Nevertheless, there are some generalities and constants that apply in using computers in education and training. Holden (1989) discusses the role computers play in the classroom. He cites the lack of influence computers have had in education. This lack of influence results because educational experts are divided on the computer's role in the classroom. While there have been some innovative and bold experiments, computers have been relegated to "drill" and passive exercises rather than leading the student in more creative and alternative ways to think about different things. O'Malley (1989) believes that we have only scratched the surface in using computers in education and training. Computers are, according to O'Malley, just beginning to take their place in education.

The possibilities are just starting to unfold. We would tend to agree. Owens (1980) cites evidence that technological changes take between 25 and 50 years to be implemented in our educational institutions. Organizational inertia (stubbornness?) resists change, and only when the old generation relinquishes control, does a new generation get to implement the technology they know and use. Perhaps schools represent the worst case scenario in implementation of technology. What makes this attitude more destructive is the fact that the public schools have a virtual monopoly on educational services. While one might choose to argue that there are other alternatives, in many cases there are no economically feasible alternatives to public education for most students. Our anecdotal evidence in several schools leads us to believe that there is extreme, and often irrational, resistance to technological changes. Perhaps our system of tenure and management of the tenure process adds to this resistance to change. Far too many educational organizations are controlled by interests vested in maintaining the status quo. Certainly, computer technology is changing at an ever increasing rate. Those who choose not to participate in the evolution of computer technology will be faced with the revolution that occurs when organizational structures get too far out of contact with the "real" world. One thing that happens in schools that pay little or no attention to the marketplace, is that the graduates of the institutions can no longer compete in the job market. Employers want and need graduates who understand and can use computers. In other words, employers want and need students who are computer literate. If schools, individually or as a group, refuse to provide computer literate graduates, then employers will look elsewhere for employees.

Others, including Collier, McGowan, and Ryan (1987), Skulley (1989), and Rogers (1988) look at the future of computers in education very positively. These authors discuss the great speed with which desktop, i.e., personal, computers have evolved, changed, and transformed the process of education. They outline and explain how the computer can and will change the process of education during the decade of the 1990's and on into the 21st century.

The expectation is that the powerhouse (80386/ 80387 and 80486) computers of 1990 will become relatively inexpensive desktop fixtures. In fact, we have seen this happen already. As this is written in mid-year 1990, we see advertisements in the trade publications for 8088/8086 machines for less than $400 and AT (80286/80287) technology based machines for less than $600. We also expect to see declines in microcomputer software. While fixed costs of development are high, more and more potential users enter the market every year. Variable costs of computer software are extremely low. Costs associated with publishing manuals and copying disks are minimal. As software companies are able to spread this fixed cost over more customers, their profitability leverage rises and expected selling prices go down as expected unit sales increases.

Examples of price declines abound. *Peachtree* published an integrated accounting software package that originally sold for approximately $800 for each of the six separate accounting modules. That $4,800 package now sells, in its third edition Peachtree III, for a street price of $149 and a list price of $199. New and improved editions of software are continuously introduced into the marketplace.

Older software programs and editions must be upgraded and improved or they simply will not sell. Software producers have to be extremely conscious of market demands, because ignoring the wants and needs of the market results in lost sales and a loss of power in the firm.

Role of the Computer in Business Education

There are literally hundreds of articles and papers about the use of computers in business education and training. Grub and Anckonie (1985) declare:

> Most responsible faculty members of a quality business school would agree that computer literacy is an essential element in the portfolio of skills that should be possessed by their current graduates .

At the minimum levels of competency, most researchers and faculty members believe that student graduates should have working knowledge of some word processing programs, spread sheet applications and analysis, some statistical applications like univariate forecasting, linear regression models, and interpretation of the results, and a basic idea of data base management programs. If we are to achieve these goals, then we must offer education and training to instructors who may still fear the computer. We must remember that many instructors were in school when it was nearly impossible for humans to interact with computers.

Only a gifted few were able to really and truly communicate with the machine on the machine's terms. Even today few have the ability to speak binary codes or low level programming languages to communicate directly with the core of the processor. Are we inferring that faculty members and trainers actually need to know how to communicate directly with the machine? Not at all, but faculty and trainers must be able to communicate with the students and employees who are going to use the machines in their work or studies.

Robinson (1985) presents a detailed discussion of how integration of the computer into business education and training programs. She states: Business educators are developing a completely new curriculum including the computer in the curriculum, which in turn demands:

- new goals and objectives
- new course titles
- new course outlines new teaching / learning strategies

- changing vocabulary content to include the new terminology
- new learning situations which include the microcomputer.

We support Robinson in her analysis of the problems and the solutions in implementing com-puter-based technology in   business education. Specifically, her recommendation or insistence on new goals and objectives, appeals to us. If we see a continuing problem with education in our society, it is a lack of goals and objectives for the programs and the curricula. Unless we, as faculty members and trainers, can decide what it is that we are supposed to be doing, we're in for a long and difficult struggle. If we cannot determine what it is that the students ought to know, and in doing so establish criteria for measuring their achievements of these objectives, our process of education and training is likely to exhibit "Topsy" like growth.

Simply declaring that "computers will be used in the accounting courses," is not likely to be produc-tive.   Many instructors will use the computer like a typewriter and give the students practice sets or "fill in the blank" spreadsheet program.   While it is an advantage to know how to type and how to fill in spreadsheets, the real advantages are gained when students learn how to set up an accounting program and how to build a spreadsheet. We agree that fill-in-the -blanks and typing exercises make an excellent beginning point, but that is exactly what they are, a starting point and not an end. An analogy would be to run the tutorial program for a desk top publishing [DTP] package like *Pagemaker*® without requiring the student to actually produce a paper or brochure using

the *Pagemaker* desk top publishing package.
Should students be required to have computers? Tyagi (1984) writes:

> As the free enterprise system continually
> moves from an industrial-based society to an
> information based society, computer literacy
> has been universally recognized as an impor-
> tant measure of quality education in business.
> . .Consequently, business students are often
> required to take courses in computer opera-
> tions.

Others, such as Dascher and Harmon, (1985)
raise issues about faculty training and requiring
computers for all students in a business curriculum.

> . . .in addition to the many pedagogical
> contributions that microcomputers can effect,
> the implementation issues concerning faculty
> training, software development, security, and
> so forth can become overwhelming. Neverthe-
> less, these issues should not deter any
> institution from considering implementation of
> a mandatory microcomputer policy at their
> school.

Ploch (1984) believes that even though the
costs of required computers for students is high, the
benefits are greater than the costs. Students react
positively to the use of microcomputers in courses.
Use of computers gives students the opportunity to
work together and increase their learning opportunities by working together in peer assisted learning

groups.

Are all results of the implementation of computers positive? There is some preliminary evidence that not all results are positive. Factors that contribute to a negative outcome are machine failures, start up efforts of developing microcomputer skills and satiation of curiosity about microcomputers.

Nevertheless, computer implementation seems to have overall positive effects on student learning. There are some negatives, but the positive effects outweigh the negative consequences. Perhaps students realize that the computer is not a cost-free resource. There is a certain amount of time and effort that must be expended to attain minimum competency. Even then, the computer cannot solve all the problems. Students still have to do some work, the computer cannot do it all!

Issues

Administrative Use of Computers

As we stated before, one of the problems entangled with the use of computers for education and training is the role and scope of the educational and training process. It seems to us that it is necessary for the managers or curriculum designers to have some goals and/or objectives before they plunge into programs or methodology without having any real idea of what it is that they are trying to do.

We think that all of us, both inside and outside the colleges and universities, have seen the results of growth (or decline) without adequate planning. We have seen, in too many institutions, senior faculty members "awarded" desktop computers that best serve as boat anchors, when the individual senior faculty member may not even know how to turn the machine on and may not care whether he or she knows how to use the machine. Schools, like most organizational units, have limited resources, and while some senior faculty do not use their machines, other junior faculty members who actually know how to use the machines do not have any access to them.

It also seems to us that the administrators, staff, and managers in the colleges and universities get first option on the supply of computers. While many of these managers use their computers to plan and forecast for the institution, many others are using state of the art machines as typewriters. These administrators take little or no advantage of the technology, but simply must be first in the pecking order of resource allocation and have all the "toys" before any of the line management and teaching faculty have access to the technology.

This seems to us like making sure that the manager of the automobile dealership has all the electronic tuning equipment before anybody out in the service shop gets access to the machinery. It doesn't make sense to us, and impedes organizational growth and organizational development. On top of that, resource misallocation creates resentment in the organization.

Establishment of Organizational / Educational Goals and Objectives

One of the most difficult decisions in academia is trying to decide what the goals and objectives of the program are! In accounting, like other school programs, academicians must decide what they believe students are supposed to learn. If, for discussion purposes, we try to establish dimensions or continua we might choose the following:

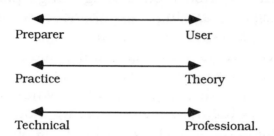

Preparer   User

Practice   Theory

Technical   Professional.

As we view the process of accounting education, it is obvious to us that different positions on these continua will result in different sets of goals and objectives for the curriculum. We would never say that all programs should have the same set of educational goals and objectives, but we would say that every program must have a set of goals and objectives. It is unlikely, at least in our opinion, that any single school will have the resources to be everything to everybody! In the futile attempt to satisfy everybody all the time, it is likely that faculty or trainers will not be able to agree on what it is that they are supposed to be doing with organizational chaos as a result.

While this chaotic scenario (Peters, 1987) is appealing to some, productivity and efficiency fall.

Crisis or chaotic management is an appealing management style. The manager is always busy "firefighting." One crisis after another arises and is "solved" or put to rest. The manager is always busy, and there is a great sense of saving the university and the program for another day. However, managers spend far too much time on day-to-day problems when they adopt the crisis management model. Little planning, planning that would avoid many of the crises, is done. When managers use the management-by-crisis model, long -range planning and strategic planning are abandoned and the organization is bound to fail in the long run.

Education is an expensive producer and consumer of scarce resources. A review of the expenditures for education should convince anyone of this. It is highly unlikely that we would ever consider building a factory without having some basic idea of what it was that we were going to produce. It only seems sensible to us that we should have some educational goals and objectives before we prepare to "educate" students.

A branch of learning theory and practice devotes its attention to the establishment of learning (educational) objectives. If we cannot define what it is that students are supposed to learn, then how can we go about deciding what it is that the teachers should teach? Bloom's *Taxonomy of Educational Objectives* (1950), establishes an ordering of learning objectives. In steps of increasing complexity and perhaps increasing difficulty, the taxonomy is:

1. Knowledge
2. Comprehension
3. Application
4. Analysis
5. Synthesis
6. Evaluation

Knowledge, comprehension, and application are learning tasks that stress memorization. Analysis, synthesis and evaluation are the thinking tasks. An ordering of learning tasks using the taxonomy affects the teachers' thinking about materials and the teaching methods used in the courses.

If the curriculum is designed around memory skills, teachers use different classroom approaches than if instruction, courses, and programs center on thinking skills. While others may argue about the relative importance of each type of learning task, it seems to us that university level students must be proficient at all six classifications of Bloom's taxonomy. It is not enough to concentrate on learning at knowledge and comprehension levels in university and college level programs. Students must be able to "pull together" or synthesize different methods or theories in problem solving. Students must be able to evaluate the quality of different solutions to problems and decide which action to select from a set of possible actions.

Contemporary education writers like E.D. Hirsch (1988) have made very critical and pointed comments about college students' lack of entry level skills. Hirsch's study demonstrates the lack of knowledge and comprehension in today's students. What are educators and trainers to do?

If these knowledge and comprehension skills are necessary for future cognitive development, then the students have to obtain them. If Bloom presents a realistic and operational ordered learning taxonomy, then educators and trainers have no choice but to help students learn these essential skills and facts at the knowledge and comprehension level before the students can undertake tasks at higher cognitive levels. As an example, if students do not know what a budget is and understand why a business organization might want to have a budget, then it is impossible to have students learn how to prepare a budget. Attempting to teach students how to use a spreadsheet program without having some idea of budgeting and organizational planning might be both ineffective and inefficient. Perhaps it is impossible to consider the coursework that teaches budgeting and spreadsheets as discreet courses when we consider effectiveness and efficiency in education and learning. We would say that it is difficult to operate in an educational environment without integration of subject material. How can one consider the functional disciplines of management, marketing, accounting, and finance without considering the business entity as a whole? It is, to us, almost insane to look at the business as a collection of discrete operating segments with no common goals and purposes. While many university organizational units operate with no coordination and no synthesis of subject material, for-profit business cannot operate without this integration — at least not for long.

We are not sure that the standardization of business curricula under the American Assembly of Collegiate Schools of Business (AACSB) necessarily brings about "better" educational institutions. We see too many instructors who have no practical business experience at all in the classroom. Mathematical modeling of human behavior and motivation is one thing, making personnel decisions about hiring and layoffs or terminations is quite another. Perhaps this insistence on "terminally qualified" instructors brings to the classroom those who might know the theory of their narrow functional disciplines, but the generalist manager is excluded. Integration of practical skills and theory is what this educational process is all about. If a faculty or academic program is anchored at one end of the continuum, it is unlikely to produce graduates who are able to get anything done in the real world business environment.

Although the last paragraph critically examines the role of the "theoreticians" in the business schools, the proponents of "on-the-job training [OJT]" cannot escape examination. While OJT appeals to students who are vitally interested in how to improve their job performance and how to solve the problems they are facing while working their way through school, such practical training is not what college and university level schools are for. We have failed if we turn our college and university programs into Schools of Philosophy, Heating, Electronics, and Real Estate. While the acronym for such an institution might be SPHERE, we would hardly say that has any real sense of direction.

Faculties, administrators, staff, and students plus those who pay the bills must work together to decide what it is that schools are supposed to do. It seems to us that the universities and colleges cannot be allowed to become trade or technical institutes whether the students want that kind of practical and knowledge based education or not. OJT is best left to employers, not to schools. The employers knows what specific skills and knowledge they want. Let the training programs help the students learn which buttons to push and which specific word processing program to use. All will benefit if this is allowed to happen.

Universities will better serve the students and

the employers if the university can help the students learn general problem solving strategies, learn how to communicate effectively and efficiently, and use mathematics in a clear and logical manner to solve problems. Can the computer help us do this? Unquestionably and unequivocally, yes! Actually the computer can help us solve both problems, the problems of OJT and the problems relating to university teaching and learning.

Solutions and Remedies

Decision makers must first determine their goals and objectives. What is it that the educational, or training program, is actually trying to do? When educators can make these decisions, the role of computers in the curriculum is much more defined, and we have a chance to plan meaningful and useful educational programs. Problem definition is not an easy task in implementing computers, but it is a necessary step. If the decision makers cannot determine what it is that they are trying to do, all further efforts are likely to be disorganized and often conflicting.

It is essential that teachers and administrators work together in deciding what role computers are to play in higher education. We were at a school where the administrators selected a computer for the academic side of the university without consulting the faculty about the availability of useful software. The administrators decided that all students would use a computer in their courses and that computers would be made available to all students. The students could either lease or buy the computer, but all entering students would have access to one of the machines.

When the faculty tried to use the computers in the classroom, there was no software available. Students used the computers like typewriters. When students used the spreadsheet programs, few actually used any of the functions, but merely typed in the information they had computed by hand. Little training was available for the faculty, and the support staff was too small to help solve problems of either faculty or students.

As the next iteration of applications became available, students were finally able to use their computers in some of their courses. Nevertheless, most of the software was of the "fill-in-the blank" variety with limited learning assistance. Students were still using the computers as typewriters.

Where do we go from here?

As we stated before, there must be a plan if we are to successfully implement computers into a college curriculum or a training program. The administrators and the faculty must work together to establish mutually beneficial goals and objectives for the programs. It is not enough to say that "we're going to use computers" in our programs. Somebody has to establish the educational goals and objectives for the use of computers.

The next step is to confirm that the faculty and the administrators are working toward achieving the goals and objectives. It is not enough to simply state that we are going to use computers in the curriculum. Wishing or decreeing that computer integration will happen, as in so many other wish and decree issues, seldom works. Issues of academic freedom continually obscure the desire for standardization of academic programs. If faculty members do not know how to use computers, these same faculty members are highly unlikely to have their students use computers in their coursework.

With current management of the tenure system, senior faculty members who refuse to "play the game" do just that. They often refuse to play by (1) awarding little or no credit to computer exercises, (2) refusing to discuss or explain computer assignments, and / or (3) not making any computer assignments at all. While little or nothing happens to the individual faculty member, the students who are expected to have the computer skills by the instructors who offer courses that follow lose out.

As in any effective management system, there has to be some method of measurement, feedback, and control to make the planning and budgeting productive. Faculty and administrators can sabotage carefully made plans when there is no mechanism for control. Someone, perhaps the course committees or the departmental administrators, has to look for compliance with the goals and objectives of the course(s).

We opt for a management system where the instructors are part of the decision making process. The instructors of various courses need to decide what is important and how this material should be presented to the students. While we do not necessarily support "standardized" instruction, there must be some common ground in say, Cost Accounting I.

Unstructured courses and required prerequisite courses without some commonalties penalize the students, not the instructors. Instructors for these common course should be able to decide which chapters will be emphasized in a 10 week quarter course, or a 15 week semester, since it is usually not possible to use the whole text in such a limited time frame.

Writing and Editing: Our experiences in higher education lead us to believe that students would benefit most by beginning computer use as soon as they enter the university. Freshman students benefit if they learn to write "on the computer." Business writing benefits from editing and rewriting. Computers make these tasks relatively simple. No more cut and paste! No more long, and short, sheets of yellow legal paper taped together into a manuscript delivered to the typist for a first draft. The computer and word processing software allow the writer to look at the work and make changes on demand. Turner (1985) cites evidence that most of those who have used word processing programs agree that they never again want to be without one.   If either the writer or the editor does not like the order of the text, block move commands rearrange the text easily, quickly, and conveniently.

> Chapnick (1989) states:
> Writing is a difficult craft. One begins with a blank page and must eventually create a piece of text.   I'm sure the copy-editing process became more important as a quality control mechanism in the manufacturing process, and this probably had some important effects on the author's relationship to the final text, but the basic steps involved in creating text were left virtually untouched by the invention of movable type. . .

By allowing for the immediate revision and

recreation of a piece of text, computers extend a writer's mental reach. The real craft of writing is in the editing. Getting down the stream of words as they are first formed in the mind is the easy part; the challenge is taking that stream and forming it into a finished piece of text. This power to reshuffle raw text, to edit, insert, delete, and then produce a brand new, clean copy, transforms the process of text creation.

Turner(1985) says that "the computer makes revision a playground instead of a punishment. We would agree.

Faculty members can benefit from word processing programs in their preparation of lecture notes and handouts. Faculty members can revise their lectures by inserting new material and deleting old or outdated material. The lecture notes can be printed and distributed if the instructor wishes to do so, and these notes used as the basis for further discussion of the material.

A student can learn to use the basic features of a full feature word processor by running the tutorial programs that accompany all the programs. Granted, it may take longer periods of time to become an expert in the use of any single word processor, but the basic skills can be learned in an afternoon. If every student is using the same word processing software, they will interact and help each other learn. The synergistic learning effects of standardized software are an additional benefit. Students, in addition to learning how the software works, will also learn from each other about writing because they will be able to review and comment on each others work before it is submitted to the instructor. A paper in *Collegiate Microcomputer* (1990) discusses Remedial English Students: Computer based instruction. O'Neill and Alperson (1989) determined that computers "work" best for drill and practice , and tutorials. Their study used several different ways of using the computer in beginning level courses in the Social Sciences. The methods considered were drill and practice, tutorials, and models or simulations. The authors found that beginning students learn more from tutorials than any of the other methods. Their research supports the hypothesis that the structure of the learning task does help students learn and that more testing of learning results in greater achievement for these beginning students. Perhaps these results can be explained in terms of Bloom's Taxonomy. If beginning students are most concerned with knowledge, comprehension, and application tasks, the computer tutorial may be a very effective way to help students learn tasks at these memory skills levels.

Composition or writing instructors may use the computer to make suggestions to the student about the form and content of the work. Instructors can make style, content, and form suggestions right on the disk. The instructor can show the students the effects of various suggestions about their writing. With these suggestions, students are able to go back and make changes and resubmit the work for further comments and editing. Word processing makes this type of assignment feasible. Changes can be made quite easily and the time it takes is minimized. All we need are sufficient machines and printers to handle the work load.

Pinter (1989) states:

Significantly, the language of computer assisted writing establishes a process view of rhetoric in the same way that the computer reflects and establishes the changing nature of learning.

Arithmetic and Mathematics:

Our teaching experiences in accounting and finance lead us to believe that college and university students are not well prepared in arithmetic or algebra or higher mathematics. Some of our research (Collier and McGowan, 1989) examines these relationships between the ability to use numbers and learning in other disciplines. If our research is generalizable, then we believe that students must be proficient in arithmetic and math to have any chance of succeeding in business programs in accounting and finance.

We believe that the arithmetic and math abilities are far more important than just predictors for accounting and finance. We believe that these basic skills are necessary, but not sufficient, for all the programs in the business schools. Perhaps it is the logical relationships that are used in the arithmetic and the math that underlie the basic number skills. Further research will examine these relationships. But for now we know that students who are not very good at arithmetic are not successful in professional accounting and finance programs.

Papers about using the computer in mathematics education appear in various journals. *Using the Microcomputer to Enhance Calculus Teaching* (Collegiate Microcomputer, 1990) discusses how an instructor might use the microcomputer to help students learn about calculus. Other papers on microcomputers in the mathematical sciences and the effects on courses, students and instructors appear in journals like *Academic Computing.*

Can students who do not have the basic skills learn them? We think that they can, and in addition, that the computer can help these poorly prepared students learn the things that they need to know. There are many programs that can help students learn these basic arithmetic skills. The Visions software products are very easy to use and consistent. A student can move from one program disk to another with minimum startup time. We know that many of these arithmetic skills are supposed to be taught and learned in elementary schools. Just because these skills are supposed to be learned in the early years does not necessarily mean that they have been. Do we doom a student to failure just because they have not obtained the entry level skills? We do not think so, and believe that one of the most important things that a computer can do for the student is to help the student improve these basic skills through application and drill. While this is not an exciting and highly technical use of computers, many students can benefit by this relatively low level application. Dollar for dollar, we may find that using the computer for remediation is extremely cost effective. Teacher time is minimized, student learning is maximized and those students unlikely to succeed will now have a chance to succeed in their chosen academic programs.

Other public domain programs can help students learn basic skills. Dr. David Lovelock, his colleagues and his students have written and published several advanced math programs. Included are programs titled Are You Ready for Calculus, Are You Ready for Business Calculus, Linear Algebra, and Are You Ready for Ordinary Differential Equations. While many of these are beyond the scope of most undergraduate business programs, some of these programs would be useful for graduate students. Reliance on quantitative methods, forecasting methodology and experimental design demands knowledge and application of many mathematical tools. Nearly all students have some difficulty in remembering and reviewing fundamental skills. Use of these programs can help students find out what it is that the do know about the subject material and also what they do not know. Both are important. If the students can find out what skills they lack, they can review the material until they demonstrate proficiency.

One problem with using computers for remedial education and basic skills review is that these programs require a relatively high level of self-motivation. We are not sure that this is a real problem of higher education, for much of the motivation in students must come from within if the student is to be successful. If students are not intrinsically interested in learning at advanced levels, there may not be any extrinsic rewards that will ensure successful completion of any academic or training programs. Businesses and schools cannot, and will not, continually reward expected behavior. Many, perhaps most, of the rewards for academic and training programs must be intrinsic, for extrinsic payoffs may come much later after the student graduates from college or is back on the job.

Spreadsheet Application

Perhaps the single most important software package for accounting and finance is the spreadsheet. Much like KleenexR and and JelloR are American trade names that identify a generic line of products, Lotus or 1-2-3 identifies a generic spreadsheet software program. Although there are many other spreadsheet packages available to computer users, some more powerful than 1-2-3, like EXCEL, and Symphony, advertisements in the help wanted sections of the local newspapers often specifically request ability to use 1-2-3.

In higher education assignments, professors often require the student to fill in the blanks in a software template designed to work with one of the spreadsheet programs. It is useful to do this once or twice, but the real skill is to design the template. Some of our previous comments about implementing computers and computer programming into higher education and training related to using the computer as a typewriter. If instructors are not careful in using spreadsheet templates, they can be part of the problem rather than part of the solution.

Students need to learn how the spreadsheet programs can be used to solve problems. Spread sheet programs can be very useful in transmitting large amounts of data about budgeting and planning to other managers. Adding another column to the spreadsheet budget gives a manager a simple comparison between the budget or plan and the actual results to date.

Yohn (1989) discusses how spreadsheet programs "combine ease of learning and operation with a powerful processing and output capability." The paper supports spreadsheet programs as excellent environments for a variety of instructional uses in economics education.

Simulations and Sensitivity Analysis

Without belittling the tremendous benefits that beginning students and employees can gain from using the computer for basic skills and training programs, the greatest benefits more advanced students get from use of computers are when they use the computer for sensitivity analysis and simulations. Sensitivity analysis allows us to see how decisions might change as measures of independent input variables change. It is, of course, possible to do a sensitivity analysis with paper and pencil. However, each analysis and each change requires the decision maker, or the student, to recalculate the whole problem. Sensitivity analysis is very time-consuming and difficult to do without a computer. However, with the computer and a spread sheet program, sensitivity analysis is easy to do. In addition, decision makers can see the results right away and compare the results quickly. Decision makers are likely to consider more alternatives if the cost of making the analysis is low and the computer spreadsheet package gives us the ability to do so.

One example of this type of sensitivity analysis is when the computer user applies linear programming model software. Several excellent public domain programs exist, and the cost of using any of the "freeware" is minimal. Linear programming models give us shadow prices, or sensitivity analysis information. By using the sensitivity analysis, a decision maker gains information about how to allocate additional resources to the production of goods or services.

Students in quantitative management courses often shy away from application of the linear programming models because they are relatively difficult to solve by hand. The computer makes application of the models quite easy. We do support teaching the theory of Linear Programming and solving at least one of the programs by hand to illustrate how the model works, but simply working the problems to demonstrate computational skills is, in our opinion, a waste of time and effort. We believe that students should know how to invert a matrix, but to invert a matrix by hand every time we need to make the calculation seems like a terrible waste of resources. We should use the tools available when we can use them effectively. One question that must be asked and answered in the use of computer software is, what are we trying to do? Are we teaching, and learning, computation? Or are we looking for application and analysis of decision models? While we might try to reach higher levels of synthesis and evaluation in our classroom problems, we often have to settle for analysis of various conditions. Sensitivity analysis allows us to do this in linear programming models. The sensitivity analysis allows us to consider how the outputs of the process might change as we change the inputs to the process.

It has always been possible to run simulations on mainframe computers. One story is that the machines were called computers because one of the first tasks they were programmed to do was to determine artillery shell trajectories. The people who used to make the calculations were called computers and the name transferred from the people to the machines.

Simulation programming has been difficult

because the user has to learn a specialized programming language like GPSS. However, we now have capabilities to do simulations within spread sheet programs like Lotus 1-2-3. @Risk, a proprietary program of Palisade Corporation, allows us to run simulations within Lotus 1-2-3. The learning curve is steep, and the graphic output improves with each iteration of @Risk. Using @Risk enables the decision maker to vary the shape and parameters of the probability distributions for independent variables and to measure the changes in the probability distribution of the output variable(s). We believe that it is important for decision makers to consider the probabilistic or stochastic nature of their quantifiable input variables in their decision models.

Humanities and Languages

Many public domain programs exist to help students learn grammar and memorize vocabulary and verbs in foreign languages. French, German, Chinese, Japanese, and Italian language programs are in the public domain. Other programs that print Hebrew characters and Chinese language characters are offered for sale in college and software bookstores.

A French language (Scott, 1990) writing program for beginners exists. It creates a task oriented creative writing situation for beginning French composition students. This program can help students develop effective writing strategies.

Other journals cited in previous sections of the paper offer reviews of humanities -oriented software. As more computer applications are developed for higher education, potential users will be able to find software that can be integrated with their teaching styles and individual student learning styles.

Conclusions and Summarization

It appears to us the computers are here to stay in education and training. Our students are expected to know how to use computers. A glance at the help wanted section of newspapers indicates that potential employers want candidates who know how to use computers. We cannot escape the inevitable. Our students and trainees will have to learn how to use computers for word-processing and for spreadsheets. College administrators and teachers must learn how to use computers so they can help their students learn the basic skills of computer literacy. Are all the results of computer literacy positive? We don't think so. One of the greatest failings of the computer revolution is the stress on lower levels of Bloom's taxonomy, or the memory skills, rather than the higher levels or the thinking skills.

Given the option of choosing between more work and less work, most individuals will choose less work (and at lower cognitive levels.) Faculty, administrators and students must recognize that using computers requires a start-up cost. That start-up cost is likely to be relatively high. If students do not learn the necessary prerequisite skills, then tasks that follow may be so difficult that students who do not obtain basic skills may be doomed to failure.

Transfer students are likely to have additional problems in programs with high levels of computer skills. Others have spoken of the problems relating to the "dumbing down" of high school and college curricula. Colleges must decide upon the role of the institution in society. How colleges view their students is one critical issue. Is the student a product or is the student a customer? While students have some of the characteristics of each extreme position, where the university positions itself on this continuum is of great importance. We believe that when students are viewed as customers, the quality of the academic programs necessarily declines. When the student is viewed as a customer, then customer satisfaction becomes the governing factor in program evaluation. As we have stated before, output measures of programs are necessary. If our primary measure is to be student satisfaction, we believe the quality of educational programs will decline further.

If administrators and faculty view the student as a product, problems can still arise. Faculty tyrants can exist where "products" are the emphasis. The human and cultural aspects of education can be ignored if faculty and administrators move too far in the "product" direction. Other problems arise in the use of computers in higher education and training. One significant problem is the reliance on the "right" answer. Evaluation level thinking, by definition, encourages thinking about relative solutions to complex problems. Computer models present single solutions to carefully defined problems. Although Artificial Intelligence (AI) computer programs are starting to address problems with multiple dependent variables, most of our computer programs give us one solution to one problem. Even though we preach sensitivity analysis and simulation, these techniques are relatively advanced and not easy to use.

We have to consider cognitive and developmental psychology research when we develop curricula and make decisions about educational goals and objectives. Faculty and administrators with responsibility for planning educational programs should review Perry's (1970) text. We have to help students grow and develop, and Perry presents a taxonomy to help us understand how students change and grow.

Computers, like automobiles, can be helpful and useful tools or cause great damage. It all depends on how we use them.

References

Academic Computing: Covering Computer Use in Higher Education; Academic Computing Publications, Inc.; 200 West Virginia; McKinney, TX 75069-4425.

Andris, J.; Exquisite Tools Exquisite Art: Using Digitizers and Paint Programs, School Arts, December, 1989, pp. 17+.

Bloom, B.S., Ed.; Taxonomy of Educational Objectives: The Cognitive Domain, Longman, New York, 1950.

Carolina State University, Raleigh N.C. 27695, V7 No.2, Summer 1989, pp. 175-182.

Chapnick, P.; Computers and Text, AI Expert, April 1989, pp. 7-8.

Collegiate Microcomputer, Rose-Hulman Institute of Technology, Terre Haute, IN 47803; V8 No.1, February 1990, pp. 47-50, 69-70.

Collier, H. and C.B. McGowan, An Empirical Examination of the Relationship between Mathematics Skills and Course Grade in Intermediate Accounting I, The Accounting Educators' Journal, V2 No. 2, University of Nevada, Las Vegas; Las Vegas, NV, 1989, pp. 78-86.

Collier, H.W., C.B. McGowan and W.T. Ryan; Microcomputers: A Successful Approach to Teaching Business Courses, Computers and Education, V.11 N.2, 1987, pp. 143-148.

Dascher, P.E. and W.K. Harmon; Mandatory Microcomputers: Pedagogy and Implementation, Journal of Business Education, January 1985, pp. 146-149.

Grub, P.D. and A. Anckonie III; B School Basics and Computer Literacy: A Time for Change, A paper presented at the Annual Meeting of the Academy of International Business, October 1985, 12

Hapgood, F.; The Magic Theatre, Omni, December 1989, pp. 114+.

Hirsch, E.D.; Cultural Literacy: What Every American Needs to Know, 1st Vintage Books, New York, 1988.

Holden, C.; Computers Make Slow Progress in Class, Science, May 26, 1989, pp. 906+.

Mathematics Software, Department of Mathematics, University of Arizona, Tucson, AZ 85721

O'Malley, C.; The Revolution is Yet to Come!, Personal Computing, October 1989, p. 115+.

O'Neill, D.H. and J.R. Alperson; Tutorial or Simulation: Exploring Relative Educational Value Social Science Computer Review, NCSU Box 8101, North

Owens, R.; Organizational Behavior in Education, Prentice-Hall, Englewood Cliffs, NJ; 1980.

Perry, W.G., Jr.; Intellectual and Ethical Development in the College Years: A Scheme, Holt, Rinehart and Winston, Chicago, 1970

Peters, T.; Thriving on Chaos, Handbook for Management Revolution, Knopf, New York, 1987.

Pinter, R.C.; The Writing Machine: The Word Processor Instituting the Writing Process, The Computer Assisted Compositon Journal, V. 4 No. 2 [1989], Johnson, VT; pp. 33-40.

Ploch, M.; Micros Flood Campuses, High Technology, March 1984, pp. 47-49.

Robinson, B.; A SuccessfulProgram for Integrating Microcomputers into the Curriculum, Journal of Business Education, March 1985, pp. 240-242.

Rogers, M.; Computers of the '90's: A Brave New World, Newsweek, October 24, 1988, pp. 52-55.

Scott, V.M.; Task Oriented Creative Writing with Systeme-D, CALICO Journal, V7 No.3, March 1990, pp. 58-67.

Skulley, J.; The power of Ideas and Information, Vital Speeches, July 1, 1989, pp. 565-69.

Solomon, G.; Computers Help Students See Art in A Different Hue, Electronic Learning, October 1989, pp. 16-17.

Solomon, G.; How To Get Better Scores: Use Computers to Help Teach Music, Electronic Learning, Nov/Dec 1989, pp. 18-19.

Turner, J.A.; A Personal Computer for Every Freshman: Even Faculty Skeptics Are Now Enthusiasts, The Chronicle of Higher Education, February 20, 1985, pp. 1+.

Turner, J.A.; Scholars Who Use Word Processing Programs Agree They Never Want to Be Without Them, The Chronicle of Higher Education, April 10, 1985, pp. 25-27.

Tyagi, P.K.; Student Reaction: Mandatory Use of Microcomputers in Business Education, Journal of Business Education, November 1984, pp. 89-92.

Walter, C.H.; Art and Computers: Is there room in the studio for both?, Design for Arts in Education, Nov/Dec 1989, pp. 18+.

Warren, K.C.; What Are They Doing With Computers?, School Arts, December 1989, pp. 20-21.

Yohn, W.P.; Spreadsheets in Teaching Economics, Social Science Computer Review, V7 No.4, Winter 1989, pp. 431-445.

Chapter 14

MICROCOMPUTER EDUCATION:

ARE INSTITUTIONS OF HIGHER LEARNING PROVIDING EFFECTIVE MICROCOMPUTER TRAINING TO FUTURE BUSINESS LEADERS?

John Lanasa
Duquesne University

As the complexity of decision making in the business environment increases, the need for the more efficient use of available business tools will increase proportionally. The business manager can be better prepared for critical situations by taking advantage of the available computer technology that has increased calculation power and speed. In addition, with the availability of inexpensive and powerful modern microcomputer hardware and "user-friendly" software, business managers now can interact directly with data and models when personally organizing information for decision making. Some business managers, however, have not been able to take advantage of all that the microcomputer has to offer.

Previously published in the Journal of Microcomputer Systems Management, Vol. 1, No. 1
© Idea Group Publishing

Most managers usually understand the basics of microcomputer technology, but often adequate analysis, selection, design, and implementation of the microcomputer-based applications are beyond the manager's abilities. On the other hand, the majority of microcomputer applications are developed by end users/managers. Some of these users normally invest tremendous amounts of time to learn the art of system application development without having any prior training in the process or any assistance from information systems personnel in their organizations. Despite the lack of adequate knowledge about the microcomputer-based application process, many have managed to utilize microcomputers to their fullest potential. Conceivably, better educated microcomputer users could have a much greater positive impact on organizations by utilizing this new technology in a more efficient and effective way.

Today's business students enrolled in colleges and universities -- the business managers of the future -- have a need to be educated about the current and future potential of microcomputer technology. However, many microcomputer courses offered at the college level may not be sufficient to respond effectively to the future needs of an increasingly demanding and competitive business world. At present, most business schools are offering microcomputer exercises as either a part of a specific discipline, such as accounting, finance, or marketing, or as a complete course in microcomputer applications. In either case, the emphasis is basically on a few limited business applications and the operation of one or more software package.

This paper focuses on the current status of microcomputer education at the college level and the future needs of business managers. In addition, it provides some direction for the better preparation of business students in dealing with microcomputer technology and its potential.

Utilizing Micros in Business

In recent years, the influx of inexpensive, powerful, user-friendly, microcomputer software packages for business, and the vast computing power of the modern microcomputer, have helped to make microcomputers powerful tools primarily useful for decision making and information management. It has been estimated that there were approximately 5.4 million microcomputers in 1984, doubling the number in 1983. Projections of the number of microcomputers in use by the year 1990 are estimated to be approximately 13 million units (Guimaraes & Ramanujam, 1986).

When reviewing the impact of the microcomputer, the true value can be realized in decision support type applications. A Decision Support System (DSS) can be thought of as a total integration between managers, microcomputer hardware and software, models, and databases whose purpose is to contribute to the decision process necessary to accomplish strategic, tactical, and operational objectives within an organization (Davis, 1988; McLeod, 1988). The technology available in modern decision support systems will allow managers to interact with data on a continual basis, and in a more intimate way (Fay & Wallace, 1987).

In addition to DSS applications, microcomputers can be regarded as a power tool for communication applications where managers can share data, information, and messages with their colleagues without the worry of location constraints. Microcomputers have been utilized for accessing electronic mail systems, electronic bulletin boards, databases, and other computers. The technology of local area networks (LANs) of the past decade has revolutionized the capabilities of microcomputer applications and use. Through networking, many organizations have managed to take advantage of microcomputer technology in a way that has shaped their competitive posture in the market place.

The Impact of Microcomputers on Information Processing

One of the challenges made to the management of traditional information processing systems is that the information systems department no longer controls all computer usage in most organizations. Therefore, the information systems manager now has the responsibility to be knowledgeable about many different aspects of the microcomputer and software support.

It has been predicted that the future information systems (IS) professional will be less of a controller and more of a support person, primarily responsible for the education of end users and offering supportive assistance toward their computing and information processing needs (Holmes, 1977; Sullivan, 1985). With an ever-increasing number of end users in organizations, more and more IS personnel will be engaged in assisting users who are engaged microcomputer applications in carrying out their functions in the organization. One can argue that the days of mainframe centralized systems are diminishing, and the future information processing system will consist of microcomputer systems connected to each other through a variety of network structures.

The existence of microcomputer end users, therefore, cannot and should not be ignored any longer by information systems professionals, but rather, the future IS professional must be well prepared to support the needs of the end users in their respective organizations.

Microcomputer Training

In the past several years the topics of microcomputer training and how business managers should be trained in the utilization of this technology have been the subject of much speculation (Karten, 1987). Many organizations have invested an enormous amount of financial and human resources into microcomputer technology hoping that this technology will assist their managers in becoming more efficient and effective in their decision making. Many of these organizations have been disappointed with the level of training available to the potential microcomputer users.

From a survey of 98 manufacturing firms, results indicated that little correlation existed between the training of the current employees and their success with microcomputers. However, the author analyzing the survey results did clarify the findings and stated that there may not have been training programs in the sample companies. In addition, the sampled personnel had various educational backgrounds. This indicates that the lack of correlation could be explained by the variations in sample. Thus, of the 64 firms who did not offer formal training, assumptions can be made that the majority of these people had some previous experience and/or education in microcomputer usage (DeLone, 1988). In order to enhance efficiency and effectiveness in training, specifically job related training, business schools need to offer all disciplines at a minimum of a micro literacy course. The education system cannot assume that the employee will receive on-the-job training. This places the burden of training on the education system.

The importance of these findings in later organizational training relates back to the responsibility placed on the business schools. Once the student leaves the formal education process there may not be time for further education, so a student should not assume that they will later supplement their educational deficiencies with managerial training in microcomputers. There are simply not a high percentage of companies who can afford to give extensive training to their employees.

The Microcomputer in the Business Curriculum

The popularity of microcomputer use in the business world has encouraged many colleges and universities to introduce microcomputer training for their students. Many of these schools began by incorporating microcomputer applications into their traditional course work, later offering new classes in the area of microcomputer applications. In response to this move by business educators, many existing textbooks in various disciplines had to be updated to incorporate microcomputer applications, and new textbooks had to be written for courses in microcomputer applications.

In the past decade, there has been an influx of new textbooks in the area of microcomputer applications written by many accomplished scholars. Although many of these books have satisfied the initial needs of business education in the area of microcomputer applications, in recent years, their inefficiency in dealing with a broader range of issues of microcomputer applications and management has become more evident. The majority of these books have been developed by either traditional IS professionals with a heavy focus on the computing side of computers and no appreciation of managerial issues inherent in the use of microcomputer technology in business, or they have been written by those who become enamored with popular software packages used with microcomputer and have failed to understand the overall value of information and the information systems' development process.

A quick review of the existing microcomputer textbooks clearly indicates that these book are strong in providing coverage of different software packages, but also offer a very narrow view. In many ways they can be regarded as simpler and more understandable versions of users' manuals which typically accompany the software packages highlighted in these books. They are not designed to equip the future business manager with a broad understanding of microcomputer technology, its potential in the business world, managerial issues surrounding management of microcomputer resources, and adequate knowledge of the process of microcomputer-based information systems development. Table 1 illustrates an overall evaluation of five microcomputer textbooks utilized in courses in microcomputer applications.

TEXTBOOK	EVALUATION
Four Common Software Tools By Tim Duffy Publisher: Wadsworth Company, 1988	- Adequate introduction to microcomputer hardware and software components - Covers four major software packages; functions as mini-manuals - Limited explanation of microcomputer potentials in business - No explanation of the role of microcomputers in business management - No information about development of micro-based information systems - No coverage of microcomputer networking concepts and applications - Not adequate for graduate (MBA) course on microcomputers
Business Applications Software By Lon Ingalsbe Publisher: Merrill Publishing Co., 1988	- Adequate coverage of four major software packages; good examples of the packages used - Weak explanations of microcomputer hardware and software - No explanation of managerial issues related to microcomputer applications and use - Much material duplicates software manuals - No coverage of micro-based information system development process - No coverage of microcomputer networking concepts and applications - Not adequate for graduate (MBA) course on microcomputers
Microcomputer Applications By Robert T. Grauer and Paul K. Sugrue Publisher: McGraw-Hill, 1988	- Provides good coverage of several important software packages - Provides coverage of " success story" case studies - Attractive illustrations and pictures - Weak explanations of microcomputer hardware and software - No coverage of micro-based application development processes and concepts - Not adequate coverage of networking concepts but good coverage of desktop publishing - Not adequate for graduate (MBA) course on microcomputers
Using Microcomputers By Wayne Spence and John C. Windsor Publisher: Times Mirror Publishing, 1987	- Good Coverage of micro hardware and software esp. communication software packages - Coverage of unpopular software packages in business - No explanation of managerial concerns of microcomputer applications and resources - No coverage of microcomputer-based information systems development processes - Not adequate for graduate (MBA) course on microcomputers
Microcomputer Applications By Larry J. Goldstein Publisher: Addison-Wesley, 1987	- Good coverage of micro hardware;very confusing with regard to software package - No coverage of managerial issues of microcomputer applications and use - Attractive illustrations and pictures - No coverage of the microcomputer-based information systems development processes - Not adequate for graduate (MBA) course on microcomputers

Table 1: A Summary of the Evaluations of a Few Microcomputer Textbooks

An issue that must be addressed by the educational system is how to train those people who will later be employed in support functions, enabling them to fully understand the process of developing micro-based information systems and deal with many managerial issues surrounding microcomputer applications and use in organizations. Often, even the student who specializes in the area of MIS (Management of Information Systems) will not be completely familiar with the issues surrounding the development of microcomputer information systems and the using managers.

The student in a non-computer field (e.g., finance, marketing, or accounting) may have limited exposure to microcomputer systems. Thus, when called upon in the business world to develop a simple information system, that person may not be adequately prepared to provide the company with a piece of work which will be useful to himself and other potential users (Keen & Woodman, 1984).

Although there is a relatively wide variety of material written for existing business computer courses, often the majority of the written material has proven to be nothing but glamorized manuals for popular software packages, representing only a narrow view of microcomputer capabilities. Because of this often narrow perception portrayed by the textbooks, some textbooks tend to serve as supplementary material to the existing documentation of popular software packages.

One approach for the better training of business students in microcomputer applications is to integrate various applications of business functions in the microcomputer course. According to an article by Karten (1987), students in training sessions learn to use micros best when they have the education tied closely to their area of specialty. For example, those people in accounting (or from the accounting department) would learn more effectively when their training material corresponded to actual accounting work.

The effectiveness of this approach is well founded in the results from a survey of 12 organizations in which the majority (approximately 75%) of the microcomputer users found themselves using spreadsheets. The average amount of time the respondents spent per week using spreadsheets was approximately five hours. The effectiveness is demonstrated in computer efficiency. By training employees to do what they will be expected to do in their everyday workplace, the employee becomes more effective which is translated into a higher level of productivity. (Lee, 1986). The importance of end-user computing cannot be stressed enough. Therefore, the end users of the future should be made aware of business potentials and managerial applications and issues of microcomputer technology.

In modern business organizations most microcomputer users can be characterized as follows:

- the main investigators of the need for the use of microcomputers,
- the selectors of hardware and software,
- the designers of application programs,
- the implementors of the programs developed, or
- the primary users of the product of these systems, which is the information.

As mentioned previously, in the study by Lee, there were strong implications that the implementation of microcomputers leads to a more effective performance by the business user. Thus, the division manager not only must consider to what extent to bring in microcomputer technology, but must also determine how to effectively implement the microcomputer systems into the existing framework of the department or division. (Lee, 1986).

In many cases, students are limited in their classroom exposure, acquiring only a procedural knowledge of how to use specific software packages instead of gaining a broader exposure to issues such as developing microcomputer information systems, networking, and managing microcomputer resources and applications. For example, when the time comes for the purchase of a new microcomputer, there will probably not be enough time for a systems analyst to become involved. Therefore, the manager who is responsible for the micro will have to make the decision as to which micro to buy in order to best meet the objectives of the company (Potts, 1984).

A new educational emphasis on the management of microcomputer applications and resources is essential. The end-user is ultimately the person who is responsible for the use of the computer and should be well exposed to the issues of technology management. Among the many challenges facing the business managers of tomorrow are:

- managing the demand for training and support,
- dealing with non-user-friendly products,
- resolving issues of incompatibility
- providing access to corporate data
- learning new micro technology
- addressing issues on data, and

- gaining and retaining management
  support   (Karten, 1987).

Unfortunately, the danger of relying only on limited microcomputer skills is that the microcomputer may never be fully utilized in many business areas. The machines may end up only being used for spreadsheets and word processing. In order to benefit from the opportunities presented by the microcomputer, the modern business person needs to be aware of the potential locked inside of their investment (Karten, 1987).

Conclusions and Recommendations

Current technology in the decision-making area of business has improved radically in the past few years and the outlook for the future indicates a continuing trend in technological expansion. However, even with the promise of such innovative support tools, there remains a challenge to bridge the gap between microcomputers in academics and their actual use in the business world. Training the business person on the job is not an effective solution. The training needs to be accomplished within the educational system, before the individual reaches the business community. Further, the training provided in microcomputer applications and management courses at the college level must correspond to actual business needs so that the future business person is more comfortable with the micro in different situations.

Within the classroom, it is essential to place more emphasis on the management of data and the end usage of micros. Once again, if the business student is well prepared and widely exposed to the microcomputer under a variety of different conditions, the student will later be more capable of synchronization with microcomputer technology as it is implemented in the business setting. In the current curriculum of most business schools, there is usually some form of microcomputer exposure, yet the student needs more than just an introduction to microcomputer software packages. The student does not need to be an IS expert; rather must be prepared to handle tasks related to the development of microcomputer-based information systems without being totally dependent upon the IS department. Even when the technical support of the IS department is available to the micro user, past studies indicate that the IS department is not capable of assuming all the responsibility for end-user demands. Here again, the business manager needs to be broadly prepared in micro technology in order to assist their department when deficiencies arise.

Microcomputer based decision support systems consist of a powerful array of decision aids that have the capability of increasing the business manager's calculational data analysis and interpretive comprehensiveness. However, as the technology has increased, so also have the demands on the business person to be more knowledgeable about microcomputers. The higher education systems must address these needs in order to prepare their business students for self-sufficiency in their future computing and information processing responsibilities.

References

Davis, M. W. (1988). *Applied decision support.* Englewood Cliffs, NJ: Prentice-Hall.

DeLone, W. H. (1988). Determinants of success for computer usage in small business. *MIS Quarterly,* 50-61.

Duffy, T. (1988). *Four common software tools.* Boston: Wadsworth Company.

Fay, Charles H., & Wallace, M. J., Jr. (1987). *Research-based decisions.* City: Random House.

Goldstein, L. T. (1987). *Microcomputer applications.* Reading, MA: Addison Wesley.

Grauer, R. T., & Sugrue, P. K. (1988). *Microcomputer applications.* New York: McGraw-Hill.

Guimaraes, T., & Ramanujam, V. (1986). Personal computing trends and problems: An empirical study. *MIS Quarterly,* 178-187.

Holmes, F. W. (1977). Information resource management. *Journal of Systems Management, 28*(12), 6-9.

Ingalisbe, L. (1988). *Business applications software.* Columbus, OH: Merrill Publishing Company.

Karten, N. (1987). Managing end user computing when the only constant is change. *Journal of Systems Management,* 26-29.

Keen, P. G. W., & Woodman, L. A. (1984). What to do with all those micros. *Harvard Business Review,* 142-150.

Lee, D. M. S. (1986). Usage pattern and assistance for personal computer users. *MIS Quarterly,* 312-325.

McLeod, R., Jr. (1988). *Management information systems.* Chicago: SRA Associates.

Potts, G. (1984). Maintaining control of microcomputer installation. *Journal of Systems Management,* 30-32.

Spence, Wayne J., & Windsor, John C. (1987). *Using microcomputers.* St. Louis: Times Mirror Publishing.

Sullivan, C. H., Jr. (1985). Systems planning in the information age. *Sloan Management Review, 20* (2), 3-12.

INDEX